How to Fix Common (and Not So Common)
Problems in a Hurry

Mac OS X
HEADACHES

Curt Simmons

McGraw-Hill Osborne

New York Chicago San Francisco Lisbon
London Madrid Mexico City Milan New Delhi
San Juan Seoul Singapore Sydney Toronto

The McGraw-Hill Companies

McGraw-Hill/Osborne
2600 Tenth Street
Berkeley, California 94710
U.S.A.

To arrange bulk purchase discounts for sales promotions, premiums, or fund-raisers, please contact **McGraw-Hill**/Osborne at the above address. For information on translations or book distributors outside the U.S.A., please see the International Contact Information page immediately following the index of this book.

Mac OS X Headaches: How to Fix Common (and Not So Common) Problems in a Hurry

1234567890 FGR FGR 019876543

ISBN 0-07-222886-5

Publisher:	Brandon A. Nordin
Vice President &	
Associate Publisher	Scott Rogers
Acquisitions Editor:	Majorie McAneny
Project Editor:	Laura Stone
Acquisitions Coordinator:	Tana Allen
Technical Editor:	Amy Hoy
Copy Editor:	Melissa J. Onstad
Proofreader:	Mike McGee
Indexer:	Jack Lewis
Computer Designers:	Lucie Ericksen, John Patrus
Illustrators:	Melinda Moore Lytle, Michael Mueller, Lyssa Wald
Series Design:	Mickey Galicia
Cover Series Design:	Ted Holladay

This book was composed with Corel VENTURA™ Publisher.

Dedication

For my wife, Dawn, who always supports and encourages me.

About the Author

Curt Simmons is a technical author, trainer, and general computing guru. The author of more than 30 books on computing and Internet topics, Curt enjoys working with groovy new operating systems like OS X. He is the author of *Windows XP Headaches*, also by McGraw-Hill/Osborne. Curt lives in Saint Jo, Texas with his wife and two daughters. Visit him on the Internet at www.curtsimmons.com.

Contents at a Glance

Contents

Acknowledgments

Thanks to Margie McAneny for the opportunity to write this book. A big thanks goes to Amy Hoy for a fine technical review and Laura Stone for keeping everything moving in the right direction. Thanks also to Melissa Onstad for her work on copyediting this book and making everything look great. Finally, thanks to my agent, Margot, and to my family for their support.

Introduction

Welcome to OS X Headaches!

Have you ever said something like "I thought Macintosh was supposed to be easy to use! Why can't I get it to do what I want!" or "OS X is driving me crazy! Nothing works the same any more!"? If you have expressed those feelings of frustration, don't worry—you are certainly not alone. OS X is a fantastic operating system; it does all kinds of tasks, it looks nice, and it's fun. However, that doesn't mean that applications never go wrong or that everything is easy.

As a technology author and operating system guru, I've suffered from plenty of OS X headaches of my own as I have tried to get things to work the way I need them to. I've learned a lot while fixing problems that I have experienced, and that is why I wanted to write this book for you. Simply put, I know all too well that grinding feeling in my temples, and it is no fun. So, why not write a book that helps people either avoid or fix OS X headaches quickly and painlessly?

In this book, you will find hundreds of headaches that you just might experience with OS X, and how to cure those headaches easily. I'll bet that if you are buying this book, you've had enough OS X headaches of your own, and you are hoping this book will come to your rescue.

That is what this book is all about—getting you the information, or cure, you need for the problem you are experiencing. You'll find that this book is logically divided into chapters that give you groups of related headaches. Each headache tells you why the problem occurs and how you can cure it, often in a simple step-by-step format. In fact, the idea is that you can pull this book off your shelf, find the problem you are experiencing, and then fix it.

You don't have to read this book in any particular order. You can read it from cover to cover if you like, or you can jump around and find the answers to headaches when you need them—the choice is yours. I don't ramble on for thousands of pages in this book; I just get to the point and help you find the cure you need. Use the table of contents or the book's index to find help on important OS X topics quickly and easily.

This book is for the beginning to intermediate OS X user—you don't have to be an OS X expert to use it. In fact, you don't need to know anything at all except how to turn on your Mac and how to use your keyboard and mouse.

To help you along the way, I've included a few special elements.

TIP   *Tips are friendly pieces of advice I have thrown in from time to time to make your work and play with OS X easier.*

NOTE   *Notes are little bursts of information that give you some additional headache cure information. You don't have to read these, but they can help you.*

PREVENTION   *Preventions are little pieces of advice that can help you avoid future headaches.*

Sidebars

I have placed a few sidebars here and there. Sidebars contain extra information about a particular subject. They can help you understand what OS X is doing and why the headache occurred in the first place. Again, you don't have to read these, but they can give you quick information without too many technical details.

Finally, what should you do if you are experiencing an OS X headache that this book does not mention? It is impossible for me to list every possible headache that can occur, so if you don't find it here, try these other options:

- Check the book's index and look for topics similar to what you are experiencing. Although your specific headache may not be listed, another headache could help you solve the problem!

- Check www.apple.com and search for your problem on Apple's site. If you have technical support available with your computer, don't be afraid to use it!

■   There are lots of newsgroups and Web sites that can help as well. See Appendix D for more information about those.

■   Finally, if you are stuck in headache land, feel free to send me an e-mail and I'll try to help you out. You can reach me at www.curtsimmons.com.

Okay, are you ready? Then let's get started. Your headache cure is only pages away....

Thanks! Enjoy the book!

Curt Simmons
Saint Jo, Texas

Chapter 1

OS X Interface Headaches

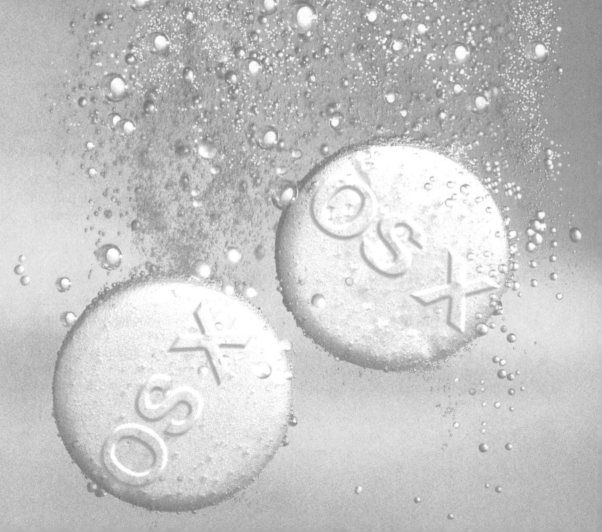

In this chapter, you'll cure...

■ Desktop setting problems

■ Dock issues

■ Finder toolbar aggravations

When you first started Mac OS X, one of the things you probably said to yourself was, "Hey, things look a little different!" Yes, they certainly do. If you have used Mac operating systems in the past, you will notice that OS X brings plenty of new features to the table. OS X version 10.2 (Jaguar) brings only more. As you started working with the new operating system, you may have felt a sense of fear and confusion—and quite possibly aggravation. After all, learning a new interface is no fun.

If you are a new Mac user, you probably started OS X, took one look at the desktop and thought, "Okay, what do I do now?" If you are new to computing, you have a big learning curve to master, and if you are moving to Mac from the Windows world, things certainly work differently.

With some exploration and practice, though, you can master Mac OS X. In this chapter, we'll get your feet on solid ground by first taking a look at the headaches and problems you have probably encountered right in front of your eyes—that's right, the interface. Can't control the Dock? Is the desktop driving you crazy? Are toolbars, screensavers, and other interface options making you pull your hair out? Don't worry; in this chapter, we take a look at the problems you're experiencing and the solutions you need!

Desktop Settings Headaches

The concept of *desktop settings* refers to what you see on the desktop—the patterns, colors, screen effects, and general overall appearance. It also includes Mac's energy-saving features as well. The good news is OS X gives you plenty of customization features and options—the bad news is that those customization features and options can drive you crazy if you haven't configured them correctly. Don't worry, though, the following examples of headaches and solutions will make your life a lot easier!

NOTE   *As you read and look at the pictures in this chapter, keep in mind that I am using OS X Jaguar (10.2). If you are not using Jaguar, some of the options may look a little different on your version, but the same basic steps and procedures apply.*

I don't like my desktop

Cause   OS X comes to you with a default desktop pattern, typically an abstract image of some kind. The purpose of the image is purely cosmetic—it's there to make your desktop look nice and add some color to your life. The problem is that we all like different things. When you first start OS X, you may hate the way the desktop looks. You can fix that easily, however, because you can change the image to another image, a solid color, or even a picture or group of pictures.

The Painkiller   In order to change the desktop picture, you need to access the Desktop settings, which are found in System Preferences. Follow these steps:

1. On the Dock, click the System Preferences icon. If you can't find it there, click Apple | System Preferences.

2. The System Preferences window appears. In the Personal section of the window, click Desktop.

3. The Desktop pane appears, shown in the following illustration. Use the Collection menu to select a new collection of images and then simply click the image that you want to use. Close the Desktop window and System Preferences.

I can't display a picture on my desktop

Cause   OS X enables you to display your own pictures on the desktop. This is pretty nifty, but in order to display a picture on the desktop, first you have to get that picture on your computer and then use your Mac to select the picture you want to display. By default, all picture files are stored in the Pictures folder, which is found in your account folder (in Users on your Macintosh HD).

The Painkiller   In order to use a desktop picture, follow these steps:

1. On the Dock, click the System Preferences icon. If you can't find it there, click Apple | System Preferences.

2. The System Preferences window appears. In the Personal section of the window, click Desktop.

3. The Desktop window appears. Use the Collection menu to select the Pictures folder (if the picture is stored in your Pictures folder) or Choose Folder to browse for the picture you want to display. If you need to choose the folder, a pop-out menu appears so you can browse for the picture, as shown in the following illustration. Choose the picture you want and click the Choose button. The picture now appears on your desktop. You can also directly drag the picture to the square area on this pane.

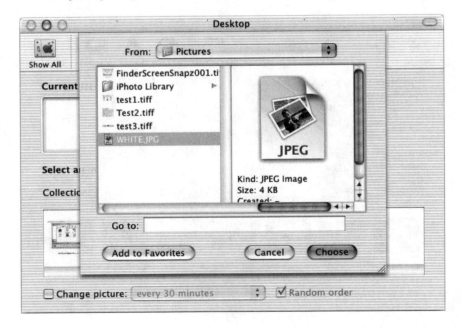

 *If you want the desktop picture to take up the entire desktop, you have to provide a picture that is large enough and has a high enough resolution to look good. You can stretch the picture to fit or tile it, but you may have to experiment a bit to get the high quality you want.*

 ## I can't display several pictures in a rotating fashion

Cause   OS X enables you to display a single picture or a collection of pictures that alternate periodically. This is a great way to view your photographs, such as a series of vacation pictures, and to remember fun events in your life. This feature works a lot like a rotating screensaver, but the changes actually occur on the desktop. To have the pictures rotate, you need several pictures located in one folder (such as your Pictures folder). Then you have to select the folder and turn on the rotation feature. The Painkiller shows you how.

The Painkiller   To use multiple pictures, follow these steps:

1. On the Dock, click the System Preferences icon. If you can't find it there, click the Apple | System Preferences.

2. The System Preferences window appears. In the Personal section of the window, click Desktop.

3. The Desktop window appears. Use the Collections menu to select the Pictures folder or locate the folder that contains the pictures you want to display.

4. Once you have made your selection, click the Change Picture option at the bottom of the Desktop window. Use the drop-down menu to select how often the pictures should change and click the Random Order check box if you want the display order to be random.

 ## The items on my screen are too large or too small

Cause   OS X can display different screen resolutions. The *resolution* refers to the size of the items that you view on the screen. The resolution also affects the quality of what you see. If the items and windows you see on the screen appear too large, you probably need to change the resolution setting. The good news is that you can change the resolution setting easily and find the one that you want with a little harmless experimentation.

The Painkiller   To adjust the resolution, follow these steps:

1. On the Dock, click the System Preferences icon. If you can't find it there, click Apple | System Preferences.

2. The System Preferences window appears. At the top of the System Preferences toolbar, click the Displays icon.

3. In the Display window that appears, shown in the following illustration, select a different resolution. Your screen changes to show you the new setting. If you do not like the setting, choose another. Notice that you can also adjust the brightness of the screen by moving the slider knob. Note too that you can adjust the colors. Typically, the colors setting should be for millions, but you can reduce the setting if the display looks odd.

TIP   *The brightness slider is available only on Apple LCD screens. If you are using an Apple ADC CRT screen, you'll see a Geometry tab.*

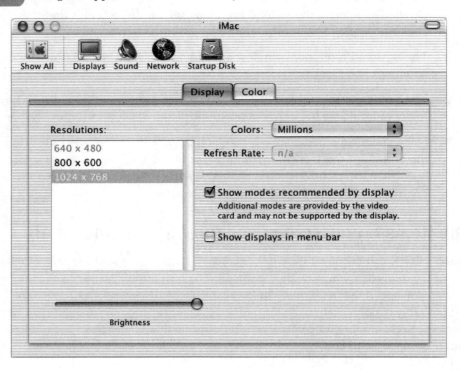

What about Display Color Settings?

You may have noticed that the Display window also contains a Color tab. The color referred to here is the color profile for your particular Macintosh. For example, if you are using a color LCD screen, your system is calibrated for that kind of screen. If you are using an iMac, the color is calibrated for the iMac. As a general rule, you don't need to change anything here because the default calibration is probably right for your computer. Keep in mind that OS X attempts to take care of you and keep you from having to worry about such items. In most cases, you don't need to do anything.

I don't like the appearance of the windows

Cause   OS X can display different window settings that affect the look of the windows you see on your screen. The default settings all fall under OS X's general appearance, but you may find that certain window behavior just irritates you. For example, the color may not be right or the scroll arrows may not work the way you want them to. Don't worry—you can adjust these settings to meet your needs.

The Painkiller   To adjust the appearance of windows, follow these steps:

1. On the Dock, click the System Preferences icon. If you can't find it there, click Apple | System Preferences.

2. The System Preferences window appears. In the Personal category, click the General icon.

3. The General pane, shown in the following illustration, enables you to change the appearance and the highlight color of the windows you see. You can also change the location of the scroll arrow, determine the number of recent items to show, and change the smooth font scaling values. You can experiment with these settings to see which ones you like best.

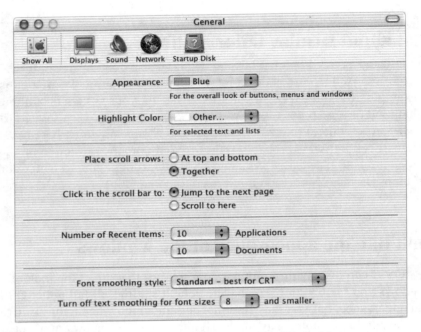

TIP   *Under the Appearance option, try using Graphite—it's a new grayscale option that many users prefer over Blue.*

I don't like the screen effect (screensaver)

Cause   *Screen effects,* formerly called screensavers, give your monitor something to display when you are not using it. You can select from several available screen effects, and you can even purchase Macintosh software that will give you many more if that is something you're heavily into.

The Painkiller   To adjust the appearance of screen effects, follow these steps:

1. On the Dock, click the System Preferences icon. If you can't find it there, click Apple | System Preferences.

2. The System Preferences window appears. In the Personal category, click the Screen Effects icon.

3. In the Screen Effects window, shown in the following illustration, select the screen effect you would like to display. You can see a preview of the screen effect in the provided box. Notice also that some screen effects have a Configure button where you can adjust the speed and other settings of the screen effect. Others simply do not provide this option; don't worry if you

don't see it for each screen effect selected. Notice that you can also select your Pictures folder. If you select the Pictures folder, the pictures found in the folder are displayed on the screen in a rotating order.

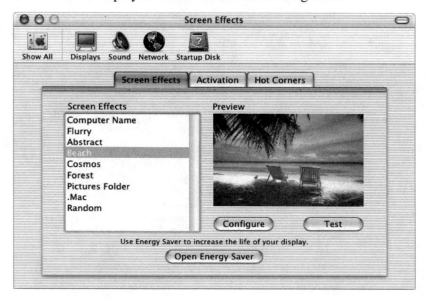

TIP   *You do not actually need to use a screen effect—they are for entertainment purposes only. In the past, an unattended monitor could suffer from "screen burn," but today's monitors are not affected by this problem.*

The screen effect starts too quickly, after a very long time, or never

Cause   The screen effect is designed to give your monitor something pretty or interesting to display when you are not using your computer. Once you stop using your computer, an internal clock tracks the time that passes. Then, at a configured time, the screen effect begins. However, you can control how much idle time goes by before the screen effect starts, or you can simply not use one at all.

The Painkiller   To adjust the amount of time that passes before the screen effect begins, follow these steps:

1. On the Dock, click the System Preferences icon. If you can't find it there, click Apple | System Preferences.

2. The System Preferences window appears. In the Personal category, click the Screen Effects icon.

3. Click the Activation tab, shown in the following illustration. Adjust the slider bar to set the amount of time you want to pass before the screen effect begins. If you do not want to use a screen effect at all, use the Never setting.

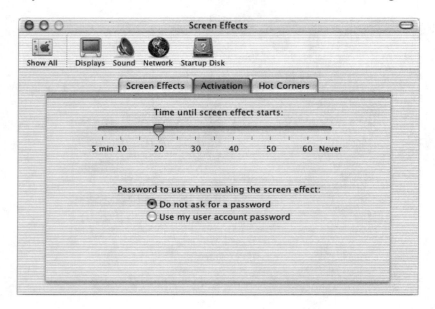

The screen effect asks me for a password every time I try to wake the computer

Cause The screen effect has a protection feature that requires a user account password to wake it from sleep. This feature, which is tied to the screen effect, protects your computer if you are away from it so that other people cannot access it. If this feature is unneeded or annoying, though, you can stop it.

The Painkiller To stop the password wake feature, follow these steps:

1. On the Dock, click the System Preferences icon. If you can't find it there, click Apple | System Preferences.

2. The System Preferences window appears. In the Personal category, click the Screen Effects icon.

3. On the Activation tab, click the Do Not Ask For A Password radio button.

Stealing Screen Effect Shots

Many of the screen effects are simply JPEG pictures that are stored in the System | Library | Screen Savers folder, but some are actual programs. If you open the Screen Savers folder, you can hold down CONTROL and click one of the folders you see there. On the menu that appears, click Show Package Contents. Another window appears listing the pictures in the folder. You can copy one of the pictures you like and store it in your Pictures folder for use as a desktop picture. Pretty cool!

TIP   *You can find a number of free screen effects for OS X on the Web. Search for them using your favorite search engine. A good place to start is www.epicware.com.*

 ## My Mac goes to sleep too soon, too late, or not at all

Cause   OS X has energy-saving features that govern when the Mac goes to sleep or whether it sleeps at all. You may find that although your computer has a screen effect, the effect never starts working because the computer goes to sleep too quickly. Or, you may feel that too much time goes by before the computer goes to sleep. Keep in mind that energy-saving features are just that—features to help you conserve power. However, if the settings do not work for you, you can easily change them.

The Painkiller   To adjust the energy savings, follow these steps:

1. On the Dock, click the System Preferences icon. If you can't find it there, click Apple | System Preferences.

2. The System Preferences window appears. In the Hardware section, click the Energy Saver icon.

3. In the Energy Saver window that appears, as shown in the following illustration, adjust the slider bar to determine how much idle time passes before the computer goes to sleep. Notice that you can configure a separate sleep time for the monitor if desired.

4. On the Options tab, shown in the following illustration, note that you can have the computer wake when the modem detects a ring or when a network

administrator accesses the computer. You also can have the computer restart automatically after a power failure. Simply click the check boxes to use any of these options if desired.

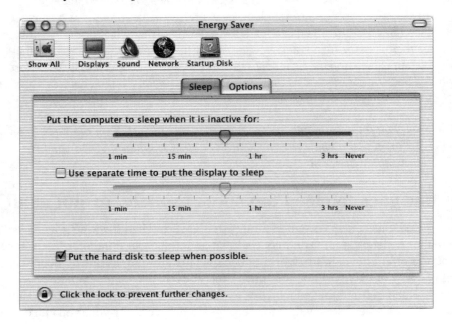

OS X Dock Headaches

OS X provides a new desktop feature called the Dock, which has been admired and cursed by Mac users since OS X's release. The *Dock*, shown in the following illustration, is simply a launcher area for programs, files you use a lot, and different disks. Residing by default at the bottom of your screen, it also contains the Trash and gives you quick access to the Finder. The Dock is divided by an almost invisible vertical bar that keeps things organized. All of the programs appear on the left of the Dock, while documents, folders, disks, files, and anything else other than a program goes to the right side.

Overall, the Dock is easy to use, but a few configuration items can be really annoying. Read on....

I can't manage stuff on the Dock

Cause   The Dock is a rather versatile OS X feature, and you can manage items on the Dock with a little practice. At first, though, how to manage those problems may not seem readily apparent. I'll admit, when I first saw the Dock, I thought, "What am I supposed to do with this thing?" The good news is that you can manage the Dock in a lot of ways, and the more you use it, the more you will like it.

The Painkiller   To manage the Dock, practice the following tasks:

- You can drag items on and off the Dock. If an item will not drag off the Dock, the item is open. CONTROL-click the item on the Dock (or click and hold down the mouse key), and a menu pops out, as shown in the following illustration. Click Quit.

- You can rearrange items on the Dock by simply dragging them around to different places. However, keep in mind that applications always stay to the left of the Dock and everything else goes to the right.

- If you need to open an item that is on the Dock, click it once and it opens. A triangle appears under opened Dock items.

- If you store items on the Dock that contain subfolders, you can CONTROL-click or just hold down the mouse key on the icon to see the subfolders. For example, as you can see in the following illustration, I keep my personal folder on the desktop for easy access to all of my files!

Pop-out menus will only display 96 items. So, if you have a folder that has more than 96 items, you can only see the first 96 from the Dock pop-out menu. The items are not gone; it is just that the Dock can't display them all.

- Programs that are open appear on the left side of the Dock automatically. They disappear once the program is closed. However, if you want to keep a program on the Dock all the time, whether it is open or closed, just CONTROL-click or hold down the mouse key over the icon when it is on the Dock and click Keep In Dock.

- You can drag any item off the Dock to remove it from the Dock (when you release your mouse key, it disappears in a cloud of smoke). However, you can't remove the Finder or Trash icon—or anything that is currently open.

The Dock is too big or too small

Cause   The Dock's default size may not work for you. The items on the Dock may be too small for you to read, or you may find that the Dock takes up too much room on your desktop. If you have a lot of items on the Dock, you may find that you can't see them all. You can adjust the Dock's size to meet your needs, though, so you need to play around with the feature to find the size that works for you.

The Painkiller   To change the size of the Dock, follow these steps:

1. On the Dock, click the System Preferences icon. If you can't find it there, click Apple | System Preferences.

2. The System Preferences window appears. In the Personal section, click the Dock icon.

3. In the Dock window, shown in the following illustration, adjust the slider bar to increase or reduce the Dock size.

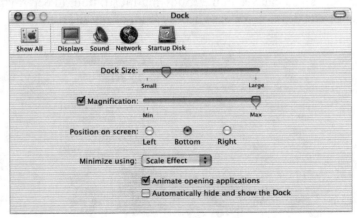

The Dock's icons are too large when I hover over them

Cause   The Dock's icons grow larger when you move over them with your mouse. This feature, called magnification, causes the Dock items to jump at you. Depending on your point of view, you may find this nice or weird. The idea is to magnify the item you are pointing at so you can see it better, then click the item to open it. However, you can adjust the magnification feature however you like.

The Painkiller   To adjust the magnification setting, follow these steps:

1. On the Dock, click the System Preferences icon. If you can't find it there, click Apple | System Preferences.

2. The System Preferences window appears. In the Personal section, click the Dock icon.

3. In the Dock window, adjust the magnification slider bar as desired. If you do not want any magnification at all, just click the Magnification selection box to turn it off.

I do not want the Dock at the bottom of my screen

Cause   By default, the Dock lives at the bottom of your screen. The idea is to give you one place at the bottom of your screen to access items. However, you might need the bottom of your screen for other items, so OS X gives you some flexibility here. You can move the Dock to the right or left side of your screen rather than the bottom (but you can't put it on top).

The Painkiller   To change the location of the Dock, follow these steps:

1. On the Dock, click the System Preferences icon. If you can't find it there, click Apple | System Preferences.

2. The System Preferences window appears. In the Personal section, click the Dock icon.

3. In the Dock window, choose the left or right radio buttons under Position On Screen.

Items minimize to the Dock too slowly

Cause   The Dock contains two effects that move items back to the Dock when they are minimized. The first option, called Genie Effect, shrinks the window so that it looks like it is shrinking to the Dock (the same way a genie would return to a bottle). However, this option takes a little longer. If the genie is too slow for you, you can set a scale option that makes the window drop back into the Dock.

The Painkiller   To change minimization to scale, follow these steps:

1. On the Dock, click the System Preferences icon. If you can't find it there, click Apple | System Preferences.

2. The System Preferences window appears. In the Personal section, click the Dock icon.

3. In the Dock window, choose the Scale Effect option in the Minimize Using menu.

> **NOTE**   *Remember, if you have several items open, you can simply click the Dock icon for the item you want to bring to the foreground. A triangle under the icons tells you what items are currently open.*

 # I want the Dock to disappear when not in use

Cause   By default, the Dock is always present. However, you can have it disappear when you are not using it. When you want the Dock to reappear, just move your mouse to its location and it reappears on the screen.

The Painkiller   To autohide the Dock, follow these steps:

1. On the Dock, click the System Preferences icon. If you can't find it there, click Apple | System Preferences.

2. The System Preferences window appears. In the Personal section, click the Dock icon.

3. In the Dock window, click the Automatically Hide And Show Dock check box.

> **TIP**   *Don't like those bouncing Dock icons when you open an item? No problem. On the Dock window, just clear the Animate Opening Applications selection box.*

Finder Toolbar Headaches

At the top of each Finder window there is the new Finder toolbar that has appeared in OS X. The good news is that the Finder toolbar is generally easy to use and is helpful in "finding" the items you are most likely to need, as you can see in the following illustration.

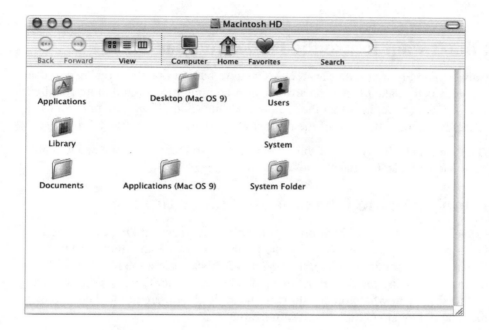

OS X gives you the following standard toolbar options:

- **Back / Forward**   As you move through different folders, you can use the Back / Forward buttons to move back and forth—just as you would when using a web browser. You can also use the Go menu to move backward and forward.

- **View**   The click-button view controls enable you to change the appearance of the folder items to icons, lists, or columns. You can click them any time to make the change, and you can use the View menu to change them as well.

- **Computer**   This option opens a window containing disk icons, the network file system, any mounted shares, and related information.

- ■ **Home**   This option opens your Home folder.

- ■ **Favorites**   This option opens your favorites list.

- ■ **Applications**   This option opens the Applications folder.

 Computer, Home, Favorites, and Applications are all found on the Go menu as well.

I don't want to use the Finder toolbar

Cause   The Finder toolbar is an OS X feature but not one that you have to use. The idea is to make navigation around your computer easier and more flexible. The problem, though, is that the toolbar takes up room. If you are pressed for space, consider getting rid of the toolbar altogether.

The Painkiller   To get rid of the Finder toolbar so that you do not see it at all, click View | Hide Toolbar.

I don't like the icons on the Finder toolbar

Cause   The default toolbar options are simply guesses that OS X is giving to you—however, you can customize the toolbar to include any items you want. When the programmers at Apple wrote OS X, they took some liberties with the toolbar by placing the default icons on it. These commonly used icons are really just to show you what you can do with the toolbar. You are not locked into using them, and they are completely customizable.

The Painkiller   To customize the toolbar, follow these steps:

1. Click View | Customize Toolbar.

2. In the Customize Toolbar window, shown in the following illustration, drag and drop the desired icons on and off the toolbar until you have the items that you want. When you are finished, click Done.

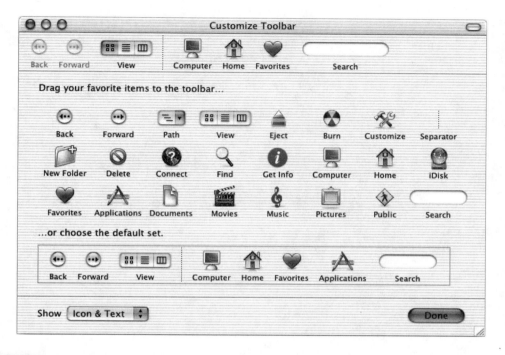

Drag your favorite items to the toolbar...

...or choose the default set.

TIP *Do you really need to save some space? No problem. In the Customize Toolbar window, click the Show menu at the very bottom and click Text Only. The icons you placed on the toolbar now appear with the text instead of the icons, which can save you some real estate.*

Chapter 2

Windows, Folders, Files, and Trash Headaches

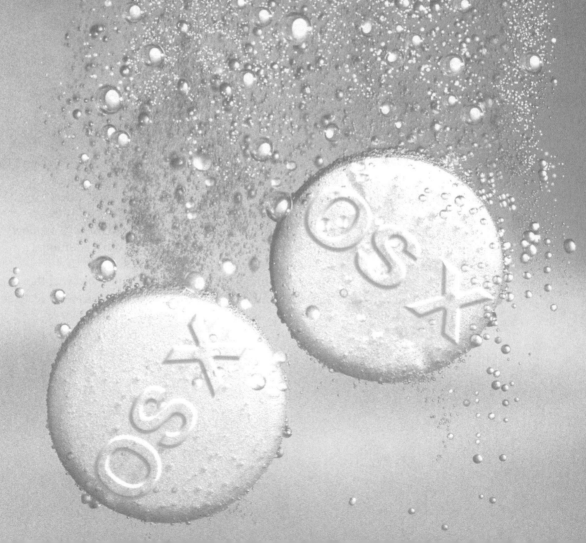

In this chapter, you'll cure...

- ■ Window aggravations
- ■ Folder and file problems
- ■ Trash troubles

As you work with OS X, a large portion of the work (and play) that you do involves the use of windows, folders, and files, as well as getting rid of items using the Trash. These items enable you to use the operating system but also to manage your own files as needed. As you might imagine, working with windows, folders, files, and the Trash isn't all that complicated, especially if you have used the Mac before. However, if you are new to the Mac, and particularly to OS X, you may run into a number of headaches that you can't cure. Most of these headaches aren't critical—they're just those nagging pains that cause you aggravation more than anything else. Don't worry, though. In this chapter, we explore OS X's use of windows, folders, files, and the Trash, and you learn how to cure those headaches in a hurry. I also throw a few cool tips and tricks your way, as well!

Window Headaches

A *window* is essentially a picture of what is inside of a folder. In a real sense, a window appears when you open a folder of some kind and shows you what is in the folder. From the window, you can open files and even other folders, if they exist in the window. If you open your Macintosh HD, you are looking at a window, shown in the following illustration. From that window, you can open additional folders, such as Applications, Users, System, Documents, and so forth. If you double-click one of the folders in the window, the window changes to reveal the contents of the new folder. You can use the Back and Forward buttons to navigate through various folders as needed—all using a single window.

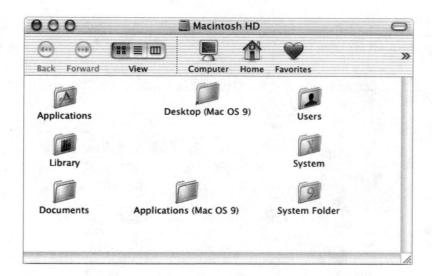

 If you are using OS X for the first time and you are a previous Mac user, the single window approach may confuse you a bit at first. In the past, when you opened a folder, you saw a window. When you opened a folder within that window, another window appeared. If you kept going, you ended up at a screen full of windows that could make you dizzy. In an effort to cut down on screen clutter, OS X opens all folders in the same window. You can use the Back and Forward buttons to move between them. This single interface is designed to make the desktop less cluttered and confusing. However, keep in mind that this feature works from one folder to the next in a hierarchy; if you open the Macintosh HD and then open the Trash, you see two different windows because those two folders do not reside in the same hierarchy.

A window seems grayed out: I can't use it

Cause   If you have two or more individual windows open on the desktop, only one window is "active" at any time. The title bar on the active window appears in color, and the title bar on the inactive window or windows appear grayed out. As you can see in the following illustration, the Macintosh HD window is active, and the Applications window is inactive.

The Painkiller   If you need to make an inactive window active so you can access resources in the window, just click the title bar of the inactive window. It becomes active and all other windows become inactive.

I see icons in my windows, but I need to see a list

Cause   OS X displays the contents of windows as icons by default. However, you have a number of options available to you on the View menu on the desktop toolbar. Market research tells Apple that most people prefer to work with icons. However, if you have a folder with a bunch of items, icons can be a real pain. For example, let's say you love digital photography (as I do). You may have a folder that holds 50 or more photos. When you open the folder, the window gives you an icon for each one of them, so you have to use the scroll bars a lot to move around and find what you need. However, if you change the view to a list, you can more easily locate what you need. You can also change the view to columns so that you can more easily move around between folders within the same window.

The Painkiller   Click the View menu and select the As List option or the As Columns option. As you can see in the following illustration (a list), the items appear with a small icon and are organized in alphabetical order by their names. If you click the arrow in the Name field, shown by the mouse pointer in the following illustration, you can even view the items in reverse order.

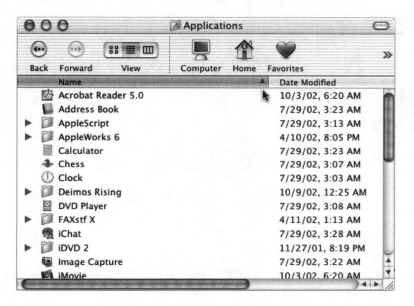

TIP

You can also use the buttons in the toolbar that indicate icon, list, and column view. Additionally, you can click and sort any of the columns in the list view.

I don't like the way windows minimize to the Dock

Cause   When you click the yellow minimize button in a window, it shrinks and collapses onto the Dock. When you need to open it again, you just click it on the Dock and it jumps back to life. By default, the minimize feature uses a Genie Effect to make the window disappear to the Dock. However, you can change this feature and use a scale effect instead.

The Painkiller   To stop using the Genie Effect, you need to edit the Dock properties, found in System Preferences. You can learn more about editing the Dock properties and how to solve this particular headache in Chapter 1.

Quick Move for Browsing Folders

As you are browsing a hierarchy of folders, the folders all open in the same window. Let's say you are five folders deep. To get back to the top, you have to press the Back button five times, right? Well, you can do it that way, but there is an easier way to move. At the top of a window toolbar, you see the name of the folder and a small icon. If you hold down COMMAND and click the name with your mouse, a menu of the previous folders pops out, as you can see in the following illustration. Just click the folder you want to return to and the window changes back!

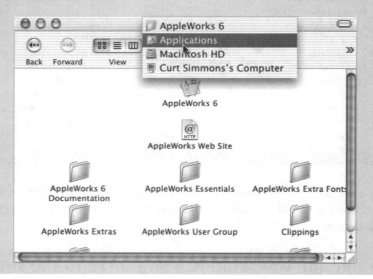

 # A window is too large or too small

Cause   Windows typically open to a default size on your desktop. However, if you have several windows open, or a particular window holds a lot of items, the window may be too small or too big. That's no problem—you can easily change the size of the window on the fly.

The Painkiller   To change the size of a window, use your mouse to grab and drag the resize box (also called the size control box) found in the lower right-hand corner of each window. When the window is the size that you want, just release your mouse.

There are no scroll bars on my window

Cause   *Scroll bars*, which appear on the right side and at the bottom of a window, enable you to scroll around within a window so that you can see all of the items, as shown in the following illustration.

However, if the window is currently displaying all of the items, no scroll bars appear because they have nowhere to scroll to, as you can see in the following illustration.

The Painkiller   This is normal window behavior, so you don't need to do anything.

I don't like the Finder toolbar

Cause   Each window contains a *Finder toolbar* at the top, which contains the Back and Forward buttons, View option, and other icons, such as Computer, Favorites, Home, and so on. The good news is that the Finder toolbar is completely customizable so that you can change it to meet your needs.

The Painkiller   See Chapter 1 for information and steps on changing the Finder toolbar.

I can't move windows around on my screen

Cause   If you have several windows open on your desktop, you may need to move them around so that you can more easily access what's inside. The trick, though, is that you can move the window only by grabbing the pin-striped portion of the title bar.

The Painkiller   To move a window, just grab any spot on the pin-striped portion of the title bar and drag the window where you want it.

I don't see a status bar on my window

Cause   Each window can display a little *status bar*, shown in the following illustration, that tells you how many items are stored in the folder the window is displaying and how much storage space is available on your computer. Some people don't like to see the status bar but others do, so you can choose whether to display it.

The Painkiller   To show or not show the status bar, click the View menu and choose either Hide Status Bar or Show Status Bar.

I want to be able to see all items in a window quickly

Cause   Windows generally open to a default size, which may show you all of the items in the window or not, depending on the number of items. If you want to be able to see all items in a window, you can resize the window to meet your needs using the resize option, or you can simply use the zoom button, which is the green button found in the upper right-hand corner of each window.

The Painkiller   Click the green zoom button and the window jumps to a size large enough to display all of the items in the window. If the window contains too many items for your desktop to display, the zoom option resizes to show you as many as possible.

Icons in my windows are too large or too small

Cause   OS X gives you a default icon size in your windows, and it even gives you one on the desktop for that matter. However, the default size may not meet your needs. That's no problem, though—you can simply adjust it.

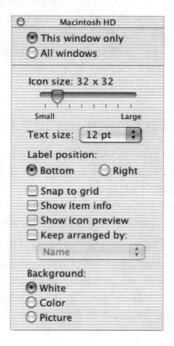

The Painkiller   To adjust the icon size, follow these steps:

1. Click View | Show View Options.

2. In the View window that appears, shown in the illustration, you can apply your changes to the current window you are using (This Window Only) or to all windows, by clicking the desired radio button. Then, simply move the slider bar to adjust the icon size as desired. You can also adjust the icon text size so that it is larger or smaller, as well. When you're done, just close the box.

I can't manage window columns in a list

Cause   You can choose to display window items in a list by clicking View | As List, or even View | Columns, if you want the column feature. When you view items as a list, the window contains the items and some additional columns with more information about those items. However, you can control what columns are used.

The Painkiller   To manage columns in a list, follow these steps:

1. Open a window and choose View | As List. Then click View | Show View Options.

2. In the View window that appears, you see the column options that are available, such as Date Modified, Date Created, Size, Kind, Version, and Comments. You can choose to display any of these (or none, if you like) by simply selecting the ones you want displayed, as you can see in the following illustration.

 List columns are too large or too small

Cause   The columns provided when you use the list feature typically provide enough room to display all of the information in the column. However, that may not be the case, and the columns more typically are so spread out that you have to scroll around a lot to see everything. However, you can easily adjust the width of the column to close up some space.

The Painkiller   On the Title of the column, you see a small separator line separating the column from other columns. Move your mouse to the separator line, which changes your mouse cursor to arrows, as you can see in the following illustration. Grab the separator line and drag the column to the left or right in order to increase or decrease the size of the column.

I don't like the order of the columns

Cause   You can select which columns you want to display in a window by clicking View | Show View Options. However, the order the columns are displayed in the window may not meet your needs. For example, you may want to see the item displayed, followed by the Comments about the item. That's no problem— you can rearrange the column order.

The Painkiller   To rearrange the column order, grab a column title with your mouse and then simply drag the column to the new location in the window where you want it to appear. Continue this process until all the columns are in the order you want.

I want to change the color of the window background

Cause   If you want to jazz up your windows a bit, you can choose a different background for the window. This option, which is available only if you are viewing your window contents as icons, enables you to choose a solid color of your choice or even a picture.

The Painkiller To change the background of a window, follow these steps.

1. Open a window and choose View | As Icons. Then click View | Show View Options.

2. In the View window that appears, you see the Background option at the bottom of the window. Select Color to choose a solid color, as shown in the following illustration, or Picture to select a picture. Click the Select button that appears and choose the picture you want to display. Once you select the picture, the window uses the image as a background picture.

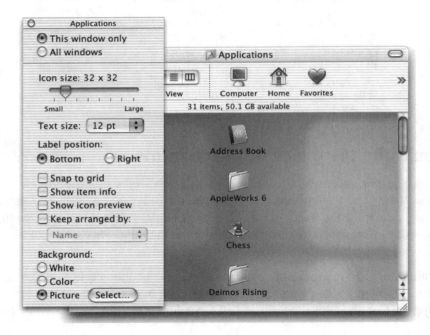

TIP *If you want the background picture to apply to all windows, click the All Windows option at the top of the View Options box, as you can see in the previous illustration.*

Managing Folder and File Headaches

Folders are simply storage locations on your Mac—they give you an easy way to organize information and keep things in a place where you can actually find them.

You can create any number of folders. You might have a folder called Finances where you keep spreadsheets concerning bank accounts and stocks, or you might have a folder called Writing where you keep letters and other files you create. Use them in any way that is helpful to you.

For the most part, dealing with folders is quite easy. However, before we get into the few headaches you may run into, you must know a few important items. Mac OS X is a multi-user operating system. This means that more than one person can use the Mac and keep all of his or her documents, files, and settings separate from those of other people using the Mac. Because OS X is a multi-user system, the Mac creates a Home folder for your account. You can find this in the Users folder, as you can see in the following illustration. Within that folder, OS X gives you a few default folders to help you get organized, such as Pictures, Documents, Movies, Music, and so forth. You can use these folders or create new ones.

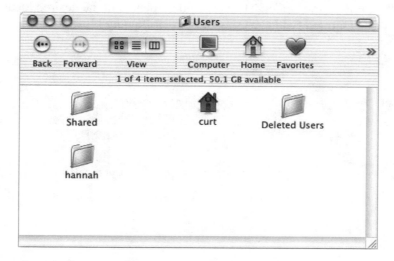

However, before you get carried away, you must also understand that OS X has two different kinds of user accounts: Administrator and Normal. If you are an Administrator, you can create new folders anywhere. If you are a Normal account user, you can only create new accounts within your Home folder. I've included an entire chapter on User Headaches, so see Chapter 3 to learn more about the limitations of the Normal account and the differences between a Normal User and an Administrator.

I can't create a new folder

Cause   In order to create a new folder, you use the File menu. If you are an Administrator, you can create a new folder basically anywhere you want. If you are a Normal user, open your Home folder in the Users folder. You can create new folders in this location.

The Painkiller   To create a new folder, follow these steps:

1. If you are creating a new folder within your home folder, open your Home folder. If you want to create a subfolder in an existing folder, open that folder as well. For example, if you want to create a new folder in your Pictures folder, open the Pictures folder.

2. Click File | New Folder. The new folder appears in the desired location and is titled Untitled Folder, as shown in the following illustration.

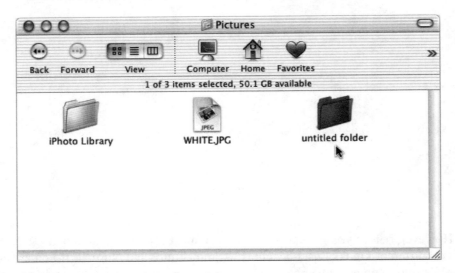

3. Double-click the folder name. A cursor appears so that you can change the name of the folder, as desired.

Folder Mania

As you are working with folders, it is good to think of an operating system folder the same way you think of a paper folder you would put in a filing cabinet. Folders are designed to help you organize and store information—but too much of a good thing tends to be more confusing than helpful. You can create as many folders as you need, and you can create subfolders within subfolders within subfolders... You get the picture. The point to remember is that folders are there to help you; if you have too many folders, they can be quite confusing. Try to keep the number of folders you use to a minimum. This makes finding data easier and helps you control "folder clutter."

PREVENTION *You can give more than one folder the same name, but you can't store the two folders in the same location. For example, you can't store two folders called Vacation in the Pictures folder, but you can store one in the Pictures folder and one in the Documents folder.*

I can't make an alias

Cause   An *alias* is basically a shortcut—it enables you to store a folder or file in a particular location but create a shortcut to it in another location for easy access. For example, let's say you have a folder called My Folder. This folder resides within your Documents folder. However, you would like to be able to access this folder from your Desktop without actually moving the folder there. The answer is to create an alias. You can make an alias for the folder, put the alias where you want, and use the alias to open the folder. The real folder still resides in the same location—you have simply created a shortcut to it.

The Painkiller   To create an alias, follow these steps:

1. Hold down CONTROL and click the desired folder or file. In the menu that appears, as shown in the following illustration, click Make Alias. Or, you

can simply hold down OPTION and COMMAND and drag the file or folder to the desired location. An alias is made automatically.

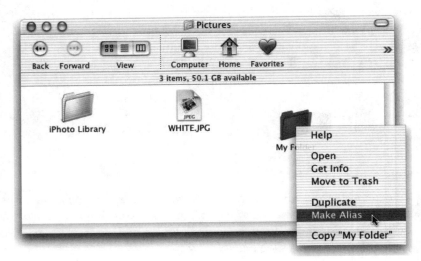

2. The Alias folder appears. Drag the alias to the desired location, such as your Desktop. Notice in the illustration that the title of the folder has changed to My Folder Alias and that a small arrow on the folder notes that the folder is an alias folder.

TIP   *Remember, you can put aliases almost anywhere for easy access—even on the Dock!*

When I try to open an alias, I get a message saying "The alias could not be opened because the original item cannot be found"

Cause   Aliases are simply shortcuts, or pointers, to the real folder or file. When you open an alias, OS X looks for the real folder or file, which must be stored where it was when you created the alias. For example, let's say you have a folder called Vacation stored in your Pictures folder. You create an alias for this folder and put it on your desktop. Later, you move the Vacation folder from the Pictures folder to a

CD-RW disk. When you try to open the alias, guess what? The Vacation folder is no longer in Pictures, where the alias says it should be. You can move aliases and target files or folders around on the same disk, but you can't move them between disks.

 *You can't copy an alias to a CD or floppy disk and then expect to be able to open the file you want. The real file is still on the hard drive, not on the CD or floppy disk!*

The Painkiller   If a folder or file that has an alias has been moved, you can either delete the old alias and create a new one or edit the alias so that it points to the correct location.

To edit the alias, follow these steps:

1. Select the Alias and then click File | Get Info. The Get Info box appears, as shown in the following illustration.

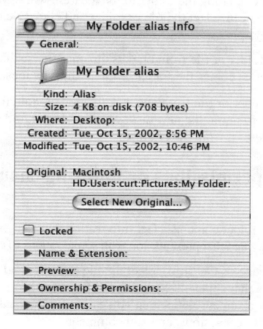

2. Click the Select New Original button. A browse window appears so you can locate the folder or file and select it. Select the desired file or folder and click Choose. This updates the alias information about the location of the folder or file.

I can't drag a folder or file to a different location, or I can't move or copy a folder or file

Cause   As you are working with folders and files, it is important to remember that a few basic rules apply and that some of these rules are different from those in previous versions of Mac OS. So, if you are trying to move or copy a folder or file from one location from another, make sure you understand how Mac OS X handles these operations.

The Painkiller   These rules apply to moving and copying:

- Dragging a folder or file from one location to another on the same disk moves the folder or file.

- To copy a folder or file from one location to another on the same disk, hold down OPTION and drag the folder to the location where you want the copy made. Or, you can select the file or folder and click File | Duplicate. Then drag the copy.

- Dragging a folder or file from one disk to another (such as from a CD to your hard drive) copies the folder or file to the new location.

- To move a folder or file from one disk to another, hold down COMMAND and drag the folder to the new disk. This moves the folder or file to the new disk and deletes it from the old disk.

 ## I can't make permissions or indexing changes to a folder or file

Cause   Each file or folder contains a Get Info feature that can give you information about the file or folder and that presents you with some options to change certain items.

The Painkiller   To access Get Info, select the file or folder and click File | Get Info. In the Info box that appears, expand the different categories as desired and make any necessary changes. Notice that you can index the contents of a folder for faster searching, edit permissions, and add comments.

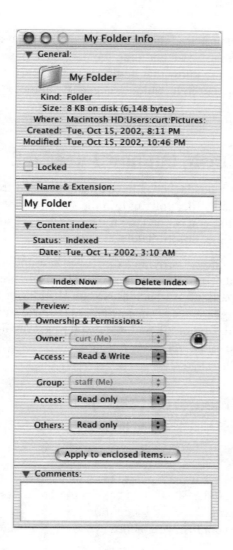

Trash Headaches

Ah, the Trash—that wonderful wastepaper basket you see on the Dock where you can get rid of items that you no longer need. The Trash is a valuable part of OS X, as it has been in previous versions of Mac operating systems. For the most part, the Trash continues to be easy to use and manage in OS X. To move items to the Trash,

simply drag them there and drop them. To get something out of the Trash, simply open the Trash and drag the item back out. In fact, OS X even lets you know that items are in the Trash by showing crumpled paper in it, which you can see in the following illustration. However, a few headaches can come your way when using the Trash. Read on...

I emptied the Trash, but now I need a file back

Cause   Oh yes, this is a headache we have all experienced from time to time. You think you no longer need a file, you put it in the Trash, and you empty the Trash. Later on, you realize that you needed the file after all. This simple human error happens from time to time, unfortunately.

The Painkiller   OS X doesn't provide a direct workaround for recovering deleted Trash items, I'm afraid. The only way to recover items that have been deleted is possibly with a third-party utility, such as Norton Utilities or Micromat Drive X. Even then, you are not guaranteed. The key tactics to make sure this doesn't happen to you are to be careful, first of all, and to consider backing up all files to a CD before they are deleted—just in case.

Quick Usage Tips for Trash

As you are using the Trash, keep the following points in mind:

- Items remain in the Trash until you empty it. Once the Trash is emptied, the items in the Trash are erased from the hard disk. To empty the Trash, CONTROL-click the Trash and click Empty Trash from the menu that appears. Or, you can click Finder | Empty Trash. A message appears asking you to confirm your action.

- To move an item to the Trash without having to drag it, highlight the icon for the item and then press COMMAND and DELETE on your keyboard.

- If you accidentally put an item in the Trash, you can open it and drag it out. If putting the item in the Trash was the last thing you did, you can either click Edit | Undo or press COMMAND-Z on your keyboard.

■ If you do not want to see the confirmation message when emptying the Trash, hold down OPTION when you click Finder | Empty Trash. Or, you can permanently stop this behavior by clicking Finder | Preferences and clearing the option to Show Warning Before Emptying The Trash, as you can see in the following illustration.

Finder Preferences

Show these items on the Desktop:
- ☑ Hard disks
- ☑ Removable media (such as CDs)
- ☑ Connected servers

New Finder Window shows:
- ○ Home
- ⊙ Computer

- ☐ Always open folders in a new window
- ☐ Open new windows in Column View

- ☑ Spring–loaded folders and windows
  Delay: ──────●────────
  Short   Medium   Long
  Press the Space bar to open immediately.

- ☑ Show warning before emptying the Trash
- ☐ Always show file extensions

Languages for searching file contents:
(Select...)

I want to make sure a file cannot be put in the Trash

Cause   Although you can't directly retrieve a deleted file, you can take some steps to make sure a file is never lost. First and foremost, consider using a CD to copy important files as a backup. As I am writing this book, I always copy each chapter to a CD as soon as I'm done. I then e-mail my editor a copy. At any given moment,

I have the original file and a CD backup of the file, and my editor has a copy as well. You can't be too careful.

However, you can also lock a file so that it cannot be moved to the Trash.

The Painkiller   To lock a file so it cannot be moved to the Trash, follow these steps:

1. Select the file and click File | Get Info. The Get Info box appears, as you can see in the following illustration.

2. Click the Locked option. This locks the file so that you cannot put it into the Trash.

Chapter 3

User Headaches

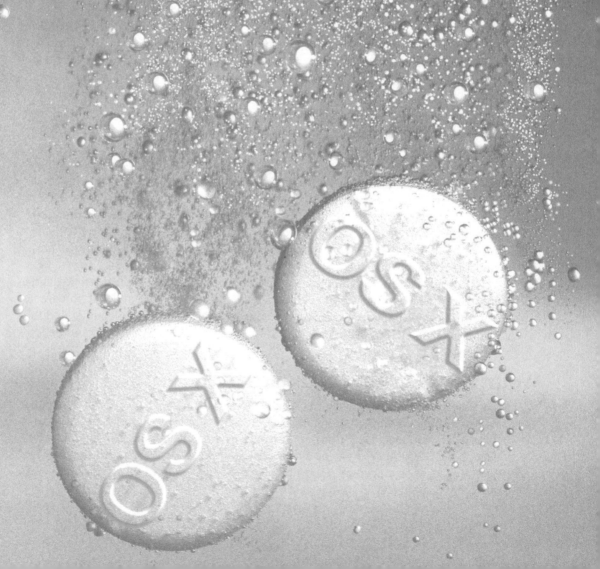

In this chapter, you'll cure…

- ■ User headaches
- ■ Multi-user environment difficulties

In the olden days of computing (OK, only a few years ago), the Mac was seen as an individual's computer. This meant you would have your own Macintosh, and that single computer was "all yours." The truth then, and certainly now, is that the Mac didn't give you a way to manage multiple users. Sure, you could have many people using the same Mac, but you all used the same desktop, often changing things and even fumbling with each other's documents, files, and other stuff. Even in a home environment where multiple family members used a Mac, they found that the single-user concept made it a lot like sharing a bedroom—everyone's stuff got all mixed up and they tended to get in each other's way.

Mac OS 9 tried to fix some of these problems by offering a users option, but OS X completely turns the tables and makes the Mac a multi-user operating system. This means that several different people can log on and use the same Mac but keep their settings and files separate. For example, with user accounts, each user configures his or her desktop and Dock settings, creates files, stores them, creates new folders, and does just about anything else. When the next user logs on, he or she can do the same without interfering with anything the first user did, and so forth. The concept of a multi-user system is certainly nothing new—in fact, all major new operating systems today (including Linux / Unix and Windows) are multi-user systems.

However, configuring and managing user accounts can be a little tricky, and a number of headaches certainly can come your way. Some are major if you are not careful. In this chapter, we'll explore the headaches you might encounter and the solutions you need to make your multi-user environment all that it should be.

Your User Account Headaches

As you are using OS X, you are using an account—even if you are not aware that you are doing so. In fact, the multi-user environment is always present; you can't turn it off. You may say, "But I am the only user of this computer." That may be true, but OS X still sees you as a user, and your personal files and settings are stored in your user account. Don't believe me? Just open the Macintosh HD and then open the Users folder, shown in the following illustration. You see a house icon with your user name listed there. That's right—you're a user after all.

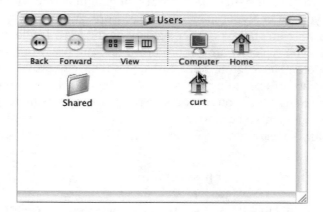

If you open your user folder, you see the folders that relate to your user account settings, such as Desktop, Movies, Documents, Music, Pictures, and so forth, as shown in the following illustration. These folders hold the settings that you make in OS X (such as your desktop, screen effect, Dock settings, and so on) and your files, such as Documents, Pictures, Movies, Music, and so forth. All of the configuration changes you make in OS X and all of your "stuff" is kept in these folders.

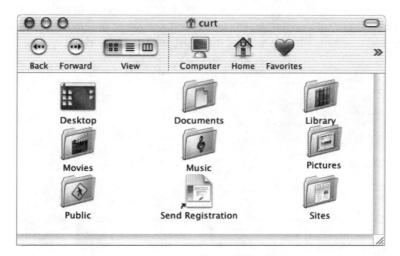

For the most part, you don't need to do anything in order to manage your user account—OS X takes care of that for you. However, a few headaches can come your way....

I can't change my password

Cause   When you first installed OS X (or if you bought a Mac with OS X pre-installed), you entered your name and a password. Although you may not have realized it, you were creating your user account on the Mac. If you are the only user of the Mac, you typically are not prompted for your password, even when you start your computer. However, in some cases, you'll have to provide the password (such as in the case of upgrading OS X to OS X Jaguar). If you need to change your password at any time, you can do so easily. However, if there are multiple users on your computer, you cannot change another user's password unless you are an Administrator. To learn more, see the "Multi-User Headaches" section later in this chapter.

The Painkiller   To change your password, follow these steps:

1. On the Dock, click the System Preferences icon. If you can't seem to find it there, click Apple menu | System Preferences.

2. The System Preferences window appears. In the Personal section of the window, click My Account.

3. The Desktop window appears, shown in the following illustration. Click the Change button to change your password. As you can see in the following illustration, you'll need to enter your existing password and then enter and verify the new password you want to use. You can enter a password hint if you want. Click OK when you're done.

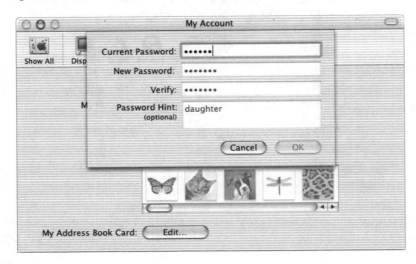

I want to change my account picture

Cause If you open the My Account option under Personal in System Preferences, you see an option to associate a picture with your password. The picture option links your account with a particular picture, which appears on the login screen when you first start OS X.

The Painkiller In order to change an account picture, follow these steps:

1. On the Dock, click the System Preferences icon. If you can't find it there, click Apple | System Preferences.

2. The System Preferences window appears. In the Personal section of the window, click My Account.

3. In the My Account window, shown in the following illustration, click a picture from the list under the My Picture box, or click the Choose Another button to select a picture of your choice. If you want to use another picture, you can also just drag the picture to the My Picture box, and OS X automatically scales it for you.

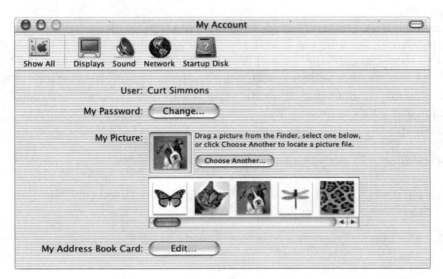

Customizing Your Account Picture

When you set your login Picture, you probably noticed that you can click the Choose Another button and select a picture that you want. The picture you select is completely up to you. In fact, here is a fun thing you can do. Use a picture of yourself, preferably a head and shoulders shot, as your account picture. You can repeat this process for other users; when the login screen appears, you only need to click the picture of yourself to log on. Of course, this doesn't do anything specifically, but it makes your Mac more customized and interesting.

OS X doesn't display the login screen when I start the computer

Cause   If you are the only user on your Mac, the system has probably configured your account for automatic login. This means that when you start the Mac, you are automatically logged in to your user account and password without any involvement from you. This is a nice feature that keeps you from having to enter your password each time you start the Mac. However, this also means that anyone else can start your computer as well. You are automatically logged in, so the Mac doesn't know whether you have started the computer or someone else has started it. So, you may want to stop automatic login from working and set it so that you have to enter your password when logging in. This is a good security feature, if you need it.

The Painkiller   To stop automatic login, follow these steps:

1. On the Dock, click the System Preferences icon. If you can't find it there, click Apple | System Preferences.

2. The System Preferences window appears. In the System section of the window, click Accounts.

3. In the Users window, shown in the following illustration, uncheck the Log In Automatically check box.

 *If you decide that you want to use automatic login again at a later time, just return to the Accounts page of System Preferences and click the Set Auto Login button. Enter your password, and automatic login turns back on.*

Multi-User Headaches

With OS X, multiple users can log onto the Mac, each keeping his or her own settings, files, documents, pictures, and most other things that make using the Mac unique. Of course, managing a multi-user environment can certainly give you some headaches, especially until your feet are on solid ground with certain concepts.

So, let's get the main concept out of the way right now. The Mac gives you two different kinds of user accounts: Administrator accounts and Normal accounts. If you installed OS X (or purchased a new Mac with it pre-installed), you entered your name and a password. OS X saw you as the first user and assigned your account as an Administrator account. An Administrator account is just as it sounds—the Administrator is the one in charge of the Mac. So, what can the Administrator do? Just about anything.

- The Administrator can create and delete user accounts.

- The Administrator can create another Administrator account.

- The Administrator can install new programs in the Applications folder.

- ■ The Administrator can make changes to all System Preferences options.

- ■ The Administrator can use the Disk Utility programs and NetInfo Manager.

- ■ The Administrator can create new folders outside of the Administrator's folder (also called the Home folder).

- ■ The Administrator can install fonts to the Library folder.

As you can see, the Administrator has the power to administer, or manage, the Mac. So what about the second account? The second kind of account is called a Normal account. The Normal account is designed for everyone who is not an Administrator. The Normal account gives a user power over his or her home folder, but not much else. The Normal user can change a few System Preferences options (such as the Desktop, Screen Effect, and so on), but outside of this, the Normal user cannot make changes that affect the whole system. In fact, the Normal user cannot even create folders outside of his or her home folder. So, is the Normal account too restrictive? Not at all—a typical user can do everything he or she needs to do, without making systemwide changes. This protects the Mac from the hands of those who should not be making changes and keeps you in control.

You might be wondering who is an Administrator on your computer. That's no problem; just open System Preferences and, in the System category, click Accounts. You see a list of accounts. The accounts that are Administrator accounts have the word "Admin" listed in the Type column, as shown in the following illustration. All Normal accounts have nothing listed in the Type column.

Understanding the Root Account

I said that Mac supports two kinds of accounts: Administrator and Normal accounts. That is not entirely true. There is a third account, hidden way down in OS X called the root account. Way down under the nice graphical interface of OS X is the UNIX operating system. UNIX has been around forever, practically, and OS X runs on top of UNIX, giving you a rock-solid stable operating system. Within this UNIX system is the root account, which is also called the superuser account. Basically, the *root account* can do anything and everything, which includes deleting and fiddling with OS X operating system files. It is designed for programmers and those deep in the trenches of OS X, not the rest of us who want to use and enjoy the Mac. So, should you use the root account? Around 99.9 percent of the time, the answer is a resounding no. Watch out—and keep out—should be your motto. However, in the interest of providing information, I'll show you how to log in to it. But beware, you can greatly damage your Mac using the root account (and even completely wreck OS X so that you have to reinstall), so exercise extreme caution if you want to use this account.

1. Log on to OS X with an Administrator account.

2. Open the Applications folder and then the Utilities folder.

3. Open the NetInfo Manager. Click the lock and enter your Administrator password.

4. Choose Security | Enable Root User. You'll be prompted to create a password for the root account.

5. Exit NetInfo Manager.

6. Log out and log back in with the root account.

I can't create a new user

Cause   When you are ready to begin using the multi-user environment by creating a new account or two, you use the Accounts option under System in System Preferences. The Painkiller steps show you how to create a new user, but if you are having access problems, you are probably using a Normal account. In order to create new accounts, you'll need to log out and log back in using an Administrator

account. If you do not have an Administrator account—that is, someone else is the
Administrator—you can't create a new user. Only the Administrator has this power.

The Painkiller   To create a new user, follow these steps:

1. Log in with an Administrator account.

2. Open System Preferences. In the System section, click Accounts.

3. In the Accounts window on the Users tab, click the New User button.

4. In the New User window, enter the name, short name, password, password
   verification, and an optional password hint, shown in the following illustration.
   You can also select a picture if you like (if not, you get a randomly assigned
   one). Notice that you have two additional options:

   ■ **Allow User To Administer This Computer**   If you check this option,
     the user becomes an Administrator, with the same power you have.

   ■ **Allow User To Log In From Windows**   If your Mac resides on a
     network with Windows computers, you can allow a network user to
     log in to the Mac from a Windows computer over the network.

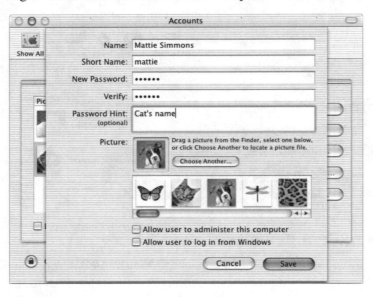

5. Click OK when you are done. The new account is created and now appears
   on the Users tab. When you log off or restart, the option to log on with this
   new account appears on the login page.

Making Passwords Strong

Passwords are only as good as their strength. If your password is so easy that people can guess it, then the guessing user can use your password to log on to OS X. Your name, spouse's name, kids' names, pets' names, phone number, and so on are all common items that are easily guessed and do not make good passwords. So, what makes a really strong password? Keep the following password strength points in mind as you are creating one:

- Effective passwords should be at least seven characters long.

- Include both letters and numbers, such as porche4785.

- The strongest passwords do not make any kind of word or recognizable number, such as jk5ri45.

- Passwords are case-sensitive, so use combinations of uppercase and lowercase letters for more strength.

Of course, you'll have to be able to remember your password, so try to create something that is complex but has some meaning to you and is easy to remember.

I can't change a user's password

Cause   Any Administrator account can change any user's password (including other Administrators' passwords), but if your account is a Normal account, you can change only your own password. To change your password under a Normal account, access the My Account option under Personal in System Preferences. Or, use the Accounts option under System in System Preferences (this way you'll only be able to edit your account, however).

The Painkiller   If you need to change another user's password (or other account data), log on with an Administrator account and follow these steps:

1. Open System Preferences and then click the Accounts option under System.

2. Select the account that you want to change and click Edit User.

3. The user's account window appears. Simply enter a new password and verify the password. Click OK.

You can also change the user's name and picture, or you can change the permission to Administrator or Normal, but notice that you cannot change the short name. This is the account name the system sees, and it cannot be changed.

I have forgotten my Administrator password

Cause   You can change the Administrator password, just as you would on any other account. Log on with the Administrator account and then use Accounts or My Account in System Preferences to change the password. However, what if you are the only user on the computer and you have forgotten your password? Or what if you have an Administrator account and a few Normal accounts, but you have forgotten your password? You cannot change the Administrator password from a Normal account (or any other password except your own), so you have two options:

■ Log on with a different Administrator account if one exists, or have another Administrator log on and change your account password.

■ If there is no other Administrator account, see the Painkiller.

The Painkiller   To change the Administrator password when no other Administrator account is available and you have forgotten your password, follow these steps:

1. Insert the OS X installation CD and start the computer. While restarting, hold down C.

2. When the installer screen appears, choose Installer | Reset Password.

3. On the Reset Password screen, click the hard drive that contains the Administrator account (usually the Macintosh HD). A pop-up menu appears.

4. Enter a new password and verify it. Close the window and restart the computer normally. Now you can log on with the new password.

 *If you are worried about forgetting your Administrator password, consider making another Administrator account with a different password. Then, write down the password and store it in a safe (preferably locked) location. Should you forget the primary Administrator account, you can use the second one to log on. However, in environments where security is a big issue, you really don't want any more Administrator accounts than absolutely necessary, so you'll have to balance your account usage with your own security needs.*

 ## I deleted a user, but now I need to recover user data

Cause If you are logged in as an Administrator, you can delete a user account by accessing Accounts in System Preferences, selecting the account you want to delete, and clicking Delete User. However, what if you delete a user and later determine that you need to recover some data? For example, let's say that the user had some documents. Once you delete the account, the documents are deleted too, right? Well, sort of. Deleted items are actually stored in a Deleted Users folder found in the Users folder. You can open it up and see the file in which the deleted account is stored.

The Painkiller If you need to recover the data from a deleted user account, follow these steps:

1. Open the Deleted Users folder, found in Macintosh HD | Users.
2. Double-click the .dmg file of the deleted user.
3. The user's account file appears on your desktop as a mounted volume.
4. Open the volume and simply drag out the items you want.

 ## I can't manage login options

Cause When you first start OS X, the default action is to provide you with a login window that shows the user's account name and the account picture, if one is selected. When you click the account you want to log in to, the other accounts disappear and a password dialog box appears for you to log in. However, you can use a couple of different options. To change the options, you must be logged in with an Administrator account.

The Painkiller   To change login options, follow these steps:

1. Open System Preferences and click Accounts in System. Click the Login Options tab.

2. On the Login Options tab, shown in the following illustration, you can select the option to show either the Name And Password or List Of Users. You can also choose to hide the Restart and Shut Down buttons. In addition, you can have the system show the password hint (if one is configured in the user's account) after three failed login attempts. You can make any desired selections here.

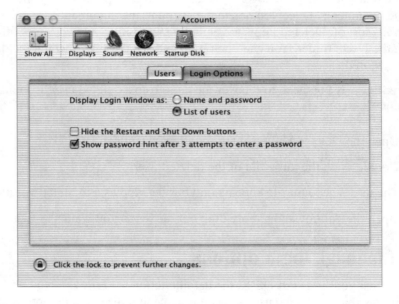

   *You may notice the click lock option in the previous illustration, which appears both on the Login Options tab and on the Users tab. If you want to make certain that no changes are made by Normal users, click the lock. To make changes, click the lock again and enter your password.*

I need to control what a Normal user can do

Cause   A Normal user can do certain things, all using his or her account and folders. However, what if you want to place even more restrictions on a Normal user? Well, you can, assuming you have an Administrator account.

The Painkiller   To place additional restrictions on a Normal user, follow these steps:

1. Open System Preferences and click Accounts in System.

2. On the Users tab, select the Normal user you want to make changes to and click the Capabilities button.

NOTE   *The Capabilities option is grayed out if an Administrator account is selected.*

3. A drop-down menu appears, shown in the following illustration. Use the provided check box options to limit what the user can do. For example, if you do not want the user to remove items from the Dock, simply uncheck the option. If you want to control the applications the user can access, select the option and clear the Allow check box next to the application the user is not allowed to use. When you're done, click OK.

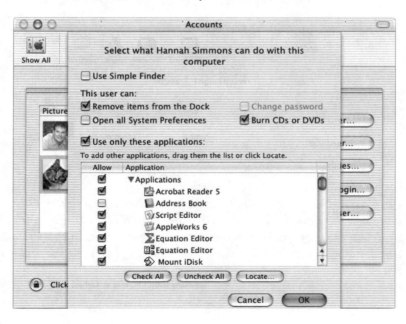

In all walks of life, flexibility usually makes things easier. Make sure you do not restrict a user from using something listed here unless you have real and practical reasons for doing so. If you are too restrictive, you'll hear a lot of complaining and a lot of "Can you help me with…" questions.

But… I need all users to access the same file!

Cause   When I mentioned that all users have their own folders and files tied to their Home folders, you may have felt your heart sink. After all, what if you have a file (or a bunch of files) that all users need to be able to access when logged on? Don't worry, this very real headache is easily cured.

The Painkiller   If you open the Users folder, you'll see a Shared folder, as shown in the following illustration. You can place any shared files and folders in the Shared folder so that any user who is logged on can access them. However, keep in mind that anyone can put files here and take files out. Make sure a file really belongs in this "free for all" folder before putting it there.

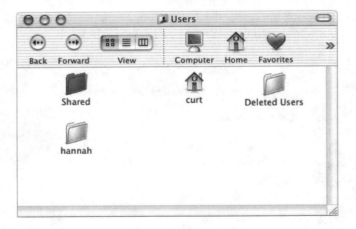

Each user also has a Public folder in his or her Home folder. Other users can open the Public folder and view the items there, but they can't change or delete them. If you have a file that you simply want to show to other users, put it in your public folder and then direct them to the folder to check it out.

Chapter 4

OS X Program Headaches

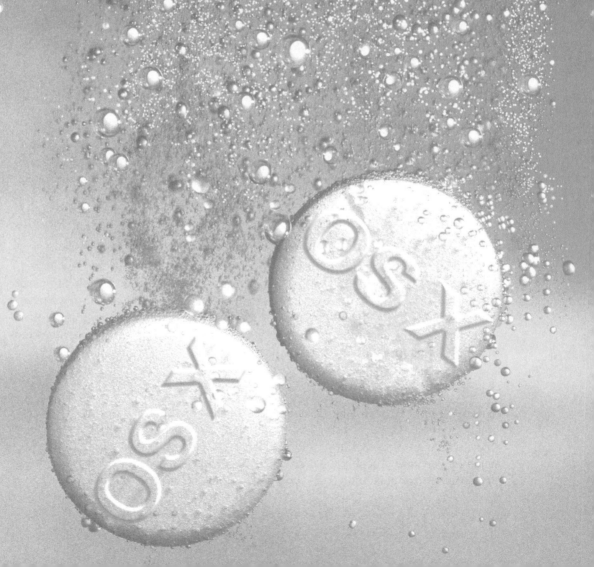

In this chapter, you'll cure…

■ Common problems with free OS X programs

■ Common problems with free OS X utilities

Without programs, a computer isn't worth much, whether it's a Mac or a PC. The good news, of course, is that you can install a number of applications and programs on your Mac, whether you purchase them from a store or download them from the Internet. The additional good news is that OS X gives you a number of free programs and utilities that give your Mac more functionality, making it more fun to work and play with. The third piece of good news is that most of these programs are rather easy to use—but if you are new to them, they can give you a few headaches along the way.

In this chapter, we take a look at those free OS X programs and utilities available on your Mac. I point out some general information about these programs and show you the headaches and painkillers, where appropriate. Most Mac programs are easy to use, so you probably won't have many problems. Nonetheless, this chapter works great as a quick primer to these programs to get you on your way. Also, some of these programs deserve their own chapters, so I'll send you to the correct chapter in this book, when appropriate.

OS X Program Headaches

OS X comes to you with a number of programs and utilities, and even a few games. If you open Macintosh HD | Applications, you can see all of those applications as well as any applications you may have installed yourself. In this section, we take a look at some of the main OS X free programs you find there. The ones you find will vary slightly, according to your version of OS X, but this chapter includes the main ones that might give you a few headaches.

Acrobat Reader

Adobe Acrobat Reader is included on OS X, as it is on most new operating systems today. Acrobat Reader is a standard reader application that reads portable document files, which are files that have .pdf extensions. If you have spent any time on the Internet, you have probably run across PDF documents—they are used for everything from online manuals to tutorials, and they provide an easy way to mix text and graphics in a document. Your version of Acrobat Reader is just that—a reader. You can read PDF files, but that's about it. If you are interested in creating PDF files with Acrobat, you can buy the full version at www.adobe.com. The reader is provided so you can read any PDF documents, regardless of where they come from. To use Acrobat Reader, you can launch it by double-clicking its icon in the Applications folder, clicking File | Open, and selecting the PDF document you want to view. Basically, the reader works like a standard word processor where you can scroll around and read the document, shown in the following illustration.

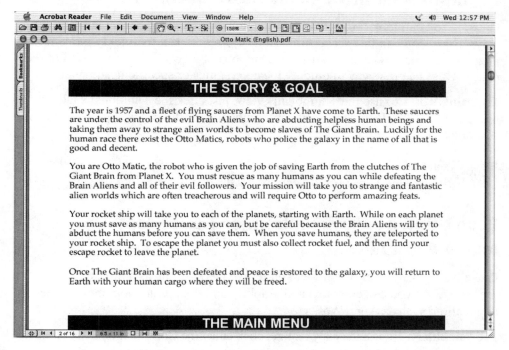

I'm having problems moving around in Acrobat Reader

Cause   Documents that open in Acrobat Reader can be a little odd sometimes, mainly because they're displayed at an unusual size or you have problems getting around and seeing all of the document at first. That's no problem, though, because Acrobat Reader gives you easy controls along the toolbar.

The Painkiller   To move around and changn text, and change the overall size. For example, if the size of the document is display the document as you read, simply use the toolbar controls to move forward and back, zoom in oed at 150%, you probably need to reduce it a bit in order to see everything. If you are having problems reading the text, just increase the size.

> **TIP** *You can view a document in full-screen mode by choosing View | Full Screen or by pressing COMMAND-L. Just hit ESC to return to normal. You can also move from page to page in the document by just pressing ENTER.*

I want to look through an entire document

Cause   You can look through an entire document very easily in a few different ways. Sure, you can just scroll through it or press ENTER to quickly move from page to page, but you can also use the Thumbnails view to see a collection of the pages. This is a great way to quickly locate graphics or specific headings.

The Painkiller   To use the Thumbnails view, just click the Thumbnails tab on the left side of the document. A list of thumbnails for the pages appears in a pane. Just click a page to go to it.

> **NOTE** *You can also use the Document menu to move around through a PDF file and the View menu to choose a variety of viewing options.*

I can't find a Save As option, or I can't copy text and graphics

Cause   Acrobat reader doesn't let you resave the PDF file as a different kind of file. However, you can copy text and graphics and then paste them into another application, such as AppleWorks.

The Painkiller   To use the copy feature, click either the Copy Text or Copy Graphics button on the toolbar and then use your mouse to select the text or graphics (you can't do both at the same time). Click Edit | Copy and then use the Edit | Paste command to paste the text or graphics into another program.

Address Book

Address Book is a cool program that enables you to store addresses, phone numbers, and other information about people. It's really very simple to use, and it is integrated to work with Mail. In fact, you can open it either from the Applications folder or directly from Mail (see Chapter 11 to learn more about Mail.).

Address Book enables you to enter addressing information for individuals and to organize those individuals into groups, as you can see in the following illustration. This way, you can e-mail a message to an entire group just by entering the group name.

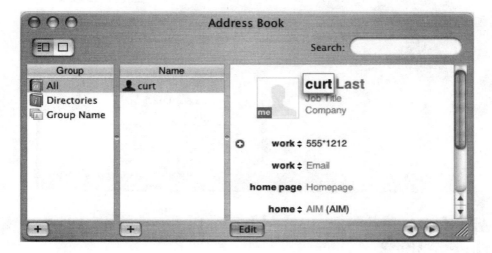

In the Address Book interface, click New (+) to add either a new group or a new person to the address book. If you add a new person, click the address areas to add the person and his or her contact information. As you can see in the following illustration, you can click the square box to add the person's picture, if you like.

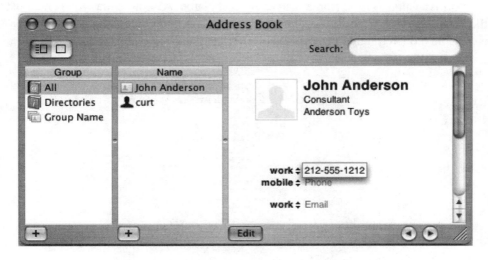

Add people in the address book to the groups that you want by simply dragging their cards to the group name, as shown in the following illustration.

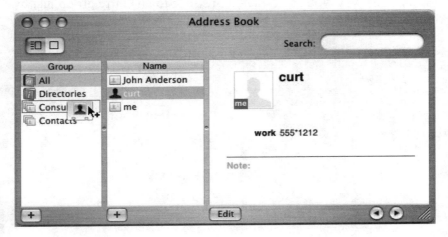

All of my cards are sorted by last name—can I change that?

Cause   Yes, you can have the name cards in your address book sorted by first or last name. Just see the Painkiller.

The Painkiller   To change the sort preference, click Address Book | Preferences. On the Preferences window, General tab, shown in the following illustration, change the Sort By value to First Name instead of Last Name. Also note that you can adjust the Font Size and Address Format here as well, and you can change how names are displayed (first name last, last name first).

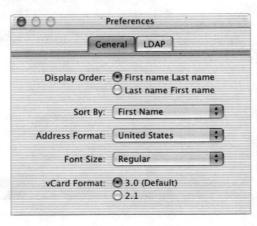

I want to customize what I put on a card

Cause   The card automatically gives you some standard fields, such as name, phone numbers, e-mail addresses, home page, and home address information. You can't really customize these, but you can add fields for phonetic names, birthdays, and instant messaging addresses.

The Painkiller   Click Card | Add Field, and choose the field you want to use in order to add it to the card.

AppleWorks

OS X gives you a complete suite of productivity applications called AppleWorks that appears on consumer Macs, such as iMacs and iBooks. In AppleWorks, you get word-processing, spreadsheet, database, drawing, painting, and presentation capabilities. You can choose the application you want to use when you first open the program. AppleWorks gives you standard toolbars and interfaces for using these applications, which you can get to know by just experimenting and using the Help files.

Calculator

The Applications folder gives you two calculator applications—the standard Calculator, shown in the following illustration, and a PCalc program that is a third-party product. Both work well and give you a number of functions you can use, including advanced functions, a paper tape, and a Speech menu that can call aloud the numbers and values as you work, which is really cool. Use the Convert command to convert a number of different values, including currency, speed, length, and so forth. You aren't likely to encounter any headaches while using the two calculators (unless you are figuring your taxes, which aren't the Mac's fault). Just use the keypad and the menus to move around as needed.

Clock

The Clock application, which is different from the Date and Time found on your menu bar, gives you a clock that resides on the Dock or floats on your desktop. The program is so simple that you won't encounter headaches. Just open Clock and click Clock | Preferences. You can choose an analog or digital clock and decide where you want the clock displayed (Dock or desktop). If you put the clock on the desktop, it floats; you can move it anywhere you want, and you can also adjust the transparency of the clock to determine how brightly it shows up.

iDVD

See Chapter 16 to learn more about iDVD.

Image Capture

Image Capture is actually a cool little program that many people ignore. The truth is that Image Capture is designed to come to life when you plug in a digital camera. You can use Image Capture to download your photos to a desired folder and to do a few tasks, like automatically turn them into a web page, or automatically scale them to e-mail size. The only headache you might experience here is that Image Capture doesn't work with every digital camera. However, it works with most Canon, Olympus, Epson, Nikon, HP, Sony, Fuji, and Kodak cameras. By default, Image Capture activates whenever you plug in a digital camera, but you can disable it if you want to use iPhoto to manage your photos. See Chapter 13 to learn more about using iPhoto.

iMovie

See Chapter 14 to learn more about iMovie.

Internet Connect

Internet Connect is a little utility you use with dial-up modems to connect to the Internet. You can learn more about Internet connection headaches in Chapter 9.

Internet Explorer

OS X includes Internet Explorer for all of your web-surfing needs. See Chapter 10 to solve any quirky Internet Explorer headaches you may be experiencing.

iPhoto

iPhoto is an ultimately cool photo-management program. Chapter 13 explores it.

iTunes

iTunes is Apple's wildly popular music-management program. See Chapter 15 to learn more.

Mail

The Mail program is your default e-mail program. See Chapter 11 to find out more.

Preview

Preview is a cool little program designed to jump to life whenever you open certain items, namely photos. You can open all kinds of picture files, including common ones like JPEG, TIFF, GIF, and also less common ones like BMP, TGA, and even older MacPaint files. Preview can also read Photoshop files and PDF files.

When you open a photo in Preview, shown in the following illustration, you can use the toolbar to see a thumbnail view, use the zoom buttons to zoom in or out, or rotate the photo.

I mentioned that you can preview PDF files, but make no mistake—you can basically view them. Hyperlinks, bookmarks, and other PDF features don't work in Preview, but if you just want to view the PDF file, it's a great program to work with. If you need all of the features of PDF files, use Acrobat Reader (explored in the "Acrobat Reader" section earlier in this chapter).

The Save As command doesn't allow me to actually "save as"

Cause   Preview lets you resave photos and files to different formats. For example, you could save a TIFF photo as a JPEG. However, to actually do this, you have to choose File | Export instead of File | Save As.

The Painkiller   Click File | Export. In the Save As drop-down window that appears, shown in the following illustration, enter a name and a place to save the file, choose the format you want from the Format menu, and click Save.

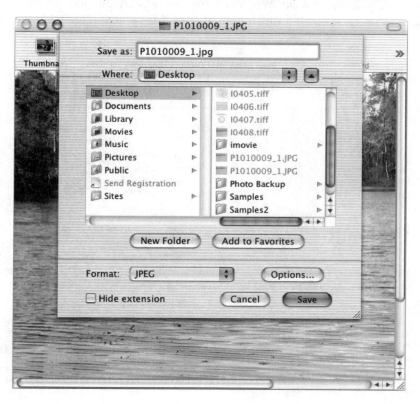

QuickTime Player

QuickTime Player is your easy-to-use player that enables you to see any QuickTime movie. See Chapter 17 to learn more.

Sherlock

Sherlock is a search tool that enables you to look for and find things on your computer and the Internet. You can even find stocks, items in the Internet yellow pages, stuff on eBay, flight information, people's e-mail addresses, and just about anything else you might want. When you first open Sherlock, you see a Channels view, shown in the following illustration, that enables you to click what you want to find.

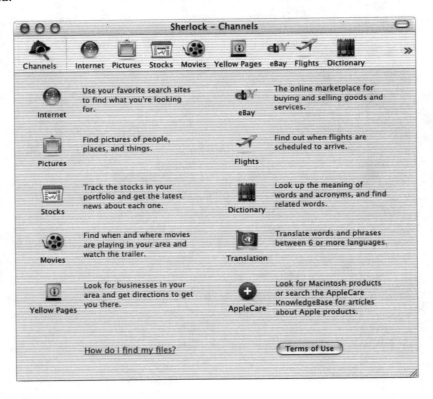

Just click the appropriate icon and enter your search criteria. For example, in the following illustration, I am looking for "iMac" on the Internet. Notice that Sherlock scans a number of standard search engines for results. This makes searching the Internet much faster than if you used a browser.

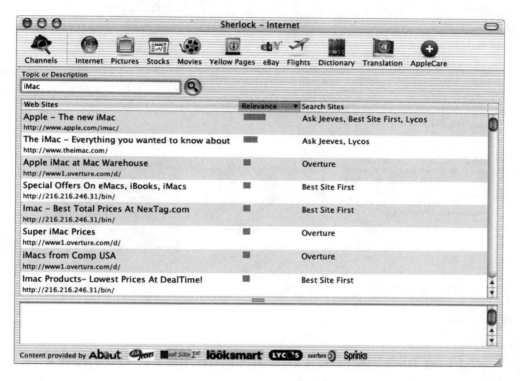

The same process works for finding pictures on the Internet, stocks, movies—you name it. Speaking of movies, Sherlock has the coolest movie locator I've seen (it's shown in the following illustration). Click Movies and enter your ZIP code in the window that appears. Select the movie and the place you want to see it, watch the trailer, buy the tickets—all in one simple window!

I want to use Sherlock to find stuff on my computer

Cause   At first glance, Sherlock channels make it seem as though you can't look for files and folders on your Mac. The truth is that OS X Jaguar contains changes that make finding items on your computer easier.

The Painkiller   To search for items on your Mac, try one of the following techniques:

■ In any finder window, such as the one shown in the following illustration, enter your search criteria and click Search.

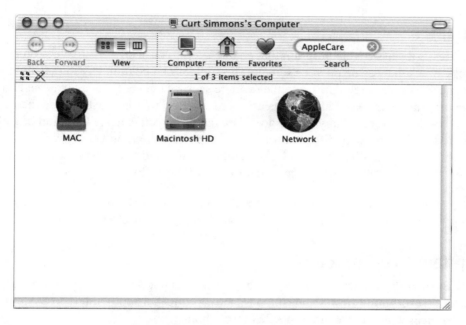

■ In Finder, click File | Find. The Find window appears, in which you can choose where to search for items and add search criteria, shown in the following illustration.

Stickies

Stickies is a classic Mac program that enables you to basically create electronic sticky notes that reside on your screen. The stickies can contain any information you need to access regularly, and they can be seen whenever Stickies is turned on. The program works as it always has and is really easy to use—just browse the menu options to see what you can do. Also, in OS X, you can use bold, italic, and colored text, along with different fonts. You can also import and export text and graphics using the File command. Use the Edit command to check your spelling. Play around with them for five minutes and you'll be a pro.

> **NOTE** *Want to create voice stickies? You can with QuickVoice 1.6, a shareware application you can download from www.apple.com/downloads/macosx.*

System Preferences

Use System Preferences to make changes to most major portions of your operating system—everything from the desktop to networking. This book refers to System Preferences again and again as needed throughout.

TextEdit

For years, the Mac has had a basic program for creating and editing text. TextEdit is that program in OS X, but make no mistake—TextEdit is a real word processor. You can format text, work with spacing and standard page-setup options, and even open up HTML documents in the program.

To prevent headaches, simply access Preferences in TextEdit | Preferences. The Preferences window, shown in the following illustration, contains a couple of items you should check out that will make using TextEdit easier.

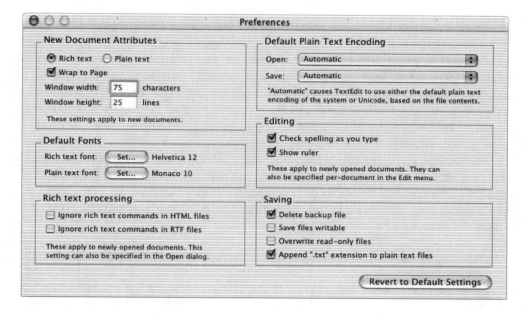

- ■ **Rich Text**   Make sure you use Rich Text. Plain text doesn't support any formatting at all, so use Rich Text for your documents. SHIFT-COMMAND-T enables you to toggle between the two modes.

- ■ **Wrap to Page**   Turning on Wrap to Page keeps your text inside your window so you can view it all at once.

- ■ **Font**   Choose the desired font—Helvetica 12 is the default font, but you can choose a different one.

- ■ **Check Spelling As You Type**   This one is a no-brainer.

- ■ **Show Ruler**   This places a rule on opened documents so you can more easily work with margins.

iCal

iCal is a very nice Apple application that was released a few months after OS X Jaguar. You may find it in your Applications folder, depending on when you bought Jaguar. If not, you can download it from www.apple.com/ical. iCal does require OS X version 10.2.2 or later, so make sure you are fully upgraded before downloading it.

As you can guess, it is a calendar application, and I have to say that it is one of the nicer calendar applications I've seen in a while. You can create multiple calendars, color-code them, be warned of conflicts, and even share them online. You can e-mail or send text messages from the calendar and even configure alerts so your Mac can let you know when an appointment is coming up. You can even send an e-mail alarm to your mobile phone or pager.

As you can see in the following illustration, iCal is really easy to use. Just use the provided interface buttons to move around between views and use the File menu to create events to add to your calendar. When you create an event, you can configure an alert, as well. The calendar is so easy that you can even drag appointments around to rearrange them!

NOTE *You may also consider reading about and downloading iSync at www.apple.com/isync. This utility also works with iCal and Address Book to synchronize data with your mobile phone, Palm, iPod, or another Mac. Check it out!*

Chapter 5

Hardware and System Headaches

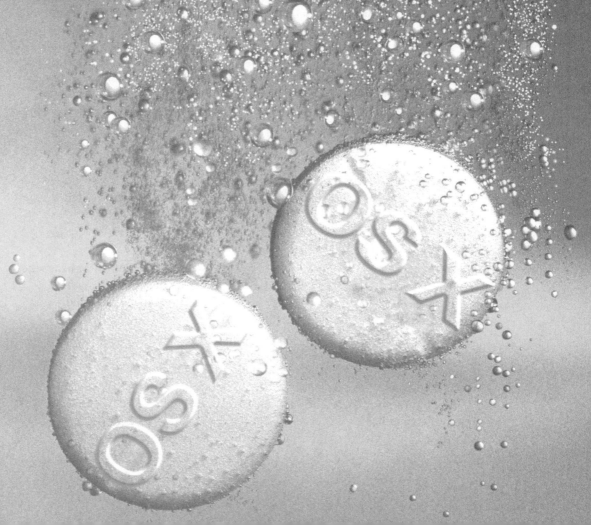

In this chapter, you'll cure...

- Problems with hardware
- Peripheral difficulties
- System settings headaches

The term *hardware* refers to any collection of devices and components that work with your Mac. Hardware includes such items as the computer's modem, the hard disk, floppy drives, CD/DVD drives, and other devices, such as printers. Hardware also refers to devices that you connect to your Mac in order to use or manage it in some way. Keyboards, mice, joysticks, and related controllers are all hardware. All of these devices, along with some additional system settings we consider in this chapter, provide different features and functions that make using your Mac, and ultimately using OS X, a fun and rewarding experience. However, what if you have problems with these items? Hardware and peripheral problems are certainly nothing new, but with OS X, they are easier to fix than ever before. In this chapter, we'll take a look at hardware and peripheral headaches, and we'll also take a look at a collection of system settings that might be causing you some problems as well.

NOTE   *You may be thinking, "Great—my printer is driving me crazy!" True enough! You may very well run into a number of printer problems, so I've included a whole chapter on printing. Go to Chapter 7 to learn more!*

Hardware and Peripheral Headaches

Unlike users in the PC world, who have traditionally experienced a lot of headaches with hardware, you have a Mac that comes to you in its own perfect state of harmony. The devices you receive with your Mac will work just fine, and you are unlikely to have any problems at all.

However, what if the devices that come with your Mac are not all you need? What if you need to use other hardware and peripherals—can you get those items to work? Probably so, if you keep two important points in mind:

Your device must be compatible with OS X and the Mac platform. You can't walk into a computer store and buy any hardware device, expecting it to work. Check the box carefully; it should say "compatible with OS X" right on it. Also, check Apple's web site for more information about device compatibility.

■ If your device is compatible, you may not need to do anything except attach the device to the Mac. OS X does a good job of detecting new hardware automatically and making it work with the Mac. However, this does not always work. In order for any device to work with the Mac, you must have a driver for that device. A *driver* is a piece of software that enables a hardware device to work with OS X. The driver usually comes on a CD-ROM or disk with the hardware device, and your Mac also has a database of generic drivers it can use. Follow the manufacturer's instructions as necessary for installing the driver. As a general rule, it is best to use the drivers that come with the device if possible.

I don't know how to install new hardware or a new peripheral device

Cause   First of all, before you attempt to install a new hardware or peripheral device, read the previous two bullet points and make sure you have a device that is compatible with your Mac. Let me give a personal example. I recently purchased an external floppy disk drive for an iMac. I know, I know, I really don't need to use a floppy disk any more. But I still like having one around. I first of all located an external floppy disk drive device that said "compatible with Mac." I then made sure the device was a USB device. Some external devices are sold as SCSI devices, an interface found on older Mac and Windows computers that has been widely replaced by FireWire. With compatibility and connection issues out of the way, I bought the floppy disk drive, which came to me with an installation CD-ROM. Once you have a device you know is compatible, what do you do next? The process is simple! See the painkiller.

The Painkiller   To install a new device, follow these steps:

1. Read the manufacturer's instructions, which usually tell you to attach the device to a USB or FireWire port as appropriate and turn it on. Most of the time, the Mac asks you to install the driver first and then attach the device.

2. The odds are good that OS X will detect the new device and that it will appear on your desktop. For example, if you connect an external device, it appears as an item or drive on the desktop. If you connect a camera, you see a window asking what you want to do, such as the one shown in the following illustration. If nothing seems to happen, you may need to install software that can use the device (as well as the device driver). Refer to the

manufacturer's instructions for installing the software that came with your device.

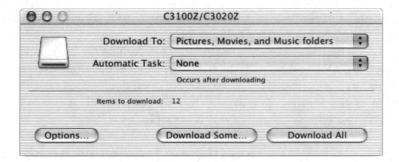

Getting More USB Ports

The Universal Serial Bus (a bus technology that allows you to connect various devices to your computer) was a great invention. After all, it's fast for data transfer, and your Mac can usually detect when you add new USB devices. Cameras, scanners, printers, mice, keyboards, video cameras, game controllers, PDAs— you name it—all are sold as USB devices these days. However, though the USB is a good thing, the Mac probably only gives you three USB ports (two of which are usually taken up by the keyboard and mouse). If you want to plug in a printer, camera, and floppy drive, what do you do? Of course, you can keep plugging and unplugging the devices as you need them, but this is a real pain.

If you are a USB junkie who needs more USB ports, you should purchase a USB hub. A hub is a little device that connects to one of the Mac's USB ports and provides additional USB connections for your other devices. This way, you can connect the devices to the hub and even daisy-chain USB hubs and devices together. Most hubs are inexpensive—a four-port USB hub will cost you under $50—but before you run out and buy a hub, check your keyboard. Another USB port or two may be hiding on the ends of the keyboard, so you may not need a hub at all.

If you do need to buy a hub, keep one point in mind. USB hubs are sold as bus-powered hubs and self-powered hubs (or both). Bus-powered hubs get their power from the Mac, whereas self-powered hubs have their own power supply that you must plug in. Bus-powered hubs are more convenient. However, if you are connecting items such as external disk drives that use a lot of power, the bus-powered hub may not be able to handle the device, and the device will not work because it lacks power. Think about your needs carefully before you buy the USB hub.

The Mac does not see my device

Cause   If you are trying to install or connect a device and the Mac pretends it is not there, there are usually three possible problems. First, the device may not be properly connected or turned on. Check the USB cable to make sure it is connected correctly to the Mac and the device, and make sure the device is turned on. Second, the device may not be compatible with OS X. Third, the device may not be installed.

The Painkiller   Check the manufacturer's instructions for installation. You may need to install the device's driver and software before the device will work. If you have tried everything, check the manufacturer's web site for more troubleshooting information.

 It is always possible that the device is faulty. See if your documentation has a support number you can call for help (don't call Apple; they will send you to the hardware device manufacturer).

 # I plug and unplug a device to and from my Mac, but I sometimes see a warning message saying "The device you removed was not properly put away..."

Cause   When you plug in a device, such as a camera, removable media drive, card reader, or MP3 player, the Mac begins talking with the device. This enables you to work with the device through the Mac and perform some action, such as downloading pictures. When you are done with the device, you simply unplug it. However, the Mac may not know that you are finished with the device and give you a warning message, such as the one shown in the following illustration.

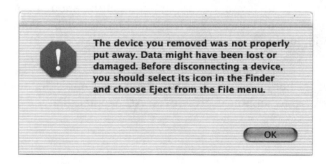

The Painkiller   You are finished with the device, so this message doesn't really matter. Just click OK. However, if you want to make sure you don't see it again and that no file corruption occurs on the device, click the Finder menu and choose Eject to eject the device before you unplug it. This lets your Mac know you are done with the device.

 ## A USB device was working—now it's not

Cause   If a USB device has previously worked on your Mac but now is not working, you can take a few troubleshooting actions.

The Painkiller   Try these suggestions:

1. Unplug the device, wait ten seconds, and then plug the device back in and turn it on.

2. If the device still does not work, try plugging it into a different USB port.

3. If the device is connected to a hub, try unplugging other items from the hub, or plug the device directly into the Mac.

4. Check the USB cable and make sure it is not damaged. Try using a different USB cable to be sure.

5. Try powering down the device and turning it back on. You can also try restarting the Mac—this sometimes fixes the problem.

 ## My printer doesn't work when connected to a USB hub

Cause   If a printer or other device that uses a lot of power doesn't work when connected to a USB hub, you are probably using a bus-powered hub rather than a self-powered hub. In this case, the printer isn't getting enough power from the bus to operate (see the previous box titled "Getting More USB Ports" for more information about hubs).

The Painkiller   Use a self-powered hub or plug the device directly into a USB port on the Mac, rather than the hub. Also, check your hub's documentation; it may already be able to support itself with an AC adapter that you can plug into a wall outlet.

My FireWire device doesn't seem to have the same kind of connection as my Mac

Cause   Your Mac uses a FireWire connection (a fast connection often used with video cameras and other devices) that accepts six-pin connections. In some cases, you may have a FireWire device that uses a four-pin connection. The two are using two kinds of connections, so you can't directly connect them.

The Painkiller   To connect the six-pin port and the four-pin device, you'll need a six-pin to four-pin FireWire adapter cable. You can find this cable at your local computer store or at any number of online computer stores.

 ## My FireWire device doesn't work

Cause   In terms of connections and installation, FireWire devices are basically the same as USB. You should be able to connect to the FireWire port, turn on the device, and have the Mac see the new device. However, in some cases you also need to install the device's software. See the manufacturer's instructions for more information, and check the painkiller here for important tips.

The Painkiller   If you are still having problems with the FireWire device, consider this:

- Make sure the device is properly connected to the FireWire port.

- FireWire connections have a limited cable connection of 15 feet or less. Make sure your cable is not longer than 15 feet.

- Don't connect the FireWire device in two ways, such as to the FireWire port and the USB port (if the device also provides a USB connection).

- As with the earlier headache concerning this same problem with USB devices, try powering down the device and then powering it back up. Also, try restarting your Mac.

 ## I have several FireWire products connected together, but performance is slow

Cause   You can daisy-chain FireWire products together. For example, you could connect a digital video (DV) camera to the FireWire port and then connect a scanner to the DV camera, and so forth. However, doing so may degrade performance.

The Painkiller   Remove items in the FireWire daisy chain to boost performance.

My CD/DVD drive doesn't do what I want when I insert a disk

Cause   When you insert a CD or DVD into your CD/DVD drive, OS X makes some decisions about what you might want to do. However, you can change this behavior using System Preferences.

The Painkiller   To manage what happens when you insert a CD or DVD, follow these steps:

1. Open System Preferences by clicking the Dock icon or by selecting Apple | System Preferences.

2. In System Preferences, click CDs & DVDs in the Hardware section.

3. In the CDs & DVDs window, use the drop-down menus to determine what happens when you insert a particular CD or DVD, as shown in the following illustration.

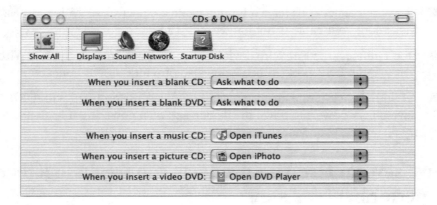

My Mac keyboard doesn't work

Cause   If the keyboard does not work at all, check the USB cable connection and make sure the keyboard is connected properly. If that doesn't work, try the painkiller.

The Painkiller   Try these options:

1. Unplug the keyboard, wait ten seconds, and plug it back in.

2. If the keyboard is plugged into a hub or is in a daisy chain, try connecting it directly to the Mac USB port.

3. If nothing seems to work, the keyboard may be damaged, in which case you need to take it to an Apple repair center. See www.apple.com for more information about authorized service centers.

 *If you are trying to use something other than the Mac keyboard, see the general USB and FireWire headaches and painkillers earlier in this chapter.*

 ## My keyboard responds too slowly or too quickly

Cause   When you first attach your keyboard, OS X makes some assumptions about how fast the keyboard and the repeat rate should work (that is, when you hold down a key, how fast the computer should respond by repeating the letter over and over). However, these assumptions might not be right for you, and you can change them.

The Painkiller   To change your keyboard settings, follow these steps:

1. Click System Preferences on the Dock, or select Apple | System Preferences.

2. Click the Keyboard icon under the Hardware icon.

3. In the Settings window, shown in the following illustration, adjust the Key Repeat Rate and the Delay Until Repeat rate by moving the slider bars. Click the provided box to test your settings.

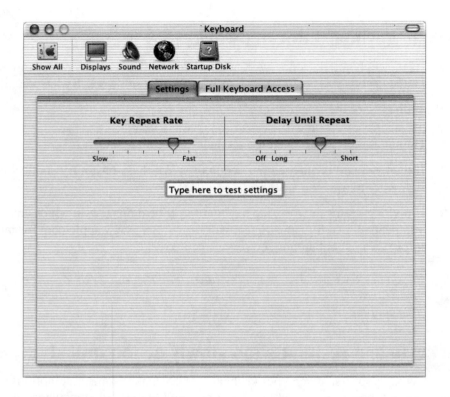

My keyboard doesn't provide very many shortcuts to manage OS X

Cause   By default, you can control the Menu Bar and the Dock with keyboard shortcuts. However, you can turn on a feature called full keyboard access. Once you turn on this feature, you can use many additional keyboard keys.

The Painkiller   To turn on full keyboard access, follow these steps:

1. Open System Preferences on the Dock, or choose Apple | System Preferences.

2. Double-click the Keyboard icon under System.

3. Click the Full Keyboard Access tab. Select the Turn On Full Keyboard Access check box, shown in the following illustration. You can choose to use function or letter keys, or you can choose custom keys to manage the menu, Dock, windows, toolbar, and utility window.

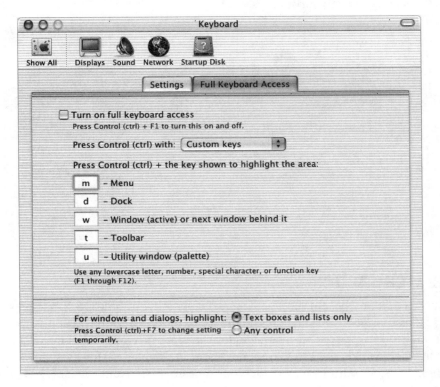

My mouse works too slowly or too quickly

Cause   OS X chooses some default settings that determine how fast your mouse movements work and how fast the double-click action responds. You can easily change these settings to meet your needs, however.

The Painkiller   To adjust your mouse settings, follow these steps:

1. Open System Preferences on the Dock, or choose Apple | System Preferences.

2. Double-click the Mouse icon under System.

3. In the Mouse window, shown in the following illustration, adjust slider bars to change the tracking and double-click speeds. Use the double-click trial box to test your settings.

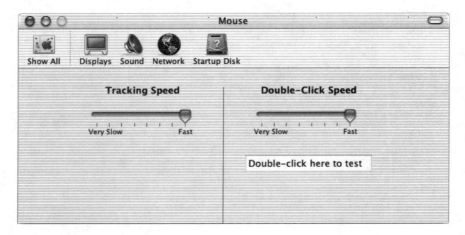

System Headaches

When you think of system settings, you probably think of how OS X operates. You're exactly right. OS X handles a number of different options that give you the functionality you enjoy. This also includes such interface options as the desktop and the Dock, which you can learn more about in Chapter 1. However, a few additional system settings may cause you some confusion and headaches. This section explores them.

I don't know how to change the date and time

Cause You can see the date and time on your Menu bar, shown as either text or a clock icon. (Click it to select the one you want. If you don't see one at all, see the painkiller.) You can make adjustments to date and time settings as needed.

The Painkiller   To adjust the time or date, follow these steps:

1. Open System Preferences on the Dock, or choose Apple | System Preferences. Or, click the time and date on the Menu bar and choose Open Date And Time, if the time option appears on your Menu bar.

2. If you opened System Preferences, double-click Date & Time under System.

3. On the Date & Time tab, shown in the following illustration, adjust the calendar date and time by clicking the desired options. If you want to set international time, click the Open International button.

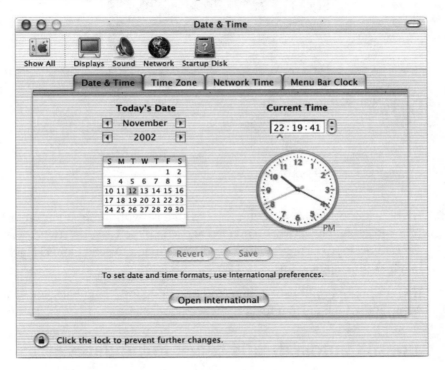

4. To set your time zone, click the Time Zone tab, shown in the following illustration. On the world map, click where you live. You'll see the closest city appear in the provided dialog box.

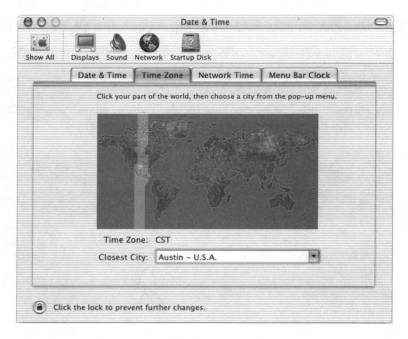

5. If you want to synchronize your Mac with a network time server on the Internet, click the Network Time tab and select the Use A Network Time Server check box. Then, use the drop-down menu to select an NTP server (such as time.apple.com).

6. If you want or don't want a time icon or text on the Menu bar, choose the Menu Bar Clock tab and make your selection.

OS X doesn't automatically check for updates from Apple

Cause   From time to time, Apple may release updates and "fixes" to OS X. These updates may include software code that fixes problems in OS X or increases its functionality. OS X can automatically check www.apple.com for updates, but you have to configure it to do so.

The Painkiller   To have OS X check for updates automatically, follow these steps:

1. Open System Preferences on the Dock, or choose Apple | System Preferences.

2. Under System, double-click the Software Update icon.

3. On the Update Software tab, shown in the following illustration, select the Automatically Check For Updates When You Have A Network Connection option, shown in the following illustration. Use the drop-down menu to select how often you want OS X to check for updates (such as daily, weekly, monthly). Weekly is a good setting here.

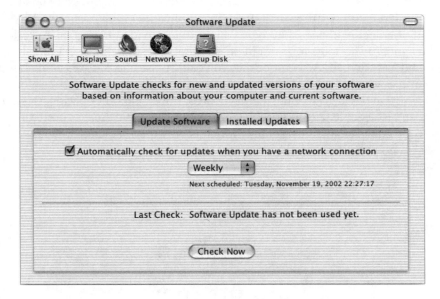

4. If you want to manually check for updates, click the Check Now button.

 *Want to see what updates have been installed? Click the Installed Updates tab.*

 # I have certain disabilities and need OS X to help me

Cause   In the past, computers were not very friendly to people who had trouble using the keyboard or the mouse, or who had problems seeing items on the screen. The good news is that all of that is changing, and OS X gives you a full palette of tools that make it easier to use if you have certain disabilities. These tools, called

Universal Access, can help you see the display, hear sounds the computer makes, and use the keyboard and the mouse.

The Painkiller   To configure Universal Access, follow these steps:

1. Open System Preferences on the Dock, or choose Apple | System Preferences.

2. Under System, click Universal Access.

3. On the Seeing tab, shown in the following illustration, click the boxes to turn zoom on or off, switch the monitor to white on black, or use grayscale. If you decide to use zoom, you can use the provided Universal Access keyboard shortcuts to zoom in on screen items so that they become large and easy to read. Also notice that you can choose check boxes at the bottom of the window to use Universal Access Shortcuts or enable access for assistive devices (specialized keyboards, mice, and other peripherals). You can also enable text-to-speech when using Universal Access preferences (this one is enabled by default, which is why the Mac talks to you when you point to items on this window).

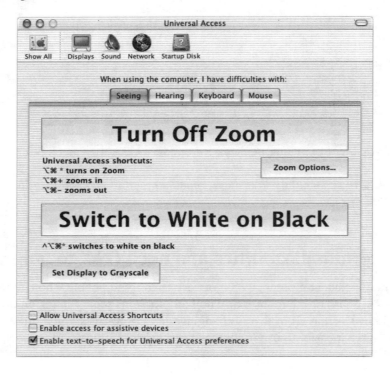

4. Click the Hearing tab if you need assistance with hearing. On the Hearing window, shown in the following illustration, you can choose to enable the Flash Screen option, which makes the screen flash as a substitute for sound alerts. You can also click the Adjust Sound button to make sound alerts much louder or softer.

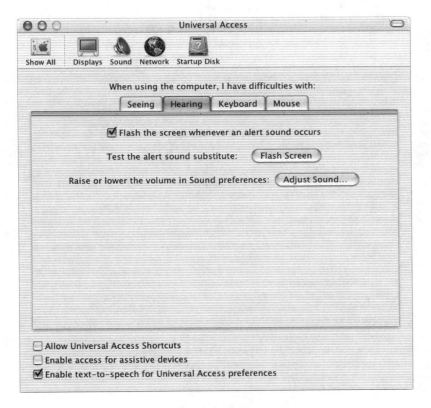

5. If you need help using the Keyboard, click the Keyboard tab. The Keyboard tab, shown in the following illustration, enables you to manage Sticky Keys and Slow Keys. Sticky Keys is helpful if you cannot press more than one key at a time (you can press, for example, Command and then press *Q* without having to press them at the same time). Slow keys puts delays between keystrokes so that you do not accidentally press keys twice. Note the available options for each and try these out.

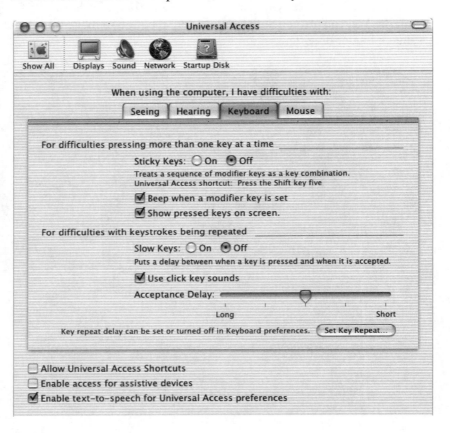

6. If you are having problems using the mouse, click the Mouse tab, shown in the following illustration. You can choose to use Mouse keys so that you can use the numeric keypad rather than the mouse. You can also adjust the slider bars to manage mouse pointer movements.

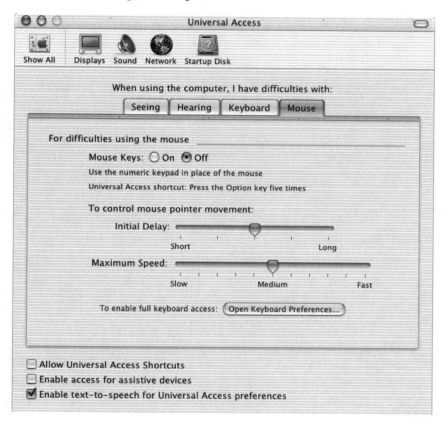

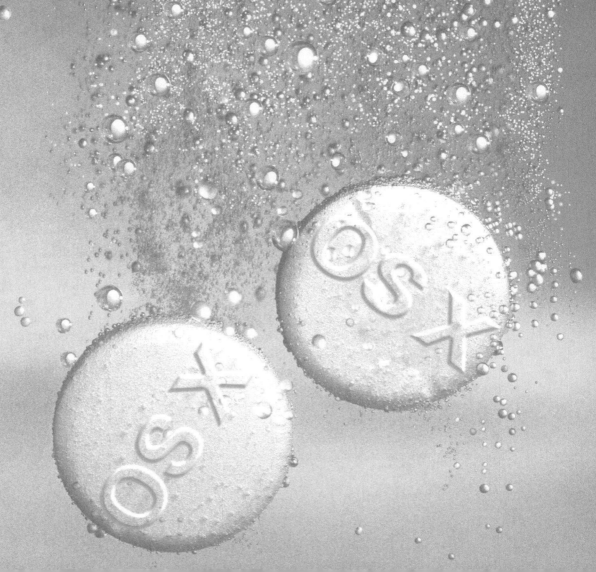

Chapter 6

Disk Headaches

In this chapter, you'll cure...

- Problems with the hard disk
- Aggravations with CD/DVD-ROM and floppy drives

In the olden days of computing, early PC users were always fumbling with hardware, trying to get certain devices to work with the PC, worrying about disk problems and the like. The Mac has always been a stable and easy-to-use operating system, most often free from the hardware headaches that came with owning a PC. The same is true today—the Mac is more rock-solid than ever, and the likelihood that you will have hardware and disk problems at all is rather small. However, the Mac isn't a perfect machine—no computer is—and you may run across some hard disk problems or aggravations with CD/DVD-ROM drives and floppy drives. In this chapter, we take a quick look at the headaches that could come your way and the cures for those headaches.

Hard Disk Headaches

The Mac's hard disk holds all of your information, as well as the OS X operating system. In other words, it is the central storage location for everything on your Mac. When the operating system runs, it uses files stored on the Mac. When you use an application or open a file, that information is taken from its storage location on the Mac.

The good news is that the hard disk is tucked away inside of the Mac and, as a general rule, you don't have to worry about it all. It takes care of itself and works when you need it to. However, there is always the potential for problems. With that in mind, OS X gives you a Disk Utility, formerly called Disk First Aid in OS 9 and previous versions of Mac operating systems. The Disk Utility program can repair most problems with the Mac hard disk. Additionally, you can use a UNIX command line utility called *fsck* (which means File System Check) that does the same thing.

So, how do you know if you need to use one of these tools? No hard rules apply, but you can bet you have a hard disk problem if your Mac freezes during startup, if you see a text command line during the startup process, if your application icons turn into folders, or if you experience other unexplained hiccups and error messages. When in doubt, run either the Disk Utility or fsck utility to fix the problem; the following two headaches and painkillers show you how.

I don't know how to use the Disk Utility

Cause   You can find the Disk Utility in Macintosh HD | Applications | Utilities. If you double-click the utility, you can find information about the hard drive and can click the First Aid tab. Here, you can verify disk permissions and repair them, as shown in the following illustration. If you need to repair the disk, restart the Mac using your OS X installation CD. Disk Utility cannot repair a disk that it resides on, so you have to run the Disk Utility from the installation CD. The painkiller shows you how.

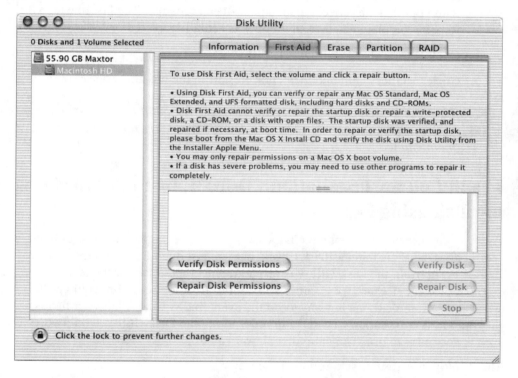

The Painkiller   To repair the disk, follow these steps:

1. Put the Mac OS X CD in the CD drive and restart the Mac. Hold down C when the Mac is restarting.

2. When you finally see the installer window, click Installer | Open Disk Utility.

3. When the Disk Utility appears, select the Macintosh HD (or any drive that is causing the problem) in the left pane and then click the First Aid tab in the right pane.

4. You can click Verify Disk if you want the utility to check for disk problems. If you already know problems exist, just click Repair Disk.

5. The repair process begins. It may take some time for the utility to check everything, but eventually the process ends. If you see a final message telling you The Volume Macintosh HD Appears To Be OK, then everything with your disk has checked out and has been repaired. The last line says Repair Complete whether anything was actually repaired or not.

6. Click Disk Utility | Quit Disk Utility.

7. Click Installer | Quit and then click Restart in the box that appears.

 *This tool is great to use when a problem occurs, but it is taxing on the hard drive. In other words, don't run the Disk Utility every night as preventative maintenance.*

 # I can't find my installation CD-ROM, or I want to check my disk using fsck

Cause   An alternative to using the Disk Utility is to use the fsck command line tool. It does the same thing as Disk Check, but you just don't have a pretty interface to look at. In truth, the Disk Utility is just a graphical interface for the fsck tool, so think of them as exactly the same. This tool is great to use if you would rather work at the command line anyway, or in the event that you can't put your hands on your OS X installation CD-ROM in order to run the Disk Utility. Don't worry; fsck is very easy to use. The painkiller shows you how.

The Painkiller   To run fsck, follow these steps:

1. Restart the Mac. When the Mac starts to boot, press COMMAND-S. This starts the Mac using the command line. You see white letters on a black background. When the Mac is finished, you see a white box at the end of the text where you can enter a command (your mouse will not work here, only the keyboard).

2. Type **fsck –y** and press RETURN (make sure you put the space between **fsck** and the **–y**. This command tells the console to fix all problems automatically. You see a readout of what the utility is checking—basically the same as the Disk Utility offered.

3. When the utility is done, you see the message The Volume Macintosh HD Appears To Be OK. If you see a message stating The System Was Modified, that means fsck found a problem and fixed it. However, you need to run the program again and again until you finally see a message saying The Volume Macintosh HD Appears To Be OK. This way, you know all of the problems have been fixed.

4. When you are done, type **reboot** and press ENTER.

I still can't boot up, or I still have problems after running Disk Utility

Cause   If you have run the disk utility and still have problems with the disk, then the Disk Utility cannot fix the problem. Your best bet at this point is to contact Apple technical support for help. The hard disk may have physical problems, in which case you need to take your Mac to an authorized Apple repair center.

The Painkiller   Check the Apple web site for more help, or contact technical support. See your Mac's documentation for details.

Floppy disk, CD-ROM, DVD, and Other Disk Headaches

Your Mac can read just about any disk—and that's great news for you. Aside from the Mac's hard drive, you can use CD-ROMs, DVDs (assuming your Mac has a DVD-ROM drive), floppy disks, Zip disks, and just about any other kind of disk (if the Mac has the correct disk drive for the disk that you want to read). In this myriad of disks and disk drives, things can get a tad confusing at first. The important thing to remember is that each of these options simply provides you with ways to store data and move it around.

The good news about the Mac is that no matter what kind of disk you are using or what drive you are using, the Mac puts your disks on the desktop. You see them there as disk icons, although your Mac sees each one as a "volume."

Disk Confusion

If this is your first Mac, or perhaps even your first computer, all of this talk about different kinds of disks may leave you scratching your head. Your Mac supports different kinds of removable disks, such as floppy disks, CDs, Zip disks and so forth. Different companies developed these different disks at different times. In a nutshell, they all do the same thing: store data. Some are much faster than others, but the basic use for any disk is to store data. So what are the differences? Check out this list:

- **CDs**   Most software today ships on CD, and CDs are the standard for data storage. A CD-ROM is a read-only CD. In other words, your Mac can only read data from it. Most computers today come with a *CD burner*—a drive that can burn data onto a CD. Burnable CDs are sold either as CD-R, which you can burn one time and one time only, or CD-RW, on which you can read and write data over and over again. Because of the flexibility of CD-RW disks, many people use them today.

- **Floppy Disks**   Floppy disks have been around for years. In order to use a floppy disk, you need a floppy disk drive. Your Mac may have one, but most newer Macs don't. Apple believes the floppy is dead, but millions of people still use them. Floppy disks aren't that flexible because each disk holds only 1.54MB of data. However, they are cheap and easy to carry. If you still like using floppies, you can buy an external floppy disk drive to attach to your Mac for around $60 (see www.macwarehouse.com).

- **Zip Disks**   Zip disks, which look like larger floppy disks, were created by Iomega. In years past, many Power Macs came equipped with Zip drives, and you can still get an external one for your Mac if you want. Zip disks can hold either 100MB or 250MB of data, depending on the kind of drive you buy, and they give you a great way to store data. (CDs have become more popular in the past couple of years.)

- **DVDs**   If your Mac has a DVD drive, you can watch DVD movies; if it has a SuperDrive, you can play and burn DVDs. A standard DVD disk can hold up to 4.7GB of data and provides a great solution for backing up or storing multimedia files.

Your Macintosh HD (hard drive) always appears on the desktop, but if you insert a CD or DVD, an icon appears there for it as well. If you insert a floppy disk, a drive icon appears on the desktop. In fact, anything that has storage, even your digital camera, the Mac sees as a disk or a drive, and it puts an icon on the desktop for you. From this point, you can open the drive, access files, store items on the drive, or do whatever you want.

Using these drives is for the most part quite easy, but a few headaches may come your way. The following sections explore them.

I have an external floppy drive, but when I plug it in, a message appears telling me that USB power is low

Cause   If you use an external USB floppy drive, you need to plug the drive directly into a USB port on the back of the Mac or into a self-powered USB hub. If you plug the drive in as a daisy chain to other devices, such as your keyboard, you are likely to see the warning message shown in the following illustration. This message just means that your Mac doesn't have enough power to run the device where you have plugged it in.

The Painkiller   To fix this problem, plug the drive directly into a USB port on the back of the computer or into a self-powered USB hub.

My floppy drive can't read a certain disk

Cause   Your Mac can read both Mac-formatted floppy disks and Windows-formatted floppy disks. If the Mac can't read a disk, the odds are good that something is wrong with it. Floppy disks, though versatile, wear out over time; if you get a message saying the disk is damaged or unusable, you know something is wrong.

The Painkiller   If the disk is damaged, you can try to fix it using the Disk Utility. It's found in Macintosh HD | Applications | Utilities. Click the First Aid tab, select the floppy drive disk, and click Repair Disk.

Every time I eject a floppy disk, I get an error message

Cause   Once you insert a disk of any kind into the Mac, the Mac begins using that disk according to your mouse and keyboard movement. If the Mac thinks it is still using the disk and you eject it, you get a warning message (shown in the following illustration). In truth, it doesn't hurt anything to eject a disk when you are done, but the Mac wants you to do it in an orderly fashion using the Finder. If you don't, you have to contend with this warning message.

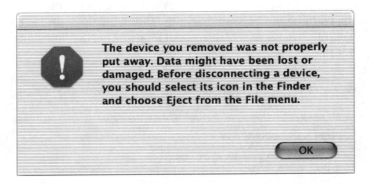

The Painkiller   To avoid seeing this message, select the disk icon on your desktop and click File | Eject. Then remove the disk from the drive. You can also just drag the disk icon to the Trash and remove the disk from the drive. When you do this, the Trash icon turns into an eject logo (because you aren't really trashing anything).

 *The eject command ejects the disk from the Mac system—not the physical disk from the disk drive.*

I don't know how to erase or reformat a floppy disk

Cause   If you need to erase all data on a disk or reformat a disk, use the Disk Utility program. It's easy.

The Painkiller   To erase and reformat a disk, follow these steps:

1. Select Macintosh HD | Applications | Utilities | Disk Utility.

2. Click Erase.

3. Select the disk you want to erase or reformat. The default format, shown in the following illustration, is Mac OS Extended. It helps your disks conserve space.

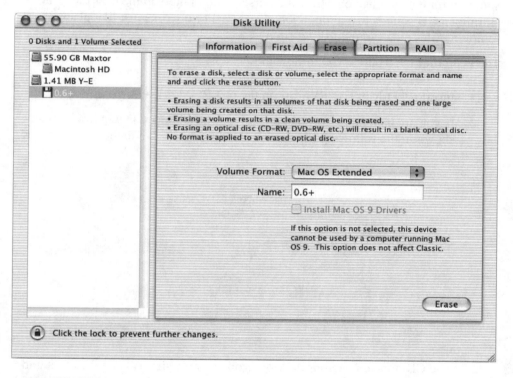

4. Click Erase.

 # A CD or DVD will not eject

Cause   You can use your keyboard to eject a CD or DVD disk, or you can use the onscreen controls to do so. However, you have probably noticed that sometimes the eject key or onscreen control doesn't eject the disk. This problem usually occurs when the Mac is still using the disk, or at least thinks it is still using the disk.

The Painkiller   To solve this problem, make sure all programs are closed and then select the disk icon on the desktop and click File | Eject. Then, press Eject to remove this disk. If this doesn't work or the disk icon doesn't seem to show up on the desktop at all, restart the Mac.

I don't know how to burn a CD

Cause   CDs are great for storing data of all kinds. In fact, CDs have become the standard for data storage on Macs and personal computers in the past few years. Burning a CD sounds like a tough job, but in reality it works just like placing and removing files on a floppy disk or Zip disk.

The Painkiller   To burn a CD, follow these steps:

1. Insert a CD-R or CD-RW disk in the CD-ROM drive on your Mac.

2. If you are using a preformatted CD, you see a blank CD window appear, shown in the following illustration. Just give the CD a name and click OK.

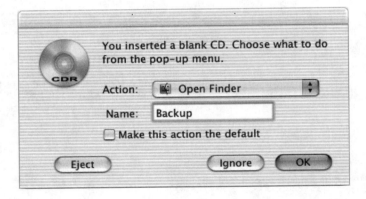

3. The CD appears on your desktop. You can now simply drag files to it and record them onto the CD. If you are using a CD-R (rather than a CD-RW, which can be used over and over again), when you are finished dragging files, click File | Burn Disc. Or, if you drag the disk icon to the Trash, a burn symbol appears. A dialog box where you can choose to burn the disk appears, as shown in the following illustration.

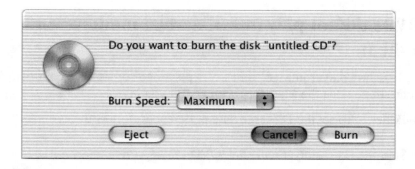

When I play a DVD, the DVD control box disappears after a few moments

Cause If your Mac is equipped with a DVD drive or an Apple SuperDrive, the DVD player comes to life when you insert a DVD movie, starting the movie in full-screen mode. At the beginning, you see a control box, shown in the following illustration. When the movie starts playing, the control box disappears after a few moments in order not to hamper your full-screen viewing.

The Painkiller To get the control box back at any time, press ESC on your keyboard.

You can also control the DVD using your keyboard. For example, use the SPACEBAR to pause playing and the arrow keys to move forward and backward through the DVD. To get out of full-screen mode, just double-click the movie with your mouse.

My DVDs do not play in full-screen mode when I start them

Cause   Like any player in Mac, your DVD player has preference controls you can use to determine what the Mac does with DVDs you insert.

The Painkiller   To set the DVD player's preferences, follow these steps:

1. Start the DVD Player and click DVD Player | Preferences.

2. On the Preferences box, click the Player tab and choose to start playing in full-screen mode and to start playing the DVD when it is inserted, as shown in the following illustration.

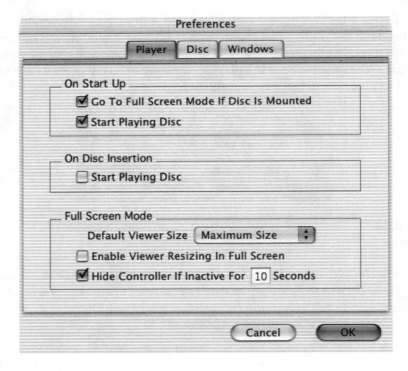

NOTE   *You can use the Disc menu to manage subtitles.*

Chapter 7

Printing Headaches

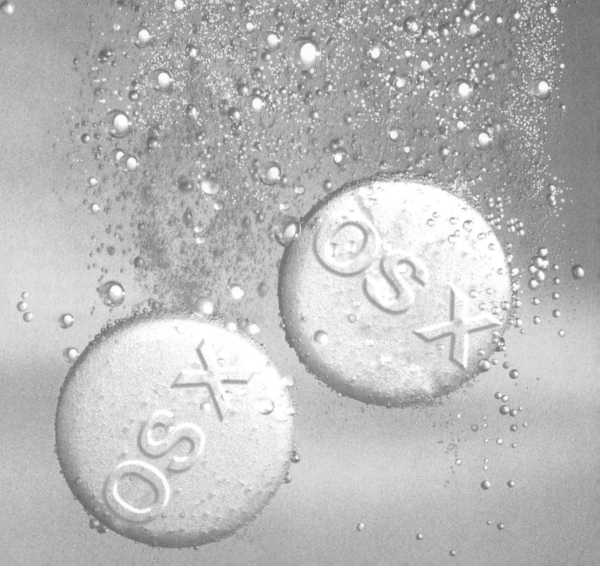

In this chapter, you'll cure...

- Problems with printer installation
- Printing problems

In the olden days of desktop computing (well, only a few years ago), it was rumored that printers would become obsolete objects. People envisioned using only electronic data in homes, in offices, and on the Internet, and they thought there would basically be no need for printing. Yeah, right.

Printing is as popular as ever—and with the new, inexpensive inkjet printers that can do a fine job when printing digital photos, almost every computer user has a printer of some kind. In fact, when you buy a new computer, you can often get the printer for free (or at least with a hefty rebate). So, printing is alive and well in the computing world, with Macintosh being no exception. The good news about printing is that printer manufacturers and operating system developers are smarter. Printers work better with computers than they ever have in the past, and OS X is no exception. You may think, "What? I've had tons of problems with OS X and my printer." That could be true, and we'll explore reasons for those headaches in this chapter!

Printer Connection Headaches

Before you can use a printer with OS X, you must install the printer on the operating system. In some cases, all you need to do is plug the USB cable from the printer into the Mac—OS X will do the rest. In other cases, you need to run a setup program from the printer manufacturer and then connect the printer to the Mac. In some cases, none of these actions get the printer to work. So, if you are having printer headaches of the connection kind, read on.

 ## I don't know how to install my new printer

Cause   Installing a new printer on OS X is an easy task. The trick to easy installation is to make sure the printer you have purchased is supported by OS X—it should say so right on the box. Once you are sure the printer is compatible with OS X, you're ready to set it up.

Understanding Drivers

Before we look at connecting your printer, you should understand one concept. When a peripheral device, such as a printer, scanner, camera, video camera, and so forth wants to play with OS X, OS X must have a driver for the device. All modern operating systems work with drivers, and OS X is no exception to the rule. A *driver* is a piece of software that enables OS X to communicate with the device. Without the driver, OS X and the device cannot communicate with each other. Keep this concept in mind as you read this chapter.

The Painkiller   To install a new printer, follow these steps:

1. Unpack the printer and locate the installation software. Although you can follow the instructions provided here, see the manufacturer's instructions as well. You'll need to install the printer cartridges, and your manual will tell you how.

2. Log in with an Administrator account.

3. Use the printer software CD to install the printer software on your Mac.

4. Follow the manufacturer's instructions for installing ink cartridges, turning the printer power on, and so forth.

5. Connect the USB cable from the printer to an available USB port on your Mac.

6. Open Macintosh HD | Applications | Utilities | Print Center. You see your new printer installed, as shown in the following illustration.

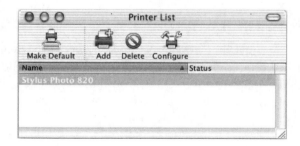

My existing printer doesn't work with OS X

Cause   Let's say you had a printer that worked fine under OS 9. You upgraded to OS X and now the printer does not work. Or, perhaps you bought a used printer that is supposed to work with OS X and it doesn't work either. Why? The issue comes back to the driver. OS X is a new operating system, completely different from OS 9. The problem with new operating systems is that software and hardware manufacturers have to play catch-up. The printer that worked fine under OS 9 may not work at all under OS X because the driver software is not compatible with OS X. So, what can you do?

The Painkiller   There is really only one way to solve this problem: you must have an updated driver. Start at the computer manufacturer's web site. Often, manufacturers will develop new drivers that you can download and install. Once you do, the printer will start working. What if the manufacturer has not developed a new driver for your printer? In this case, I'm afraid you are out of luck. It's time to buy a new printer.

    Are you dying to still use your old ImageWriter, StyleWriter, or LaserWriter models? Sorry, those printers all use Apple's LocalTalk technology, which is no longer supported under OS X.

 ## I need to install a network printer

Cause   If you are on a network, there may be a network printer that you want to use. The network printer is physically connected to another computer, but you can access the shared printer over the network and use it, just as though it were connected to your computer.

Printing from OS 9

What if you have a printer that works fine in OS 9 but doesn't work under OS X? You can still print to that printer from within OS 9. Of course, if you create files that you want to print in OS X, you'll need programs in OS 9 that can open and print them. If you're faced with this option, try saving your files as PDF files in OS X and using OS 9 to print them.

 *You must have permission to use the network printer. Don't assume that just because a printer exists on the network you have permission to use it.*

The Painkiller   To connect to a network printer, follow these steps:

1. Open Macintosh HD | Applications | Utilities | Print Center. Click Add on the toolbar.

2. A window appears where Directory Services is selected. You see any printers available on the network in the dialog box. If you don't see any printers, click the Directory Services drop-down menu and choose AppleTalk. This network protocol can locate other AppleTalk devices on the network.

3. When you locate the printer you want to use, select it in the list and click Add.

 # I need to connect to a TCP/IP printer on my network

Cause   If you are working in an office network of mixed Mac and Windows / Linux computers, you are probably working on a network that uses *Transmission Control Protocol/Internet Protocol* (*TCP/IP*) as the protocol for communications. TCP/IP is a very popular protocol used in most large networks and even on the Internet. Printers shared on the network can also use IP, so in order to connect to an IP printer, you'll need to provide the IP address to OS X. Your network administrator can help you get the IP address.

The Painkiller   To connect to an IP printer, follow these steps:

1. Open Macintosh HD | Applications | Utilities | Print Center. Click the Add button on the toolbar.

2. A window appears where Directory Services is selected. Click the drop-down menu and choose IP Printing instead of Directory Services.

3. In the IP Printing window, shown in the following illustration, enter the printer's IP address. You can also select the printer model from the

drop-down menu if required. Again, refer to your network administrator for details.

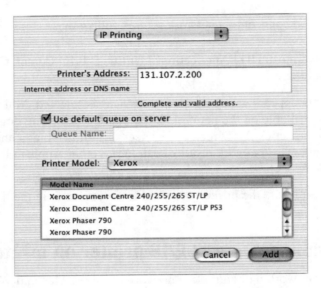

I installed the software and have my printer connected, but OS X doesn't see the printer

Cause   If you are certain that a printer driver compatible with OS X is installed and the printer is connected, you may just need to tell OS X how the printer is connected, such as by USB or FireWire, or even through Ethernet, as some laser printers connect. Each of these ports, available on the back of your Mac, can connect with printers, but most printers use the USB port.

The Painkiller   To manually tell OS X where the printer is connected, follow these steps:

1. Open Macintosh HD | Applications | Utilities | Print Center. Click the Add button on the toolbar.

2. A window appears where Directory Services is selected. Click the drop-down menu and choose the location of the device, such as USB, FireWire, and so on.

3. The printer should now appear in the window. Select it and click Add.

 *If all else fails, be sure to check your printer documentation and the manufacturer's web site. You may even be able to call the manufacturer's technical support line to get extra help with the printer installation.*

Printing Headaches

Once you have the printer connected, all you have to do is print, right? In most cases, yes; however, as you work with your printer, you may run into a number of headaches along the way. Fortunately, OS X makes solving most of these headaches easy. Read on.

 ## I have two printers installed, but OS X doesn't print to the one I want

Cause   When you have more than one printer installed, OS X chooses one of them to be the default printer—the printer OS X uses unless you tell it otherwise. The default printer is usually the first one you installed, but if you want a different printer to be the default printer, you can change the default selection.

NOTE   *Why would you use two printers? Some people who do a lot of printing might have an inkjet printer for default printing but also have a laser printer for certain print projects. They use the inkjet printer most of the time, so it can simply function as the default printer. When they need the laser printer, they can select it.*

The Painkiller   To change the default printer, follow these steps:

1.   Open Macintosh HD | Applications | Utilities | Print Center.

2.   Select the printer want to use as the default printer in the list and click the Make Default button.

TIP   *If you have read several headaches in this chapter, you have probably noticed that the Print Center is used quite a bit to manage printers and print jobs. If you don't want to wade into the Utilities folder every time you need it, just drag the Print Center to the Dock for easy access.*

NOTE   *If you ever decide to decommission a printer and use a new one, you can easily remove the old printer by opening the Print Center, selecting the printer you don't want, and clicking Delete.*

I can't manage how a file is printed

Cause When you print a file, you can change some options that determine how the file prints. They are readily available to you when you click File | Print from any application. The following painkiller shows you what you can do.

The Painkiller To manage a print file, follow these steps:

1. Open the file and click File | Print.

2. The standard print window appears, as you can see in the following illustration. By default, the Copies & Pages option is selected. You can determine how many copies you want to print and whether or not to print all pages of the file.

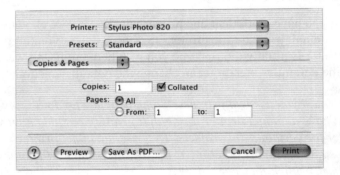

3. If you choose Layout from the drop-down menu, you determine the layout direction of the print job, shown in the following illustration. Also notice here that you can add a border to the printed page if you like.

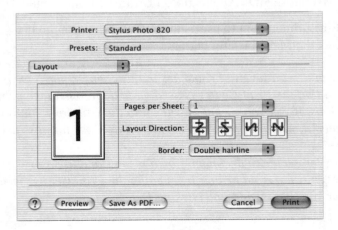

4. If you choose Output Options from the drop-down menu, you can choose to save the print job as a file in the PDF format.

Steps 5 and 6 may not appear as options, depending on the kind of printer you are using. They typically appear for inkjet printers, but not all manufacturers provide these setting options.

5. If you choose the Print Settings option in the drop-down menu, shown in the following illustration, you can choose the kind of paper you are using, choose between color ink or black ink, and choose a setting to determine the resolution of the printed file.

You normally don't need to change these settings unless you are trying to print high-quality photos on photo-quality paper.

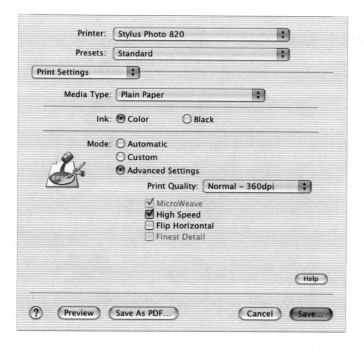

6. If you click the Color Management option in the drop-down menu, you can adjust the color used when printing. These settings may be helpful to you when printing photographs.

7. Finally, you can also select a Summary option where you see a listing of the settings you have chosen.

8. When you are done, you can save your settings or just click Print to print the file.

I need to make sure a file is printed at a certain size and scale

Cause　Aside from the options you can manipulate when you choose File | Print (see the previous headache), you can also make some adjustments to the way your file prints by choosing File | Page Setup.

The Painkiller　To adjust the page setup options, follow these steps:

1. Open the file and click File | Page Setup.

2. In the Page Setup window, shown in the following illustration, you can adjust the paper size, orientation of the print, and scale (which is set to 100% by default). Click OK when you're done.

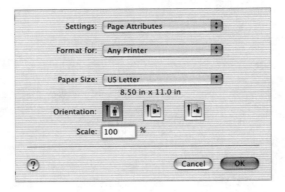

3. If you are working with custom paper sizes, choose the Custom Paper Size option in the Settings drop-down menu. Click the New button and enter the correct sizes and margins for your print job, shown in the following illustration.

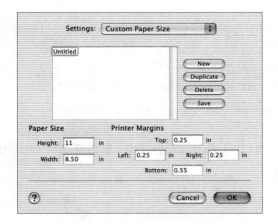

If you are printing on photo-quality paper, notice that you have that option listed in the Paper Size drop-down menu.

I have sent several files to the printer, but now I need to stop them from printing

Cause   If you send a job (or several jobs) to the printer, you can also stop the jobs from printing, or even place them on hold, even though you have already clicked Print. To do this, you must return to the Print Center.

The Painkiller   To stop a job from printing, follow these steps:

1. Open Macintosh HD | Applications | Utilities | Print Center.

2. In the Printer List window, double-click the printer.

3. In the Printer window, also called the print queue, shown in the following illustration, do one of the following:

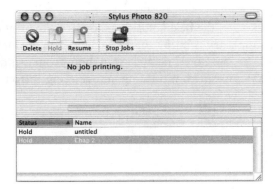

- Click the Stop All Jobs button to stop all jobs. This places all jobs on Hold. Click the Start Jobs button to restart all jobs.

- Select a job and click the Hold button to hold a particular job. When you are ready to print it, click Resume.

- To delete a job, just select it and click Delete.

When I try to print something, I get a Communication Error message

Cause   If you get a Communication Error message, like the one shown here, the computer has lost communication with the printer.

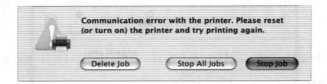

The Painkiller   Check the cables and make sure the printer is plugged into the Mac. Also, make sure the printer's power is on.

   If the message persists, something is probably wrong with the driver. Try reinstalling the driver software.

A print job fails to print

Cause   Sometimes, a particular print job will fail to print. This can be caused by a corrupt print file or by some kind of communication error between the Mac and the printer. When this happens, a dialog box appears telling you that a printer error has occurred.

The Painkiller   In this case, the best solution is to open the print queue, delete the failed print file, and simply try printing the file again. (See the earlier "I have sent several files to the printer, but now I need to stop them from printing" headache for details on stopping a document from printing and deleting it from the print queue.)

Problems of the Printing Kind

You may experience a few other print problems, all of which are the printer's fault rather than OS X's. Here are a few quick fixes for common problems:

- **Bad color or streaking appear**   If you are printing graphics and the color seems to be coming out wrong, it's simply time for a new ink cartridge. As the ink runs low, you see color distortion.

- **Printing text has jagged lines**   You probably need to align the printer cartridges. This is a process the printer runs in inkjet printers to make printed text look good. See your printer documentation for instructions.

- **Faint lines appear on the printout**   The nozzle that distributes inkjet ink may be dirty. Many inkjet printers have a Nozzle Check utility you can run from the printer software. See your documentation for details.

- **Paper jams with photo-quality paper**   Photo-quality paper is thicker than standard paper, and if you put too much in the paper tray, you may get paper jams. Try using only a few sheets at a time to solve the problem.

- **Streaked, light, or branded printing appears**   The ink cartridge is low and needs replacing.

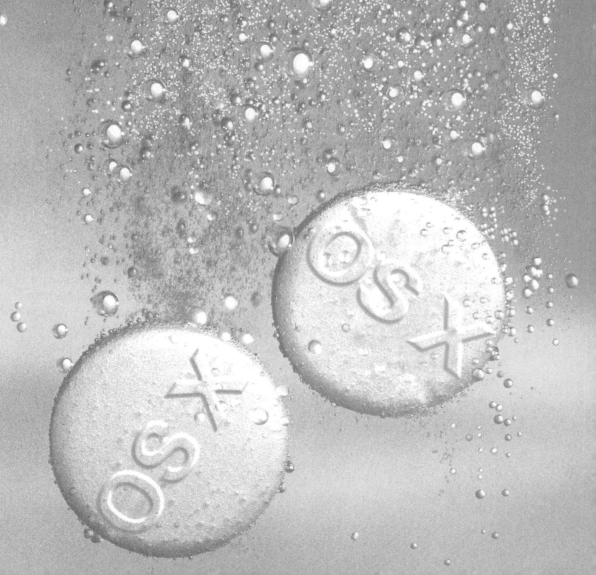

Chapter 8

Application Headaches

In this chapter, you'll cure…

■ Application installation headaches

■ Application usage problems

Applications, also called programs, are pieces of software that run on any computer operating system. In fact, operating systems like OS X are made up of a core program that makes the operating system do its thing and a bunch of applications that give you functionality you want and need. Acrobat Reader, iPhoto, AppleWorks— even Chess—are all applications. It's no secret that applications are really the heart of computing. After all, without them you wouldn't be able to do much with your Mac. Apple develops some of the applications you might use, and third-party vendors write and sell most of them. You can purchase applications you want on CDs, or you can even download and install them from the Internet.

The good news is that installing and managing applications in OS X is easier than ever before. OS X is more stable, and applications generally work better than they did in OS 9. However, that does not mean no headaches are lurking in the background, so this chapter explores the common application headaches and how to kill the pain!

Application Installation Headaches

All applications installed on OS X are installed by default in either the Applications folder or the user's home directory. The Applications folder, found in Macintosh HD | Applications, shows you all of the applications available to you. Some applications, such as Disk Copy, are stored in the Utilities folder, found in the Applications folder. From the Applications folder, shown in the following illustration, you can double-click a program to launch it. Or, if the application is stored in a folder, you can open the folder first and then launch the application icon. Aside from using the Applications folder, you can install programs directly to your Home folder—but this keeps any other users on the Mac from using the program.

 Of course, OS X gives you more ways than one to start an application. You can also simply click a program's icon on the Dock, if it is listed there. You can select the application's icon and press COMMAND-O. You can also select the application's icon and click File | Open. Or you can open any file that is associated with that program. For example, if I run Photoshop Elements, I could just double-click a Photoshop Elements file to open the program.

However, aside from the applications OS X provides for you, you can download or purchase any others you want and install them on your Mac. The following headaches and painkillers address installation problems that might come your way.

I want a certain application, but I don't know whether it will work on my Mac

Cause   Applications are written for certain operating systems. Some are written for Macs, others for Windows, Linux, and so forth. Aside from operating systems, applications are also written for certain versions of operating systems. For example, some applications were written for OS 9 and previous versions, and some are written specifically for OS X.

The Painkiller   In order for you to install and run a program on your Mac, the program must be written for the Macintosh operating system. Generally, you can't install Windows programs on your Mac without specialized software, but the good news is that OS X can run just about any Mac program. What about programs for OS 9 and earlier? No problem! OS X can open and read those programs. When you launch an OS 9 application, OS X opens a simulator called Classic so the new operating system can run these older programs. So, what can you install? For the most part, you can install any software that's compatible with OS X or OS 9 on your Mac. If you are shopping for software, be sure to check the box for compatibility. It should tell you that it is compatible with Mac right on the box.

TIP   *Some applications say "Compatible with Windows and Mac" on the box. Does this mean the software is so versatile that it can work anywhere? Not really. These programs simply have versions of the software for Windows and Mac on the same CD. This saves consumer confusion and saves the company from having to print up different boxes for the two versions.*

Cocoa, Anyone?

As we are talking about applications in OS X, and if you are discussing your Mac with other Mac users or checking out web sites, you may hear the terms *cocoa, carbon*, and *Classic* thrown around. Never fear, here's what those crazy words mean.

- **Cocoa**   A cocoa program is one that is written from scratch for OS X. The software company has used the OS X specifications to create the program specifically for the operating system. Cocoa programs generally arrive on the scene after OS X's release in brand-new programs.

- **Carbon**   A carbon program is actually an OS 9 program that has been updated for OS X. In other words, the software company didn't throw out all of the old OS 9 code but simply updated it for OS X. Carbonized programs don't have access to all of OS X's functions as the program would if it were written as a cocoa program, but carbonization saves software companies a lot of time and money in program development. In fact, many of the programs that came bundled with OS X are actually carbonized programs, including iPhoto, Internet Explorer, and even the Finder.

■ **Classic**   Classic programs have not been updated for OS X at all. They contain the same programming that was used under OS 9. Some software companies simply do not update their existing software, or you may want to use a program from a company that is no longer in business and cannot update the software anyway. That's no problem; OS X can still run these programs for you through a simulator called Classic, although this mode is less stable than the OS X environment.

I don't know how to install an application from a CD

Cause   If you buy an application from a regular store, it will most likely come to you as a CD. You typically launch the CD and follow the installation instructions that appear, and OS X does the rest for you. In some cases, you can drag the drive icon that appears on the desktop when you insert a CD to your Macintosh HD and the installation routine starts up.

The Painkiller   To install an application from a CD, follow these steps:

1. Insert the CD into the CD drive. An icon for the drive appears on your desktop. Double-click the icon to open it.

2. In most programs, a folder opens where you see a number of icons and folders, shown in the following illustration, and even some Read Me files. You should open and read the Read Me files for important installation and update information. When you're done, just close the files.

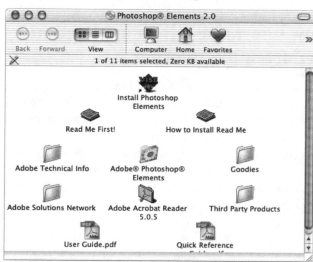

3. When you're ready to install the application, just click the Install icon that appears in the folder. This starts an installation routine. You may have to answer a few questions and read and accept a license agreement, such as the one shown in the illustration. You may also be asked where you want to install the application (Applications folder or Home folder). In addition, you may need to enter the Administrator's name and password because, by default, Normal users are not allowed to install software.

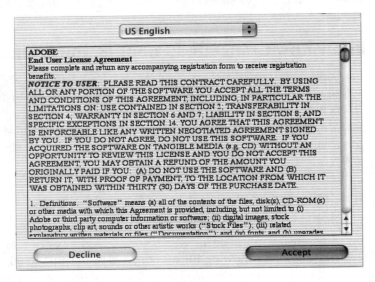

4. Continue to follow the installation instructions to complete the installation.

I don't know how to install an application I downloaded from the Internet

Cause   You can download a great number of free and cool applications from the Internet. Once you download them, they arrive on your desktop in a package form. Basically, this means that the contents of the application's installation folder have been compressed so that it does not take you an eternity to download the program. The package you see on your desktop may have a .sit extension, as shown here, which means it is a StuffIt file. Or, it may have an extension of .tar or .gz. These extensions note the file is compressed using a UNIX program. OS X uses UNIX under its hood, so this is just fine, too.

sound_studio_205.sit

The Painkiller   To install a downloaded application, follow these steps:

1. Double-click the downloaded icon. You see a dialog box showing you that OS X is decompressing the download.

2. Once the download is decompressed, a folder for it appears on your desktop. Open the folder.

3. Double-click the installation icon in the folder to start the installation, or open and read the Read Me files if any are available. From this point, installation continues, and you may have to answer a few questions or provide the Administrator name and password. Follow the steps until you are finished.

OS X will not let me install an application in the Applications folder

Cause   You're probably logged on with a Normal account. Normal account users can only install applications into their Home folders—not on the systemwide Applications folder.

The Painkiller   In order to install an application in the Applications folder, you need to log in with an Administrator account. If you do not have an Administrator account, you need get help from someone who does. See Chapter 3 to learn more about user headaches.

An application fails to install, or I get a bunch of error messages during the installation

Cause   If an application fails to install or you get failure messages during the installation, the CD you are using is probably bad or, in the case of a downloaded application, the download is probably corrupt.

The Painkiller   If you have bought a CD and are having these problems, contact the manufacturer's tech support line. In the case of a download, try downloading the application again and starting over.

 *If a program requires the support of some other program, or some specific system requirements must be met, the installation could also stop. Be sure to read the program's installation documentation for details.*

 # I need to make sure an application uses the Classic environment

Cause   OS X does a good job of deciding which applications should use the OS X environment and which applications need to use the Classic environment. However, in some cases you may want to make certain that an application opens in Classic so that helper applications or plug-ins can be used. In this case, you can configure the application to open in Classic.

The Painkiller   To make an application open in Classic, follow these steps:

1. Open Macintosh HD | Applications, or open your Home folder if the application is installed there.

2. CONTROL-click the application's icon and click Get Info. Or, select the application's icon and click File | Get Info.

3. In the Get Info window, select the check box to open the application in Classic. Close the Get Info window.

 # How do I quit an application?

Cause   When you are finished using an application, you can choose to quit the application, which just closes it. The good news in OS X is that virtual memory is handled so well that you can keep a number of applications open as you wish. In fact, some people who use certain applications a lot simply never close them. However, if you want to quit an application, you can easily do so.

The Painkiller   To quit an application, click File | Quit. If you have any unsaved work from the application, you are prompted to save your work.

Application Usage Headaches

Once an application is installed, you can open and use the application, create files, and do anything the application provides whenever you want. Different applications do different things, so you need to see the application's help files for specific troubleshooting steps if you are having problems. Also, concerning OS X applications and utilities, see Chapter 4 for additional help. The following headaches and painkillers focus on general application usage problems you are likely to run into.

An application stops working or stops responding

Cause   If you are working with an application and it suddenly stops working or responding to keyboard and mouse input, something has happened to the program and caused it to lock up. This problem doesn't happen very often with OS X applications, but you may see it from time to time when you are using OS 9 applications. The only thing you can do is force the application to quit so you can get control again. Doing this causes you to lose any unsaved work within that application, though.

The Painkiller   To force an application to quit, use the following steps:

1. Click the Apple menu and select Force Quit.

2. You can also press COMMAND-OPTION-ESC, or you can hold down OPTION and click the application's icon on the Dock. This opens a window where you see a Force Quit option. Once you've forced an application to quit, you can simply start it again and go back to work.

If some of your programs seem to work intermittently, you probably have too many applications open and are taxing the Mac's RAM. See the previous headache about quitting applications.

A file doesn't open with the right application

Cause   Files are created with applications, and when you double-click a file to open it, OS X uses the default application for that file. For example, if you open a JPEG picture file, the Preview application opens the file. However, what if you want a different application to open the file. For example, let's say I install Photoshop Elements and I want Photoshop Elements to open when I double-click a certain picture file. In this case, you can use Get Info to change the file's application association. This change tells OS X to open the file with the application you choose.

 *An application must be able to read the file type in order to open it. For example, you can't open a Quicken file using Photoshop Elements. Just keep in mind that applications can only open and read the types of files they were created to open and read.*

The Painkiller   To change a file's application association, do this:

1. CONTROL-click the desired file and click Get Info, or select the file and click File | Get Info.

2. In the Get Info window, expand Open With and select the application you want to use to open the file, as shown in the following illustration.

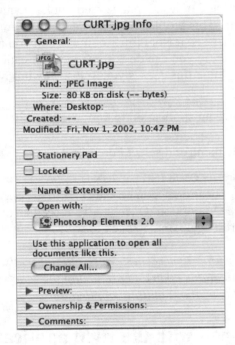

3. More easily, you can CONTROL-click the file's icon, point to Open With, and select the application you want to use. However, this option is a "once only" feature. The next time you open the file, it opens with the default application. To change the association permanently, use the Get Info option, as described in Step 2.

I want certain applications to start automatically when I log in

Cause   If you use certain applications regularly, you can configure OS X to start those applications automatically when you log in. This is just a customization feature that helps you get your applications up and running automatically instead of opening each one individually.

The Painkiller   To configure applications to start when you log in, use the following steps:

1. On the Dock, click Preferences, or choose Apple | System Preferences.

2. In the Preferences window, click Login Items, found in the Personal section.

3. In Login Items, click Add. Then, select the applications that you want to start when you log in and click Add.

4. The applications you selected now appear in the Login Items window, shown in the following illustration. To have an application start but stay hidden when you log in, click the Hide check box. You can also drag items around to determine the order in which they start.

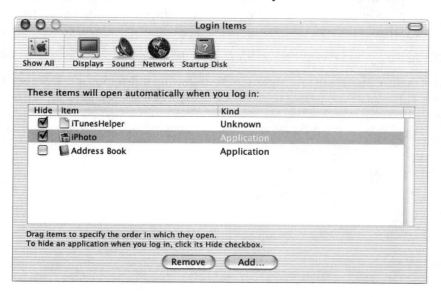

5. Close System Preferences when you're done.

If you want to prevent the applications from opening when you log in, just hold down SHIFT immediately after you click the Login button.

I have several OS 9 applications open, and they have all stopped working

Cause   If you are using several OS 9 applications, Classic mode is started to run those applications. However, in some cases, when an application stops working, it makes the other OS 9 applications stop working, too. It's a real pain, yes, but it does happen. In this case, you need to Force Quit all of the applications or Force Quit the Classic environment altogether to shut the applications down.

The Painkiller   To Force Quit the OS 9 applications, use the following steps:

1. To Force Quit the individual applications, see the "An application stops working or stops responding" headache previously in this chapter.

2. If you want to stop the Classic environment, thus quitting all OS 9 applications, click System Preferences on the Dock or choose Apple | System Preferences.

3. In the System Preferences window, click the Classic icon in the System section.

4. In the Classic window, shown in the following illustration, click Force Quit. This causes you to lose unsaved data in all OS 9 applications that are open.

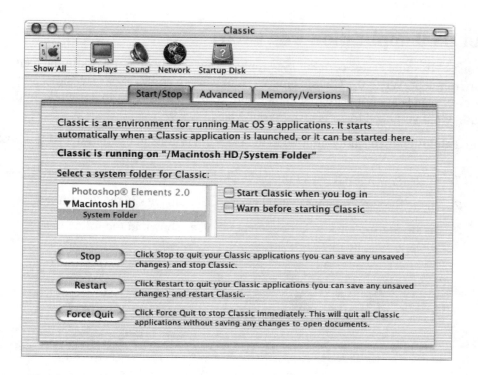

 ## I want the Classic environment to start automatically when I log in

Cause   If you are using several OS 9 applications, you can have the Classic environment start automatically whenever you log in. You can also configure the applications to start automatically, which starts the Classic environment. See the "I want certain applications to start automatically when I log in" headache earlier in this chapter.

The Painkiller   To start the Classic environment automatically, use the following steps:

1. Click System Preferences on the Dock or choose Apple | System Preferences.

2. In the System Preferences window, click the Classic icon in the System section.

3. In the Classic window, click the Start Classic When You Log In check box option.

An OS 9 application won't start

Cause   In some cases, certain OS 9 applications simply do not work in the Classic environment. When the Classic environment is used, some OS 9 extensions and control panels are not started, and therefore some applications do not work. In this case, what you need to do is restart your Mac in OS 9.

The Painkiller   To start your Mac in the OS 9 environment, use the following steps:

1. Click System Preferences on the Dock, or choose Apple | System Preferences.

2. In the System Preferences window, click Startup Disk in the System category.

3. In the Startup Disk window, select OS 9, as shown in the following illustration, and click Restart.

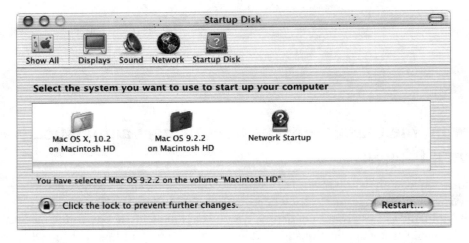

4. The Mac starts in OS 9. When you're done using the OS 9 application, return to Startup Disk, select OS X, and restart your computer.

I don't know how to move around between applications

Cause   If you have several applications open at the same time, you can easily move between them using the Dock. You can also hide open applications by pressing COMMAND-H.

The Painkiller   The Dock is your best source for switching between running applications. You can learn more about the Dock in Chapter 1.

Chapter 9

Internet Connection Headaches

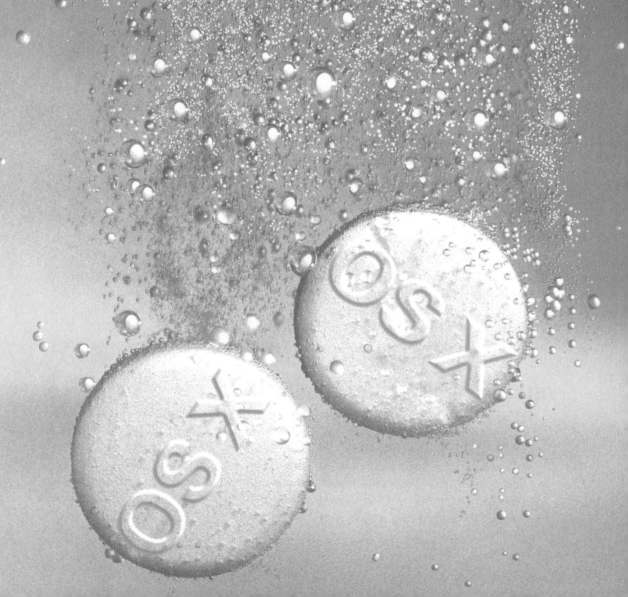

In this chapter, you'll cure...

■ Problems with Internet connections

■ Modem issues

The *Internet*, which is the world's largest network, has become an important force in all of our lives. I remember back in the mid-1990s when I was using a PowerMac with a whopping 16MB of RAM. I bought my first 28.8-kbps modem and set up my first Internet connection. The connection cost $6 per month and gave me five hours of Internet access each month. I remember remarking, "Why would I ever need more than five hours a month?"

Now, of course, you use 56-kbps modems, or you can use a broadband connection if one is available in your area. In terms of using the Internet, I use it hours every day. In fact, as a freelance writer, I do all of my work and communication with my editors over the Internet, and I would not be able to survive without it. In fact, your Mac came to you with an internal modem built in, and it is ready for the Internet. The Internet is no longer seen as a cool option but as a standard part of having a computer. Although the Internet is still a baby in terms of technology, it has grown by millions of computers and has more features and services than ever. In fact, I buy more stuff from the Internet now than I do at most brick-and-mortar stores (I even bought most of my kids' Christmas presents online this past year).

The Internet is a vital part of computing, and you'll no doubt want to be connected so you can take advantage of all the Internet has to offer. However, for all the great things OS X brings to the table, it is not the easiest computing system to use to create an Internet connection. You may have some difficulties when creating and using your Internet connection. Never fear, though, that's why I wrote this chapter!

Internet Connection Headaches

The good news is that OS X has everything you need to create an Internet connection. The bad news is OS X doesn't give you a handy assistant to guide you through the process of creating that connection. You have to do it manually by entering the correct settings for the connection. Although not difficult, the process can be a bit confusing if you are not that familiar with Internet connections. Don't worry, though. In this section, I'll show you how to create the Internet connection, how to dial the connection, and how to solve a few aggravating headaches.

Now I said OS X doesn't have an assistant to help you set up your Internet connection, but that is not entirely true. When you started OS X for the first time, there was a little assistant to help you set up your Internet connection. If you didn't set up the connection at that time, you can still find the little assistant lurking deep in OS X. It is located in Macintosh HD/System/Library/CoreServices/Setup Assistant.

Understanding Types of Internet Connections

If the concepts of dial-up and broadband connections leave you scratching your head, don't worry. Here's the skinny:

- **Dial-up**   A dial-up connection uses your Mac's modem to dial a phone number that connects you to an Internet server (also called a PPP Server, or Point-to-Point Protocol Server). You access the Internet over the phone line and through this server. Modems are limited to 52-kbps transfer by FCC regulations, with the reality being about 48 kbps or less. So, modem access is the slowest type of Internet access today, but it also is the least expensive and most popular. Most dial-up plans cost between $10 and $25 each month for unlimited access, depending on what Internet Service Provider (ISP) you decide to go with.

- **DSL**   DSL is a broadband technology that gives you fast Internet access. You don't have to dial a phone number because the connection is always present. DSL uses a standard phone line, but it works at higher frequencies so it doesn't interfere with analog phone calls, and it provides digital service, often at 500 kbps and up. The speed of DSL depends on where you live, if it is available at all. DSL costs between $30 and $50 each month, and you'll need a special DSL modem for the connection (which is usually provided free with your ISP subscription).

- **Cable**   Cable is another type of broadband technology, also giving you around 256-kbps transfer and up. Cable Internet uses television cable. A cable modem is used for the connection. The cable connection is always on, so no dialing is involved. Like DSL, cable connections cost between $30 and $50 per month.

- **Satellite**   You can also use a satellite connection, which works like DirecTV. Satellite connections are not as popular as DSL and cable, but they can provide you with 400–600–kbps transfer or even better. You'll have to find a satellite provider that supports Macintosh systems, and the service can cost upward of $100 a month. You'll also have to pay for the satellite dish and setup, which can cost you another $500 or so.

How do I get an Internet Account?

Cause   This headache often occurs when people new to the Internet first try to understand how to get an Internet connection. Here's the deal—the Internet is a free network, but you have to pay a company called an Internet Service Provider (ISP) to give you a connection. Once you select an ISP, you open an account with it in much the same way you would open a phone account. Depending on the kind of service you purchase, such as dial-up, DSL, cable, and so on, you pay a certain monthly fee to them. The ISP provides you with information and instructions about how to set up the account on your computer. Specifically, it provides you with a username, password, and, if you are using a dial-up account, the numbers you dial to access the ISP's servers.

The Painkiller   Depending on where you live, there are probably a number of ISPs competing with each other. If you need to find an ISP, start with your phone book's yellow pages. Call the companies and ask them about their plans, rates,and so on. Most ISPs give you at least one e-mail address, and a few even give you web space so you can set up a home page if you like. Some ISPs offer better deals than others, so shop competitively and be sure to solicit advice from friends and family who live in your area.

I don't know how to set up my dial-up Internet connection

Cause   As I mentioned, OS X doesn't give you an easy assistant to help you set up your Internet connection (except for the little assistant buried down in OS X), but all you have to do is plug the information your ISP gives you into the correct place, which I'll show you how to do in the Painkiller.

The Painkiller   Make sure the documentation provided by your ISP is handy and follow these steps:

1. Click System Preferences on the Dock to open it.

2. In the Internet and Network category, click Network (not Internet).

3. In the Show drop-down menu, select Internal Modem.

4. On the TCP/IP tab, shown in the following illustration, you can manually enter the Internet Protocol addresses of some servers your computer uses to communicate on the Internet. However, for most connections, you can accept the default of Using PPP instead of entering anything here. Check your ISP's instructions—if it doesn't tell you to do anything here, leave this tab alone.

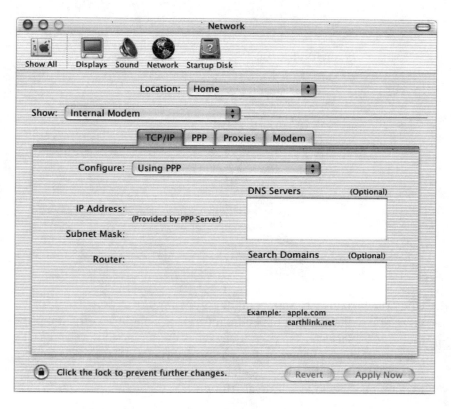

5. Click the PPP tab. The PPP tab is where you plug in the information provided by your ISP, shown in the following illustration. Enter your ISP's name, your account name, and your password as provided to you by your

ISP and then enter the phone number your Mac should call when connecting to the Internet. If your ISP provides optional numbers in the event the first number is busy, enter the optional number as well. If you do not want to enter the ISP password every time you connect, click the Save Password option.

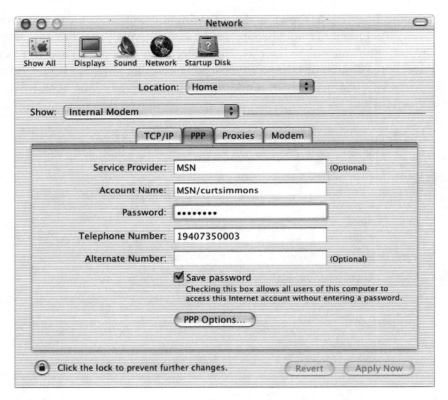

6. Click the Proxies tab, shown in the following illustration. The Proxies tab gives you a place to enter specific information about servers that provide the Internet services listed. You can enter the server address and TCP port—but the good news is that you probably don't have to do anything here. Check your ISP documentation. Unless it specifically tells you what to enter on this tab, don't do anything.

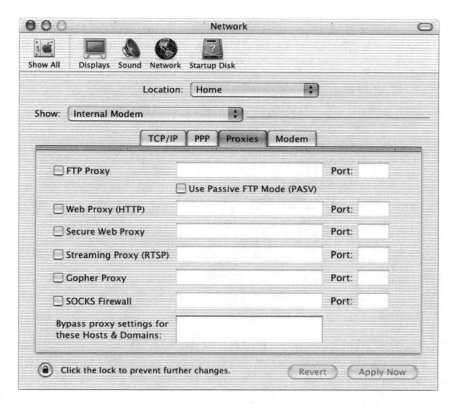

7. That's it! Click Apply Now.

I don't know how to dial an Internet connection

Cause   To start an Internet dial-up connection, first make sure you have the connection configured (see the previous headache). Then you can start the Internet connection using the Internet Connect program in your Applications folder. You can also configure your connection to start automatically whenever you open an Internet application, such as Internet Explorer or Mail.

The Painkiller   To use Internet Connect, follow these steps:

1. Open Macintosh HD I Applications I Internet Connect.

2. In the Internal Modem window that appears, shown in the following illustration, click Connect. Notice that you can have the connection status appear in the menu bar by clicking the check box.

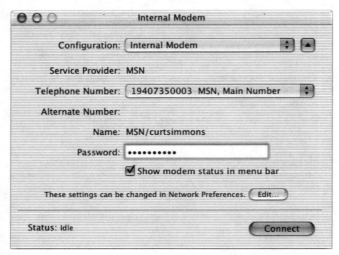

3. Once the connection is established, the window shows the connection status and the amount of time you have been connected, as shown in the following illustration. Click Disconnect to stop the connection.

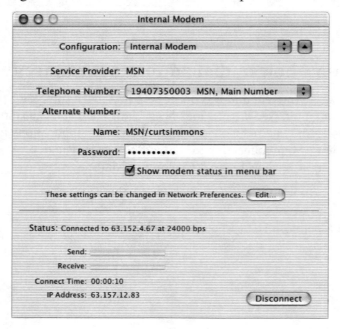

 *If you chose to display the modem status in the menu bar, you see a phone icon and the amount of time you have been connected. To disconnect without returning to the Internet Connect window, click the phone icon on the menu bar. A menu appears. Click Disconnect.*

 # I don't know how to set up my broadband connection

Cause   Broadband connections such as cable and DSL typically connect to an Ethernet port on the back of your Mac. An Ethernet port is a networking port typically used when networking computers together, but broadband connections may also use this port. Once they are connected and set up, you do not have to dial a connection. You are always connected, so start the Internet application you want to use.

The Painkiller   To set up your broadband connection, follow the instructions provided by your ISP. Each ISP is a little different, so make sure you follow the instructions—and don't hesitate to call their help line if you are having problems. For the most part, though, you simply follow the same steps as you would when setting up a dial-up connection. See the "I don't know how to set up my dial-up Internet connection" headache for more information.

 # My dial-up connection does not start when I start Internet applications

Cause   OS X can start a dial-up connection for you when you first open an Internet application, such as Internet Explorer or Mail. This way, you don't have to worry about dialing the connection each time. However, you have to enable this feature.

The Painkiller   To configure OS X to start a dial-up connection when you start an Internet application, follow these steps:

1. Open System Preferences.

2. In the Internet and Network category, click Network.

3. Click the PPP tab.

4. Click the PPP Options button.

5. In the drop-down window that appears, shown in the following illustration, select the Connect Automatically When Needed check box. Click OK and

click Apply Now. The connection starts automatically when applications need it.

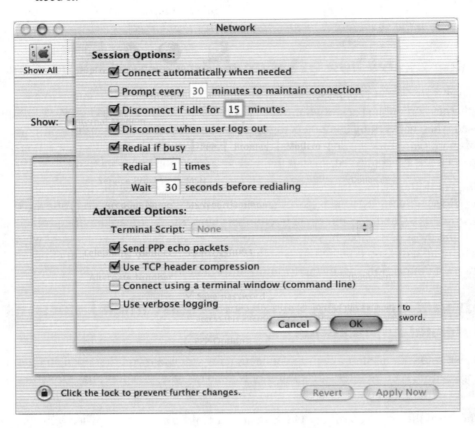

You may find it helpful to display the dial-up connection on the menu bar so you can see what is going on with the connection. To enable the dial-up icon on the menu bar, enable the option in the Internet Connect interface as discussed in the "I don't know how to dial an Internet connection" headache earlier in this chapter.

My dial-up connection keeps trying to connect when not in use

Cause   If your dial-up connection is configured to connect when needed (see the previous headache), it tries to connect whenever an application needs data from the

Internet. If you are not using any applications, the odds are good that one of them is open and trying to use the Internet.

The Painkiller   Use the Finder or the Dock to make sure all Internet applications are actually closed.

My connection keeps asking me whether I want to stay connected

Cause   In order to keep you from forgetting about your connection and leaving your computer connected unnecessarily, OS X can prompt you every 30 minutes or so with an annoying dialog box asking whether you want to stay connected. If you don't want to see this dialog box, you can stop it.

The Painkiller   To stop the autoprompt feature, follow these steps:

1. Open System Preferences.

2. In the Internet and Network category, click Network.

3. Click the PPP tab.

4. Click the PPP Options button.

5. Uncheck the box that says Prompt Every x Minutes To Maintain Connection. Click OK and then click Apply Now.

My connection disconnects itself if I leave the computer idle

Cause   In order to keep you from forgetting about your connection and leaving your computer connected unnecessarily, OS X can automatically disconnect the connection for you after a certain amount of idle time has passed (the default is 15 minutes). However, you may find this behavior annoying, in which case you can stop it.

The Painkiller   To stop the autodisconnect feature, follow these steps:

1. Open System Preferences.

2. In the Internet and Network category, click Network.

3. Click the PPP tab.

4. Click the PPP Options button.

5. Uncheck the box that says Disconnect If Idle For x Minutes. Click OK and then click Apply Now.

My ISP dial-up is sometimes busy, but my Mac doesn't try to redial for me

Cause   A common problem when using dial-up accounts is the famous busy signal. During peak usage times, you may have to try to dial the ISP a few times in order to get a connection. If you have to do this a lot, you really should call your ISP and complain. However, an occasional busy signal is to be expected. The good news is you can configure OS X to automatically redial for you and keep trying to get connected.

The Painkiller   To use automatic redial, follow these steps:

1. Open System Preferences.

2. In the Internet and Network category, click Network.

3. Click the PPP tab.

4. Click the PPP Options button.

5. Select the Redial If Busy check box and enter the number of redial attempts you want the Mac to make. You can also change the 30-second wait value between dialing attempts if you like. When you're done, click OK and then click Apply Now.

My connection is slow or fails often

Cause   Regardless of whether you use a dial-up connection or broadband connection, you may experience slow service from time to time. This often happens during peak usage times when your ISP is busy or the Internet sites you are trying to access are busy. There's nothing you can do about this, but if you notice that your service is regularly slow or you get a lot of disconnects with a dial-up account, you need to call your ISP about the problem.

The Painkiller   Contact your ISP for help.

I can't connect to any web sites

Cause   Once you are connected to the Internet, you can use Internet Explorer or any other web browser to access web sites. If you can't seem to access any web sites at all, you should check a few things.

The Painkiller   Take a look at these things:

1. Make sure you are connected. Even if you open Internet Explorer, you must be connected to the Internet before you can access any web sites.

2. Check your ISP's documentation. In order to access web sites, your computer must be able to access Domain Name System (DNS) servers on the Internet. Your ISP may require that you enter the addresses of some DNS servers for the connection to use.

3. Make sure you are typing the web address correctly. Web addresses work by using domain names, such as www.curtsimmons.com. You must enter the address correctly to access a web site.

 *Having problems using Internet Explorer? See Chapter 10 for more help.*

 ## I need to use more than one dial-up connection

Cause   Don't confuse your modem with a dial-up connection. Your modem is simply the hardware that uses the connection. You can configure more than one connection to use the same modem. Why would you? Here are two common examples:

- You use a Mac at home and one at your office. Your office provides dial-up access. You want to use an Internet connection at home but also dial-up to your office as needed.

- You travel with your Mac. When at home, you want to use a certain Internet connection. When you travel, you want to use an Internet connection provided by your company.

The Painkiller   To use two different dial-up connections, you have to use two different locations. Follow these steps:

1. Open System Preferences.

2. In the Internet and Network category, click Network.

3. In the Location menu, your current setting probably shows Automatic. To create a new dial-up connection, you need to create a new location setting. Click the menu and select New Location, as shown in the following illustration.

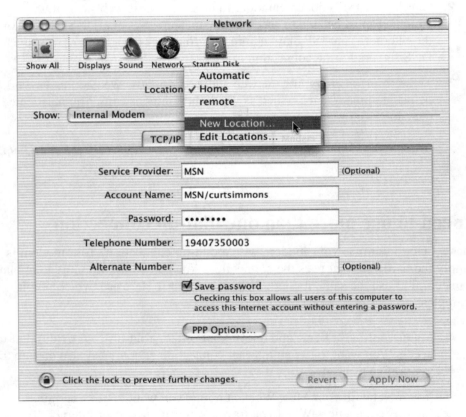

4. In the new location dialog box that appears, enter a new location name (such as "office" or "remote") and click OK.

5. Now, edit the TCP/IP, PPP, and Proxies tabs as needed for the new location. Click Apply Now when you're done.

6. Depending on the connection you want to create, return to the Network window and select the desired location from the menu. Or, for a faster location switch, choose the Apple menu, point to Location and then select your current location, as you can see in the following illustration.

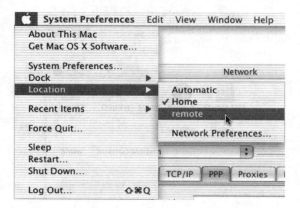

 # I have both a DSL connection and a dial-up connection—how can I control the one that is used?

Cause   You may have two connections that can be used for a single location. For example, you might have a DSL or cable connection and even a dial-up connection configured for backup purposes. You probably want to use the DSL connection only, but if the DSL connection goes down, you can use the dial-up connection. OS X can be aware of both connections or both ports and use them according to need.

The Painkiller   All you really have to do is tell OS X which order you want connections to be used. To configure the order, follow these steps:

1. Open System Preferences.

2. In the Internet and Network category, click Network.

3. In the Show drop-down menu, select Network Port Configurations, as shown in the following illustration.

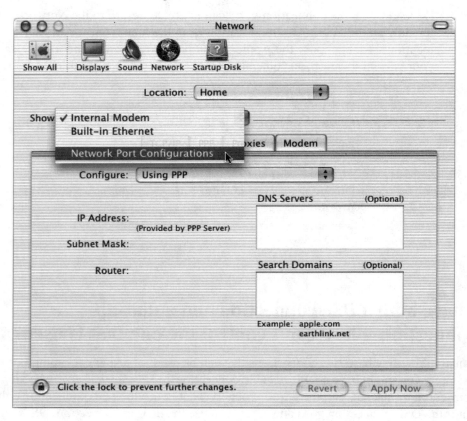

4. In the Network Port Configurations window, shown in the following illustration, you see the current ports for the location. You can drag the connections around until they are in the order that you want to use them. Click Apply Now when you're done.

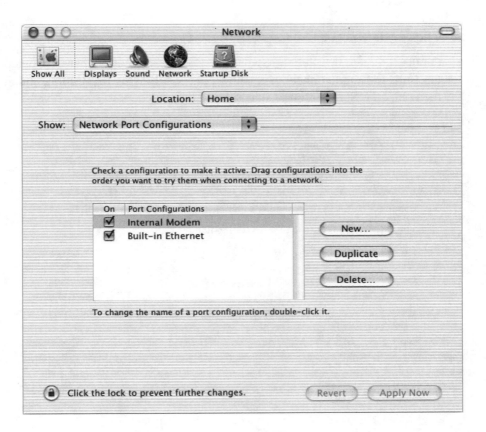

 # I don't know how to share my Internet connection

Cause   You may have a network of other Macs but only a single Internet connection. For example, let's say you have three Macs at your home or office that are networked. However, only one of the Macs has an Internet connection. You want all Macs to be able to use the Internet connection. Can you do it? Yes.

The Painkiller   To share an Internet connection, follow these steps:

1. Click System Preferences on the Dock, or choose Apple | System Preferences.

2. In the Internet and Network Category, click the Sharing icon to open it.

3. Click the Internet tab.

4. On the Internet tab, click the Share The Connection With Other Computers On Built-in Ethernet check box, shown in the following illustration, and then click the Start button to start sharing the connection.

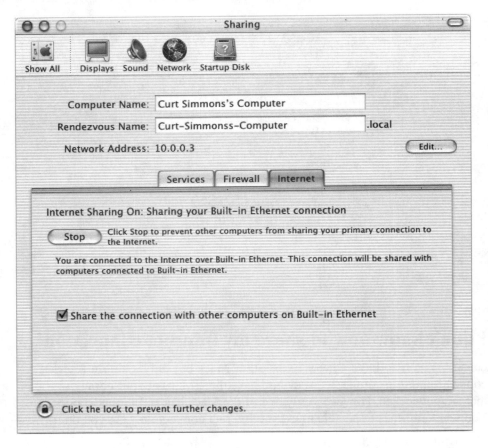

Modem Headaches

Your Mac came to you with an internal 56-kbps modem already set up and configured. Using this modem, you are not likely to experience any headaches at all. However, you can also use an external modem that you connect via a USB port. If you have chosen to use a different modem, you may have compatibility problems. If you are using a different modem, you need to make sure the modem is compatible with Macintosh systems. Otherwise, you typically don't have to change any settings.

If you open System Preferences and open Network, you can select Internal Modem from the Show menu. Then, click the Modem tab, shown in the following illustration. You'll see your modem selected in the Modem menu. You also see some settings that apply to your modem, such as Enable Error Correction And Compression and Wait For Dial Tone Before Dialing. You should not need to change these standard settings on your Mac. One helpful feature if you are using one phone line for voice and Internet calls is the Notify Me Of Incoming Calls While Connected To The Internet. This setting enables the Mac to play a sound alert if you get an incoming voice call while you are connected.

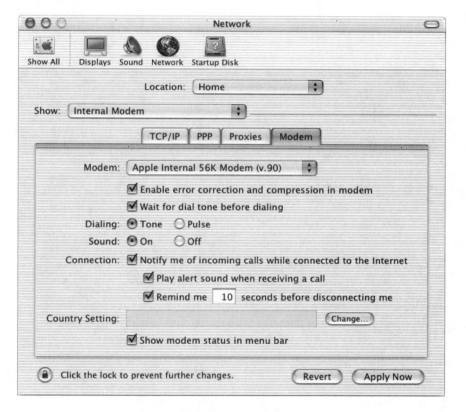

If you are using a different modem, click the Modem menu option to select the modem that you are using. You can configure any of the necessary items for that modem. Refer to your modem documentation for details and additional troubleshooting tips.

Chapter 10

Using the Web

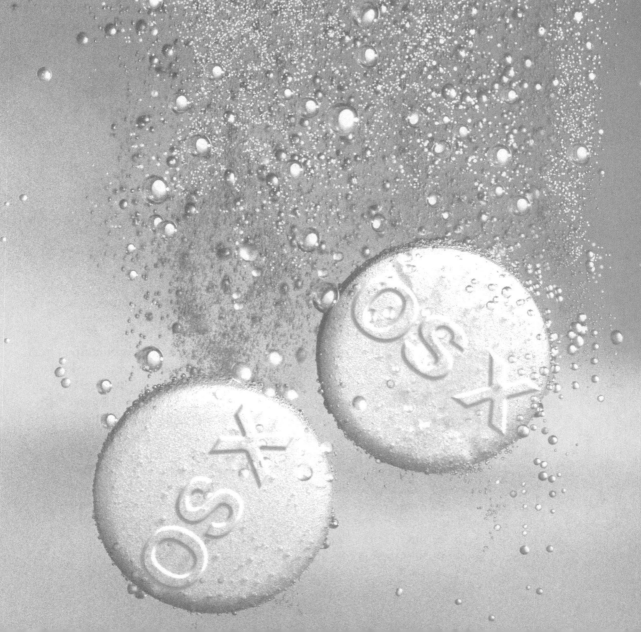

In this chapter, you'll cure…

- ■ Problems with Internet Explorer
- ■ Questions about iTools

In order to use the Internet, your Mac must have an Internet connection configured. (You can learn more about configuring and troubleshooting Internet connections in Chapter 9.) Once you are connected to the Internet, what do you do next? If you are new to the Internet, and the Mac for that matter, you need an application called a *browser* to connect to web pages and access resources on the Internet. For e-mail, you'll need an application called an e-mail client. OS X gives you both of these: Internet Explorer and Mail. This chapter focuses on Internet Explorer, but you can learn more about the Mail application in Chapter 11.

Why Internet Explorer? Internet Explorer is simply a web browser produced by Microsoft. It is arguably the most popular browser in use today, but it is not the only browser. In fact, you can download and install other browsers on OS X, such as Netscape or Opera. However, Internet Explorer is included on your operating system, and I bet that most of you are simply going to use Internet Explorer. This chapter shows you how to cure those aggravating Internet Explorer headaches you may have experienced so far, and it also takes a look at Apple's new web site called .Mac, where you can do a lot of cool things as a Mac user.

Getting to Know Internet Explorer

If you are new to the Internet and to Internet Explorer, this section is for you. If you have been using Internet Explorer and are comfortable using the browser, skip to the next section where we will get into some headaches you can easily cure.

So, is this your first time with Internet Explorer or using the Internet? In this section, we'll take a quick tour of the Internet Explorer interface, and you'll be surfing in no time. First things first: you should understand what a browser does. When you use the Internet, you access web pages. These pages are made up primarily of a computer code called HyperText Markup Language (HTML). The browser's job is to download that code and basically assemble it so that you see those cool web pages with all of their text and pictures. Depending on the web site, you may also use streaming video or audio and any number of features that make your surfing experience fun. Internet Explorer, which I'll call "IE" from now on, can interpret all of this information for you so you can use the Internet however you want. IE's job is to help you get around the Internet and to display the web pages you want to see.

Find IE on the Dock (it looks like a big *e*). Just click it to get started. If you are using a dial-up connection and you configured it to dial automatically, the connection launches and IE connects to a default home page. If you did not configure your dial-up connection to start automatically, you can manually launch the connection. See Chapter 9 for more information about configuring Internet connections. Once IE loads the home page, you see the home page in the IE window along with toolbars that can help you navigate the Web, as you can see in the following illustration.

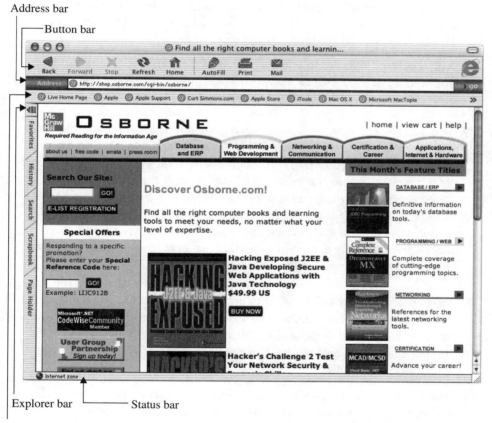

Address bar
Button bar
Explorer bar
Status bar
Favorites bar

As you can see in the previous illustration, Internet Explorer is made up of a standard interface with some different portions and toolbars. They include the following:

- **Button bar**   The Button bar appears at the top of IE by default, and it contains standard buttons you can use when navigating the Web. The Back and Forward buttons let you move between web pages you are looking at. You can also use the Stop button to stop loading a page and Refresh to have IE reload a page. The Home button takes you to the default home page, and AutoFill can help you automatically fill out web forms. In addition, you can print a page and e-mail a page easily using the buttons provided. You can also customize this toolbar for your needs; see the "Internet Explorer Headaches" section for more information.

- **Address bar**   The Address bar gives you a place to type Internet addresses you want to access, such as www.osborne.com or www.apple.com. Simply enter the address and click Go, or just press RETURN.

NOTE   *A complete web address is made up of four parts: the protocol, the service, the web site name, and the domain. For example, a complete address is http://www.apple.com. HTTP is the protocol used, www (World Wide Web) is the service, Apple is the site name, and .com is the Internet domain. The good news is that modern browsers like Internet Explorer do not require you to type http://www—this information is simply understood by the browser, so all you have to type is the site name and the domain, such as apple.com, osborne.com, and so forth. This feature saves you some time and makes browsing much easier.*

- **Favorites**   The Favorites bar lists favorite web sites that you can access. To access these sites, just click the Favorite's name, and you can automatically jump to those sites. "But, these aren't my Favorites!" you might be saying. Don't worry. You can change them, and I'll show you how in the next section.

- **Status bar**   The Status bar is a tiny bar that appears at the bottom of IE. It simply tells you what is going on with the current page (loading, errors, and so on).

- **Explorer bar**   The Explorer bar appears on the left side of the browser by default, and it allows you to access some IE features, which we'll take a look at in a moment.

Surfing the 'Net

All right—you have IE open and you are connected to the Internet. To begin surfing, you can simply enter a web address in the Address bar. Remember that you don't have to type http:// or www, just the name and the domain (apple.com, for example, is all you need). Once you enter the address, IE locates the web site and downloads the site's home page for you. At this point, you can read the site information provided. Within the site, you'll see *hyperlinks*, which are links to additional pages within the site or links to another site. When you click a hyperlink, the new page you requested is located and loaded for you. To go back to the previous page, just click the Back button. To go forward to a page you have already visited, click the Forward button. If you are looking for a particular site but don't know the address, visit a search engine, such as yahoo.com, dogpile.com, msn.com, netscape.com, or any of the many others, and search for the site. Or, more easily, just click Search in the Explorer bar (see the next section). In the event that a site you enter is not found on the Internet (or if you misspelled something), you see the Not Found page, as you can see in the following illustration. Just type a new address in the Address bar and press RETURN to go somewhere else. That's all there is to it!

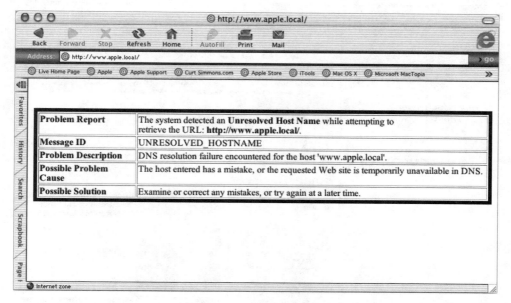

Using the Explorer Bar

The Explorer bar lives on the left side of IE by default, and it provides access to some specific items that can help you use the Internet and keep things organized.

You see tabs for Favorites, History, Search, Scrapbook, and Page Holder. If you click an item, a browser pane pops out so you can access and manage the items as desired. To close the browser pane that appears, just click the item name again.

Favorites

The Favorites list is a place to store sites that you access often. This is a great way to easily access your favorite sites and a great way to keep track of sites without having to remember their names. For example, let's say you find an Internet site that gives you a certain Christmas cookie recipe. The site name might be www.worldsgreatcookies.com/recipes/christmas.html. Rather than having to remember all of that and type it in the Address bar, you can just add it to your Favorites, give it a friendly name that you like, and simply click it when you want to return to the site again. As you can see in the following illustration, the Favorites feature enables you to easily add and delete sites as needed, and you can use the Organize button to create folders to group Favorites together.

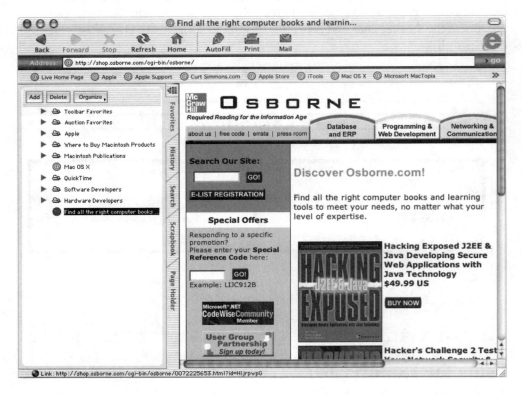

History

The History, shown in the following illustration, keeps track of all of the web sites that you visit. You see the current day's History as a link listing and the previous days' listings as folders you open. This helpful feature gives you a way to find a web site you recently visited (if you didn't add the site to your Favorites). The History list keeps track of 300 web site visits. Then they start getting dropped (oldest sites are dropped first). You can, however, change how many web site visits the History remembers or completely clear the History. See the "Internet Explorer Headaches" section for details.

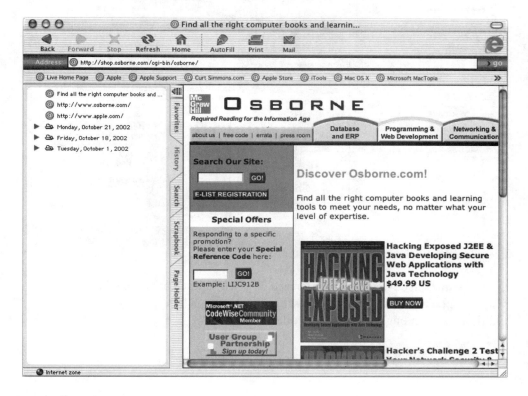

Search

If you click the Search tab, a connection is made to msn.com, where you can simply search within your web browser for items you want to locate. Use the radio buttons, shown in the following illustration, to find a web page, a person's address, a business, and so forth.

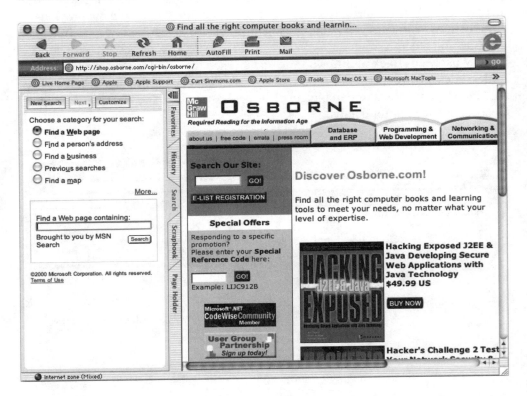

You can even customize the interface by clicking the Customize button. A window appears, shown in the following illustration, where you can select additional search engines to use in your search.

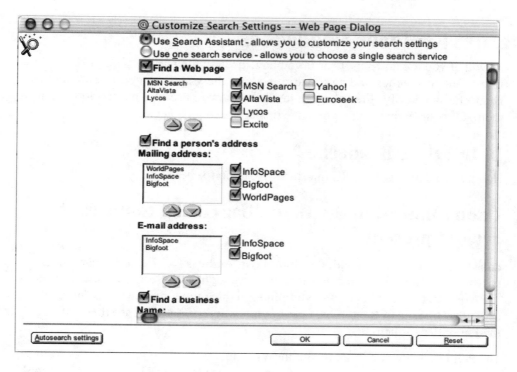

Scrapbook

The Scrapbook option at first appears like Favorites, but there is one big difference. Favorites stores a link to a web site that you visited. When you click Favorites, the page reloads. The Scrapbook, however, stores the page locally so that you can view it without having to reload. This is a great feature if you are using a dial-up connection and want to view a page when you are not online.

Page Holder

The Page Holder feature gives you a quick and easy place to hold the main page of a page that contains a bunch of links. You can click through the links and open the Page Holder to easily jump back to the main page.

Internet Explorer Headaches

Now that you are an IE user (or if you have been in the past), you are likely to run into a few headaches and aggravations along the way. The good news is most headaches are easily cured—if you just know how to use Internet Explorer to solve them. Of course, that's why you have this book, so let's get started!

IE Interface Headaches

Having problems with the IE interface? Read on for help...

I don't like all of the IE toolbars or all toolbars are not present

Cause   IE provides you with the Button bar, Address bar, Favorites bar, Status bar, and Explorer bar. You can use all of these toolbars, select only certain ones that you want, or use none of them (although this might make web surfing a little difficult). If some of the toolbars get in your way, or you don't see them all, see the Painkiller for help.

The Painkiller   Open IE and click the View menu. You see menu listings for the toolbars in IE. Bars with checks next to them appear in the IE interface. If you don't want to use a bar, simply click it to remove the check. If you want to use one that is not selected, simply click it.

The Painful "IE Is too Slow" Ailment

IE works like any web browser on the market today. As HTML data arrives from your connection, IE interprets the code and displays the web page to you. Of course, the speed at which IE can display a page to you depends on the speed of your connection; IE can only display data as fast as it gets it. So, if you think that IE is slow, the real culprit is usually your connection supplying the data. This headache generally occurs with dial-up accounts, and there isn't much you can do about it. If using the Internet is really, really slow, see Chapter 9 for some potential help with slow Internet connections. However, I'm afraid that dial-up connections simply do not work as fast as you might want them to (especially with today's graphics-intensive web sites).

I don't like the default selections on the Button bar

Cause   The Button bar presents you with some default selections. The folks at Microsoft have made some general assumptions about the items you might like to see on the Button bar. However, if you don't like what you see, you can customize the Button bar to meet your needs.

The Painkiller   To customize the Button bar, follow these steps:

1. Open IE and choose View | Customize Toolbars.

2. The options for buttons and toolbars appear in the IE interface, as shown in the following illustration. You can drag and drop icon options out of the window to the toolbar, and you can simply drag any toolbar icons that you don't want to the Trash. You can also choose a Default or Basic set of icons. When you're done, click the Back button. You can return to this page and make additional Button bar changes at any time.

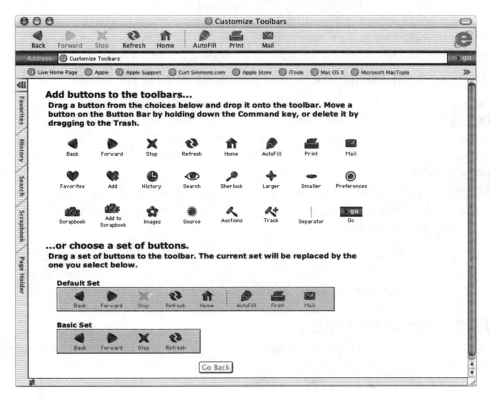

Don't like the color used on the buttons and the Address bar? No problem, just click View | Browse Color and select a new color.

I don't like the items on the Favorites bar

Cause   As with the Button bar, the Favorites bar has some default listings. They include access to the Apple site and a Microsoft site for Apple products (of course), but you can change all of these easily.

The Painkiller   To change the items on the Favorites bar, follow these steps.

1. If you want to remove an item from the Favorites bar, simply CONTROL-click the link on the bar you don't want and hit DELETE. Notice that you can also edit the name of the link here. This does not change the link itself, but it gives you a way to enter a friendlier name that makes better sense to you.

2. To add a site to the Favorites bar, first access the site by entering its address in the Address bar. Then, open Favorites and click Add. You'll see a Favorites icon appear for the site in the Favorites list. Afterward, drag the icon to the Favorites toolbar for easy access.

The text on some web sites is too small to read

Cause   Your screen resolution and the general size of the text at a web site all impact how big or how small the letters are on any particular web site. From time to time, some web sites may be difficult to read because the lettering is so small, especially if they contain a lot of text. The good news is that IE gives you a quick text zoom feature.

The Painkiller   To use the text zoom feature, click View | Text Zoom and select a zoom value. Also note that you can use COMMAND and + or – to zoom the text back and forth at any time.

You can use the default character set used by IE, which is Western (Latin1), or a variety of other character sets. Just choose View | Character Set to see the options available to you.

IE Preferences Settings

IE contains a number of default preference settings that govern how IE behaves. For the most part, the default settings are all you need to have a great surfing experience. However, a number of settings may get on your nerves or simply not meet your needs. The good news is that you can change them. Read through the following headaches and painkillers to find a quick solution to the problem you're having!

I want a text-only toolbar setting, and/or I don't want to use AutoComplete

Cause   By default, IE uses a text and icon toolbar setting so that the toolbar can display both text and icons. However, you might want to see only icons or only text. Additionally, IE tries to complete web addresses for you automatically as you type. When you type a web address, AutoComplete remembers the address and tries to finish it for you. This may be a help or hindrance, depending on your point of view.

The Painkiller   To change the toolbar and AutoComplete usage settings, follow these steps:

1. Open Internet Explorer and click Explorer | Preferences.

2. In the Internet Explorer Preferences window that appears look in the left pane and expand the Web Browser section by clicking the arrow. Click the Browser Display bullet.

3. In the right pane, shown in the following illustration, you change the Toolbar Style to icon only or text only by using the drop-down menu. If you don't want to use AutoComplete, click the check box to deselect it. Notice that you can also deselect Show ToolTips here if you like. Click OK when you're done.

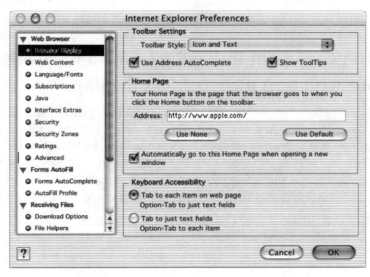

Every time I open IE, it automatically goes to Apple's web site—I want it to go to a different web site

Cause   IE comes to you with a default home page, which is www.apple.com. Every time you open IE, it will default to this home page and open it for you. However, you may not want to start at Apple's home page each time you open IE. No problem! You can choose the home page you want to start at, or you can choose none at all.

The Painkiller   To change the home page, follow these steps:

1. Open Internet Explorer and click Explorer | Preferences.

2. In the Internet Explorer Preferences window that appears, look in the left pane and expand the Web Browser section by clicking it. Click the Browser Display bullet.

3. In the right pane, click in the Address dialog box and enter a new address for the home page you want to use. You can start at any web address you like, so just enter what you want. If you don't want IE to open a home page at all, click the Use None button. Click OK when you're done.

Why would you choose not to have IE open a home page? If you have a slow connection and you like to start at different web sites when you open IE, you can save the wait time to download the default home page by simply using none at all. This keeps from having to wait (or press Stop) before you begin surfing. When you use none, a blank IE window opens where you can just use the Address bar to enter the address you want to go to.

I want to use certain link colors, or I am having problems with web page content display

Cause   IE gives you some default options for displaying links. It provides unread and read links with different colors, and all links are underlined by default. Also, you can choose from a number of page content settings, such as Show Pictures, Animate GIFs, Show Frames, and so on. For the most part, you should leave these settings alone as long as they give you the best web surfing experience. However, if you are having problems with certain page elements, you can disable them.

The Painkiller   To make changes to links and page content, follow these steps:

1. Open Internet Explorer and click Explorer | Preferences.

2. In the Internet Explorer Preferences window that appears, look in the left pane and expand the Web Browser section by clicking it. Click the Web Content bullet.

3. In the right pane, shown in the following illustration, click the link color boxes to change the default link colors. You can also select or deselect any of the check box options under Page Content and Active Content. Remember not to change these settings unless you are trying to solve specific problems. Doing so disables web content features that you might actually like.

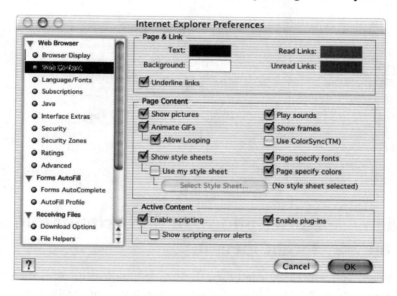

I need to view web sites that use different languages

Cause   IE gives you the option to view sites in different languages when sites provide those different languages. You can also specifically adjust the font and size of the characters used to display the languages.

The Painkiller   To make changes to languages, fonts, and sizes, follow these steps:

1. Open Internet Explorer and click Explorer | Preferences.

2. In the Internet Explorer Preferences window that appears, look in the left pane and expand the Web Browser section by clicking it. Click the Languages / Fonts bullet.

3. In the right pane, shown in the following illustration, you can add languages and order them according to the ones you use most often. Also, use the Fonts and Size section to make changes to the default fonts and sizes used so that web pages will be easier for you to read.

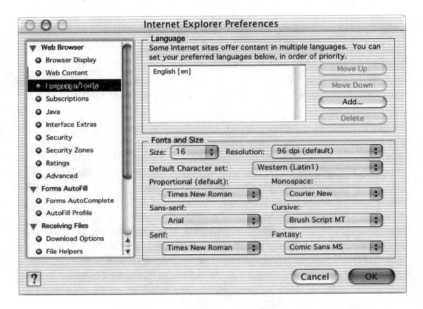

I need to use Subscriptions, or Subscriptions do not work the way I want them to

Cause   When you add a Favorite in IE, IE records the Favorite and you simply click it to load the web page. However, what if you are using a site that changes frequently, such as every day or even every hour? The problem, then, becomes accurate content. The site might have changed, but you still may be looking at content that is six hours old. This problem is common with information sites, such as news and stock sites. The good news is that IE gives you a Subscription feature that enables you to subscribe to a site and have IE check it for changes periodically. Of course, you'll have to have a live Internet connection for this feature to work very well (because IE can't check for sites when you are not connected).

The Painkiller   To subscribe to a site, follow these steps:

1. Open IE and access the site you want to subscribe to.

2. Click Favorites menu | Subscribe.

3. A subscription dialog box appears asking whether you want to subscribe. If you click Subscribe, the default subscription options are used (described later in this headache). If you want to customize the subscription, click the Customize button.

4. If you choose to customize, a window appears, shown in the following illustration. It contains several tabs so you can customize the subscription. You can manage the subscription, provide an account (if the site requires you to log on with an account name and password), create a schedule, configure a notify option that lets you know when there are changes, and have IE download the site for offline viewing. The options here are self-explanatory—just configure the ones you want to use and click OK.

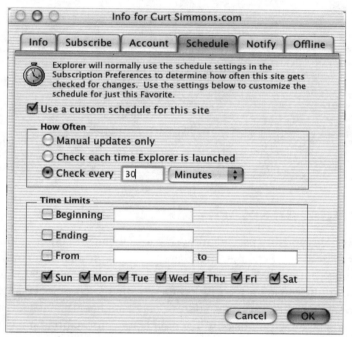

If you do not customize a subscription, IE uses some default settings that tell it how to manage the subscription. To change the default subscription settings, follow these steps:

1. Open Internet Explorer and click Explorer | Preferences.

2. In the Internet Explorer Preferences window that appears, look in the left pane and expand the Web Browser section by clicking it. Click the Subscriptions bullet.

3. In the right pane, shown in the following illustration, choose the time period that IE should use to check for site changes. You can also configure how IE notifies you when a site has changed. When you're done, click OK.

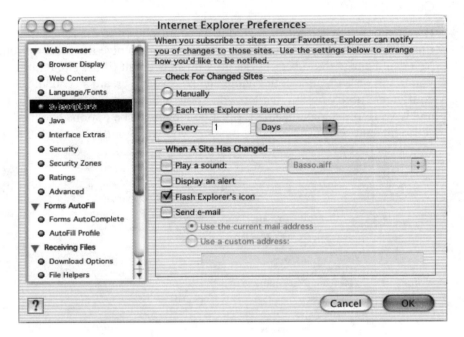

 # I keep getting IE security alert dialog boxes

Cause Web sites typically use secure web pages when you enter certain kinds of private information. For example, if you are buying a product at an online store, the store should set up a secure communication link between the site and your computer, most often using a security protocol called Secure Sockets Layer (SSL). You can then safely enter your name, address, phone numbers, credit card information, and so forth to make the purchase. When you enter information on a site or web form that is not secure and click Submit, IE gives you a warning dialog box. However, if you don't want to see these warnings, you can disable them. Before you do, be careful—the security warnings may make you think twice before entering personal information that is transmitted in an insecure way.

The Painkiller To stop the security warnings, follow these steps:

1. Open IE and click Explorer | Preferences.

2. In the Preferences window, expand Web Browser in the left pane and click Security.

3. In the right pane, shown in the following illustration, you can deselect the alert check boxes as desired. Click OK.

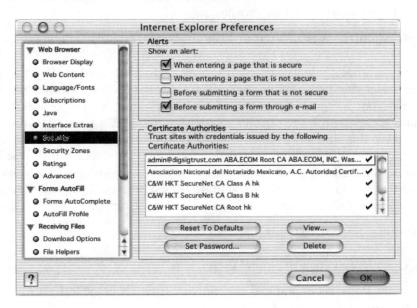

 *Remember, these security warnings are there to help you, so disable them at your own risk!*

 # IE's security settings are too high or too low for me

Cause   IE uses a somewhat complex method to determine what content is secure and what content is not secure. The default settings are generally the best for most users, so think about your needs carefully before you change them. IE works by configuring security into zones. It sees an Internet zone, an Intranet zone, a Trusted Sites zone, and a Restricted Sites zone. You can configure the security you need for each zone or even create a customized security setting for the zone. Following are the default zones:

■   **High**   The High setting is the most secure setting, but it is the least functional. This setting will not allow certain scripts, ActiveX controls, and other interactive content to work.

- **Medium** Medium is the default setting. It will allow all Web content to work, but it prompts you before running any potentially dangerous content, such as scripts and ActiveX controls, along with some interactive content.

- **Low** The Low Setting is the least secure. All Web content works, and you will not see any warning messages.

- **Customize** Use this setting to apply custom security settings.

However, what if you use a certain security setting but need a different setting for a particular site. For example, let's say you use the Medium setting, but you also access your company's web site, which has several ActiveX controls in use. You know these controls are safe, so you don't want to see a security warning when you use this site. In this case, you can add those sites to the Trusted Sites zone, which basically provides an exception to the security zone rule. These sites you enter are safe, and IE will not prompt you. The reverse is also true, you can add sites that you know are unsafe to the Restricted Sites zone for extra security. The Painkiller shows you how to configure all of these options.

The Painkiller To configure IE security, follow these steps:

1. Open IE and click Explorer | Preferences.

2. In the Preferences window, expand Web Browser in the left pane and click Security Zones.

3. In the right pane, shown in the following illustration, select the security setting you want to apply to the Internet zone and click OK (Medium is the default).

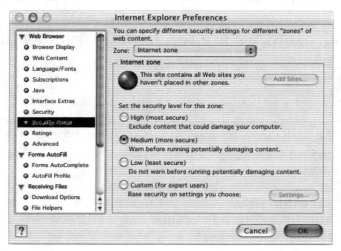

4. If you want to create custom settings for the zone, click the Custom radio
button and click the Settings button. The Internet Zone window appears,
shown in the following illustration. Review the available settings and use
the drop-down menus to select the settings you want to apply for each
security option. Click OK when you're done.

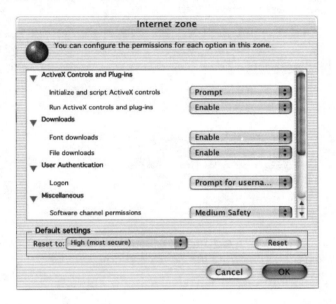

 *Make sure you think about what you are doing before you use a custom
setting. You may inadvertently allow content that is not secure!*

5. If you want to use a Trusted Sites Zone, click the Zone drop-down menu
and select Trusted Sites Zone.

6. Choose a security level for the zone (the default is Low) by clicking the
desired radio button.

7. Click the Add Sites button. In the Trusted Sites Zone window, click the
Add button and enter the site address. Click OK. Continue this process

until you have added all of the sites you want configured for this zone, as shown in the following illustration. Click OK when you're done.

 *You can create Restricted Sites zone entries in the same way: just choose Restricted Sites zone from the Zone drop-down menu.*

 The History is too long or not long enough, or I want to manually clear the History

Cause   IE maintains 300 web sites in the History. Once you go over 300, IE deletes the oldest sites. However, you can raise or lower the History setting, and you can also delete the History with a one-button click.

The Painkiller   To change History settings, follow these steps:

1. Open IE and click Explorer | Preferences.

2. In the Preferences window, expand Web Browser in the left pane and click the Advanced item in the list.

3. In the right pane of the window, change the History value as desired. If you want to clear the History, just click the Clear History button, shown in the following illustration.

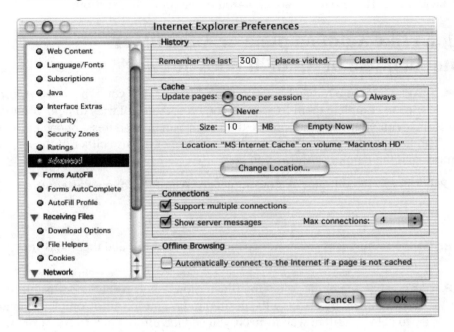

The cache is too big or not big enough

Cause   IE keeps web sites that you visit in a *cache*, which is a temporary storage location, so that IE can load them faster when you visit the site again. The default size of the cache is 10MB. If you want to use more or less of your disk space for caching, however, you can change this value. If you are not really worried about it, the 10MB default is fine.

The Painkiller   To change the cache, follow these steps:

1. Open IE and click Explorer | Preferences.

2. In the Preferences window, expand Web Browser in the left pane and click the Advanced button.

3. In the right pane of the window, change the entry in the Size box to whatever you want.

IE Usage Settings

Aside from interface and preference settings, some IE usage settings might give you headaches. These settings are explored in the following sections.

I don't like AutoComplete or AutoFill, or AutoComplete or AutoFill does not work

Cause   AutoComplete remembers web site addresses that you type in the Address bar and tries to complete them for you as you type. AutoFill tries to help you fill in web forms with your personal information, such as name, address, phone number, e-mail address, and so forth. You can choose to use or not use either of these features, and the Painkiller shows you how.

The Painkiller   To configure AutoComplete or AutoFill, follow these steps:

1. Open IE and click Explorer | Preferences.

2. In the Preferences window, expand Forms AutoFill and then click the Forms AutoComplete button.

3. As you can see in the following illustration, you can enable or disable AutoComplete by clicking the desired radio button. AutoComplete can also try to help you fill in web forms if you add the information to AutoComplete. Click the Add button and enter the information, such as your name, address, and so forth. You can add as many items as you like so that AutoComplete can help you. Click OK when you're done.

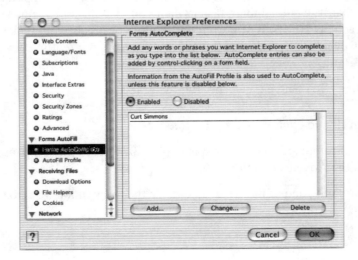

4. To set up AutoFill, click the AutoFill button in the left pane of the window. You see an AutoFill Profile. Enter the information in that you want AutoFill to help you with. Click OK when you're done.

When I download something, it always goes to my desktop

Cause   By default, when you download something, IE tries to put the download on your desktop for easy access. However, if you want downloaded items to go to a different folder, you can change this option.

The Painkiller   To change the default location for downloaded files, follow these steps:

1. Open IE and click Explorer | Preferences.

2. In the Preferences window, expand Receiving Files and click the Download Options button.

3. In the Download Folder portion of the window's right pane, click the Change Location button and select an alternate folder for downloads. Click OK when you're done.

About Cookies and IE...

In the Internet world, a *cookie* is a small text file that Internet sites use to communicate with your computer. Different kinds of cookies are in use on the Internet—some are just called *site cookies* and function with your computer during a session with the web site. Some are used at online stores when you buy something. Cookies are a necessary part of today's Internet, but they can be a security issue because a cookie can contain potentially personal information. IE provides a way to step up your security with cookies; look in Internet Explorer Preferences under Receiving Files. You can use the settings here to prompt you when a site requests a cookie so that you can choose to use the cookie or decline it. However, keep in mind that cookies are used a lot—you may see a lot of dialog boxes asking you about cookie usage. If you want to learn more about this feature, see the IE Help option and search on Cookie.

About iTools...

While we're on the subject of using the Internet, I want to point out a cool feature www.apple.com provides for Mac users. It's called iTools, and it is basically a set of web tools that are designed to "extend your digital life," as the web site says. They are available at www.mac.com, as shown in the following illustration. From the iTools site, you can...

- ■ **Use Webmail**   Apple's web mail gives you a storage location for web-based mail. As in other web mail solutions (Hotmail, Yahoo, and so on), you have a full set of features and a given amount of storage space.

- ■ **iDisk**   Need some extra storage room? That's no problem because iDisk is an online center where you can upload store files on .Mac servers. This is a great backup solution!

- ■ **Home Page**   Drag and drop your own home page or use the quick tools here to create your own in a matter of minutes.

- ■ **iCards**   Create and send personalized e-cards quickly and easily!

- ■ **Anti-virus**   Your stuff is automatically protected by McAfee's anti-virus software.

All this stuff is great, but it will cost you around $100 for the year. You can sign-up for a free trial at www.mac.com.

As I mentioned, you can sign-up directly at www.mac.com or use System Preferences. Open System Preferences and click the Internet icon. You see the option to log on with your iTools username and password. Or you can sign up by clicking the Sign Up button. This just takes you to the same www.mac.com web page so you can sign up for the trial membership or the real deal. You can also access your iDisk online storage, e-mail, and web data from this location.

This book focuses on headaches, so I'll not proceed any further with a tutorial. In fact, you really don't need a tutorial, and you're unlikely to experience any headaches at all. iTools is so easy to use and problem-free that, well, you'll never need a painkiller! Just keep in mind that iTools has a lot to offer you, so you should at least get the free 60-day trial and check it out!

I know, I know, I just said iTools is great, and it is. But if you don't want to part with your money, remember that the Internet is full of similar features for free. Web mail, home pages, e-cards, and disk storage: you can find all of these items for free at various web sites (just perform searches to find them).

Chapter 11

Using Mail

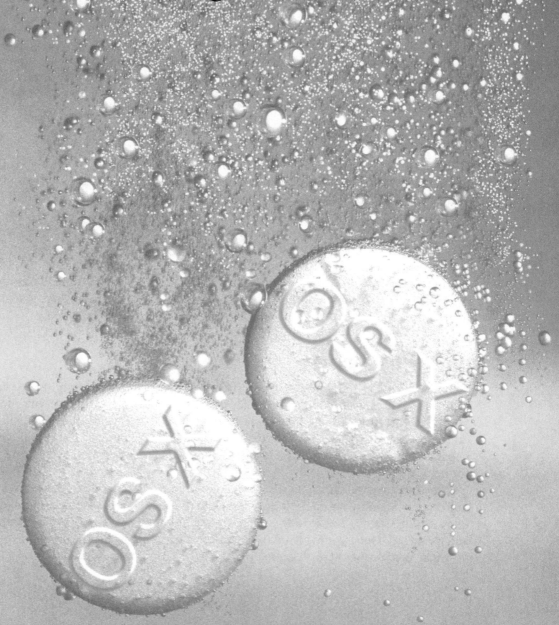

In this chapter, you'll cure...

- ■ Account problems
- ■ Hassles with sending and receiving mail
- ■ Mailbox issues
- ■ Junk mail reception

The e-mail revolution has taken us all by storm. Only a few years ago, e-mail was reserved for computer geeks who had nothing better to do than talk to each other using computers, but no longer! In fact, e-mail is so popular that millions upon millions of e-mail messages are sent every single day. My mom even has an e-mail address, so I know e-mail has really arrived!

All kidding aside, e-mail is a great communications solution. It is fast and easy, and you can send all kinds of items, including pictures, files, and even programs. You can send mail to multiple people at the same time, and with your monthly Internet account, you can send as many messages as you like at no extra charge. Virtually all businesses use e-mail as a major communication method—in fact, I do most of my work over e-mail.

The good news is that OS X gives you a Mail program that enables you to use and manage e-mail. It's fun, powerful, and all you need. In this chapter, we explore the Mail program found in OS X, paying close attention to the headaches you are likely to run into!

Account Headaches

E-mail works through your e-mail account. The Mail program, along with your username and password, contacts an ISP mail server to download your mail to you. Your ISP assigned you your e-mail username and password, so see your ISP documentation for details. If you do not yet have an ISP, you need to sign up with one in order to access the Internet and get set up with a mail account. See Chapter 9 for details.

Once you have an e-mail username and password, you can set up the Mail program to begin retrieving your mail. Simply click the Mail icon on the Dock, which looks like a postage stamp. You see a few windows that prompt you to enter your username and password. Once you've done that, you can start using Mail. Or, if you have set up a mac.com account (see Chapter 10), the Mail program uses a mac.com e-mail account for your mail.

Once the Mail interface opens, the server is contacted and any mail that you have is downloaded. You can see in the following illustration that the mail you receive appears in the upper half of the window. You see who the mail is from, the subject of the message, and the date the mail was received. If you select a message, the message appears in the lower half of the window. You can also double-click a message to open the message in its own window. On the right side of the window, you see a pull-out drawer containing your In box, Out box, Drafts folder, and the messages you have sent (click the Mailboxes button to make the drawer appear).

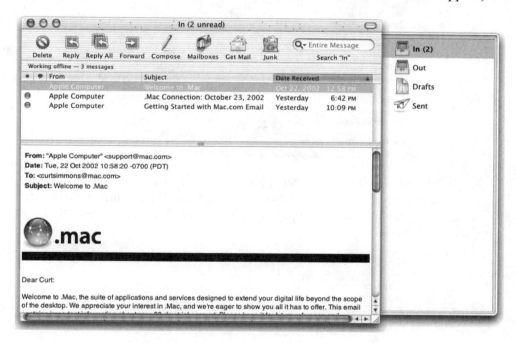

NOTE

If you are new to e-mail, spend some time playing around with the interface. As you can see, you can do most things using the Button toolbar. Don't be afraid—experiment and learn!

OSX HEADACHE   I need to make changes to my account

Cause   Once you have your Mail account set up and working, you probably will not need to make any changes. However, what do you do if your ISP decides to assign you a new password? In this case, you need to access an Accounts window to edit your account. This is easy, though, and the following painkiller shows you how.

The Painkiller   To edit your e-mail account, follow these steps:

1. Open Mail and select the Mail Menu | Preferences.

2. In the Accounts window that appears, shown in the following illustration, select your e-mail account and click Edit.

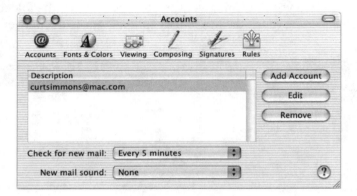

3. In the drop-down window that appears, shown in the following illustration, make any necessary account changes. Follow the specific instructions your ISP has provided for making changes to your mail account. Click OK when you're done.

I need to use more than one e-mail account, or I need to configure a new e-mail account

Cause   You may have more than one e-mail account. For example, let's say that you set up a mac.com e-mail account, but you also have a mail account with your ISP (such as myname@myisp.com). You want to use both e-mail accounts with your Mail program. Or, maybe you have switched ISPs and now you need to get rid of your old e-mail account and set up your new one. Both of these tasks are easy—just follow the painkiller steps.

The Painkiller   To create a new mail account, follow these steps:

1. Open Mail and select the Mail Menu | Preferences.

2. In the Accounts window that appears, select any mail account that you want to permanently delete and click Remove. If you don't want to remove an existing e-mail account, but simply create another one, go to Step 3.

3. To create a new account, click the Add Account button.

4. You see the Account drop-down window appear. Follow your ISP's instructions for creating the new mail account. You need to enter a name, e-mail address, the mail server, password, and so forth. Again, your ISP should provide you with all of this information. Click OK when you're done.

 *If you are using more than one mail account, Mail will automatically check for mail on both accounts. If you don't want Mail to check both accounts, click the Advanced tab, where you can deselect the option to Include When Automatically Checking For New Mail.*

Mail tries to check automatically for e-mail, but I use a dial-up connection

Cause   The Mail program tries to help you by checking the server for new mail every five minutes. However, if you are using a dial-up connection, you may not like mail trying to dial out and check for you, or you may want a longer interval between mail checks. No problem! You can easily change this behavior.

The Painkiller   To change how Mail checks for e-mail on the server, follow these steps:

1. Open Mail and select Mail Menu | Preferences.

2. In the Accounts window you see the drop-down menu to Check For New Mail. The default is every five minutes, but you can change this to a longer value—or choose Manually if you do not want the Mail program to check for you. Note that you can also choose to play a sound when new mail arrives.

I can't get Mail to check my Hotmail/Yahoo/Netscape (or other web mail) account

Cause   The Mail program can get two different kinds of mail. The first is POP (Post Office Protocol) mail. *POP mail* is the typical e-mail used by an ISP. Your Mail program contacts the ISP and downloads the mail to you, where you then read and work with it. The second kind of mail is called IMAP (Internet Mail Access Protocol). *IMAP mail* leaves the mail on the server, but you can read and use it within your Mail program. This feature lets you check your mail from any computer—all you have to do is log in. IMAP mail is not used as much as POP, although it does provide some additional flexibility. Mac.com mail is IMAP mail. The third kind of mail out there is called web mail. Web mail, like Hotmail, Yahoo mail, Netscape mail and so forth, is also stored on a server, and you work with the mail through a web browser (such as Internet Explorer). Mail is not equipped to handle these kinds of accounts, so I'm afraid you can't use the Mail program to check your web mail.

The Painkiller   There's no way around this frustration—you have to keep using your browser to read and manage web mail.

   *Some ISPs provide a way to check web mail through their mail servers. You may have to pay for an upgrade to get this service, if it is offered at all.*

I need to import mail from a different program

Cause   If you used a different e-mail program, such as Outlook Express or Netscape, before using Mail, you can use Mail's Import feature to import the mail from those older programs. You can also determine what e-mail folders you want to import.

The Painkiller To import mail, click File | Import. In the Import Mailboxes window, shown in the following illustration, choose the type of mailboxes that you want to import and click the Next arrow. Depending on your selection, Mail will try to locate the old mailboxes and import the mail folders that you want. Just follow the instructions that appear.

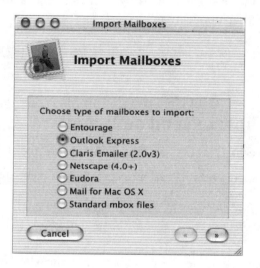

 *If you have mail on a different computer (even Windows) that you want to import to the Mac and the Mail program, you can use the old program to export the mailboxes as a standard mbox file. Move the exported file to the Mac and use Mail to import it. See your old mail application's Help files for more information about exporting your mailboxes.*

Working with E-mail Headaches

Once your accounts are set up and working the way they should, you can start sending and receiving e-mail. This section looks at some common (and not so common) e-mail headaches that may come your way.

 ## I can't check for new mail messages

Cause The Mail program automatically attempts to check for new Mail messages when you open mail. If you are not connected to the Internet, you see a message telling you that the mail server cannot be found. If you have an always-on broadband connection, such as DSL, Mail will check when it opens, and it can continue checking automatically at certain intervals if you have configured it to do so.

The Painkiller   To check for e-mail, connect to the Internet and click the Get Mail button on the toolbar. If you want Mail to check automatically at certain intervals for you, see the previous headache titled "Mail tries to check automatically for e-mail, but I use a dial-up connection."

TIP   *You can also manually check for mail by pressing COMMAND-N.*

I don't know how to send an e-mail

Cause   Sending an e-mail is easy! See the painkiller for the steps.

The Painkiller   To send a new e-mail message, follow these steps:

NOTE   *In order to send and receive mail, you have to be connected to the Internet. I assume for this headache and for those that follow that you are connected.*

1. Open Mail and click the Compose button on the Mail toolbar.

2. A New Mail message window appears, shown in the following illustration. Enter the e-mail address of the person you want to send the mail to in the To line. You can enter multiple addresses if you want, and you can Carbon Copy (CC) other mail recipients by entering their addresses in the CC field. Enter a subject for the message and type your message in the provided dialog box. When you are done, click Send.

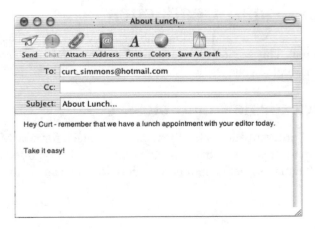

If you are connected to the Internet when you send the message, Mail sends your message right away. If you are not, Mail holds the message in the Out folder until you are connected and the mail is sent.

You can directly access e-mail addresses from your Address Book when you are typing a new message. Just click Address in the toolbar to open your Address Book, and see Chapter 4 to learn more about the Address Book.

 # How can I respond to e-mail?

Cause   When you receive an e-mail from someone, you can read the e-mail, delete it, store it in a folder, or respond to it. You can respond to the e-mail in one of three ways:

- **Reply**   If you select the mail message and click the Reply button on the toolbar, you can then type a reply message to the sender. This message goes only to the person who sent you the e-mail.

- **Reply All**   If the message was sent to you and a few other people (including those who were CC'd), you can click Reply All and send a message to everyone who received the message. For example, I recently received a message from a friend telling me that a virus was found on her computer. The message explained that she had to delete a file in order to rid the computer of the virus. As it turns out, the virus was a hoax, and all those people she sent the message to did not need to delete the file. So I just Replied All and told them what to do. This sent the message to everyone my friend sent the first message to.

- **Forward**   This option lets you forward to someone else a message you have received. Simply click Forward and enter the recipient's e-mail address (or recipients' e-mail addresses) that you want to forward the message to. You can also type an additional message to accompany the forward if you want.

The Painkiller   To use Reply, Reply All, and Forward, simply select the desired message and click the button you need on the toolbar. Type your message and enter an e-mail address if you are using a Forward and click Send. That's all there is to it!

About the Subject Line...

The Subject line is your place to tell the person you are sending the message to what the e-mail is about. However, you should keep a few Subject line "rules" in mind:

- **Keep it short**   E-mail programs have a limited amount of space to display the Subject line, so keep the subject text short and to the point.

- **Keep it meaningful**   The purpose of the Subject line is to let the recipient know what the e-mail is about.

- **Keep it specific**   Try to be specific when typing a subject. "Vacation info" is a better Subject line than "Hey Bob!" The user knows what the e-mail is about without having to guess.

I can't send an attachment

Cause   Attachments are files that you "attach" to an e-mail message. When you send the message to the recipient, the attachment goes along, too. This is a great way to exchange pictures, files, applications—you name it. You can easily send an attachment using Mail; the following painkiller shows you how.

The Painkiller   To send an attachment, follow these steps:

1. Open a new mail message and enter the e-mail address (or addresses) you desire and the subject, and type any text you want.

2. You can attach a file to the message by clicking the Attach button on the toolbar, browsing to the desired attachment, and clicking Open. You can also just drag and drop the attachment onto the message. The attachment appears in the message, as you can see in the following illustration. When you're done, just click Send to send the message with the attachment.

3. If you decide that you don't want to send the attachment after you have put it in the mail message, that's no problem. Just drag it out of the message and to the Trash (this does not delete your original file on your computer, so don't worry).

Pictures, by default, show up in the mail message as the picture. However, you can change the view so that the attachment shows up as an icon by CONTROL-clicking the attachment and clicking View As Icon.

I need to send multiple attachments

Cause   You can send multiple attachments in a single e-mail using the same steps presented in the previous painkiller.

The Painkiller   To send multiple attachments, simply drag and drop the attachments or use the Attach button to attach them. You can select several attachments at the same time by holding down COMMAND and selecting the items.

NOTE   *Mail doesn't offer a compression feature, but you can compress items with a program, such as StuffIt Lite, before sending them in order to reduce transmission time. StuffIt Lite is shareware, and it is available for download at www.aladdinsys.com.*

 *Adding attachments to an e-mail increases the size of the mail, thus requiring more time to send and download it. This may be no problem for you if you are using a broadband connection, but if you send files to people who use modems, be careful of overwhelming them with big files that take practically forever to download.*

I want to change the formatting of a particular e-mail

Cause   When you send e-mail, you can send two kinds—Plain Text and Rich Text. Plain Text gives you just plain text: you can't use different fonts or colors, and you can't bold or italicize anything. Rich Text mail gives you the same basic formatting options you would see in any word processing program. However, keep in mind that if you use Rich Text, not all people you send the message to get the formatting. Some e-mail systems and clients simply don't support Rich Text mail, in which case the user you sent the e-mail to sees only Plain Text formatting.

The Painkiller   To use Plain Text in your message, just click Format | Make Plain Text. To make e-mail text Rich Text, click Format | Make Rich Text. Then, on the mail message toolbar, use the Fonts and Colors options to change the fonts and colors used in the mail message.

I want all of my mail messages to be formatted in a particular way

Cause   If you are using Rich Text mail, you can change the formatting of any mail message using the Fonts and Colors options on the mail message toolbar (see the previous headache), or you can choose a default setting that applies to all mail messages.

The Painkiller   To choose default formatting settings, follow these steps:

1. Open Mail and click Mail | Preferences.

2. In the Preferences window, click the Fonts and Colors button. Use the drop-down menus, shown in the following illustration, to change the default fonts and colors used in your mail messages. The selections you choose here apply to all new mail messages you receive (although you can override the settings in the message with the Fonts and Colors buttons on the mail message toolbar).

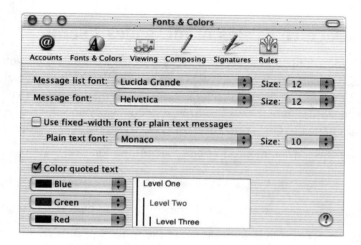

How do I redirect a message?

Cause   Mail gives you a message Redirect option. Redirect is a lot like forwarding a message, but when you redirect a message, it is forwarded to the person you specify as if it comes from the original sender. This essentially takes you out of the picture and makes the message look like it came from the original sender directly.

The Painkiller   To redirect a message, simply select the message you want to redirect and click Message | Redirect Message. Enter the desired e-mail address in the To line and click Send.

Don't assume, however, that you can redirect a message and be "invisible." The redirected mail may say "redirected by...".

What is bouncing a message?

Cause   Mail gives you a cool little feature called message Bouncing. Basically, when someone sends an e-mail to another person, the mail arrives. If the e-mail address was wrong, the message bounces back to the sender. If you receive mail from someone you don't want to receive mail from, you can select the message and bounce it back to the sender. This will create the appearance that the sender has an incorrect e-mail address. This may help reduce the amount of junk mail you receive.

The Painkiller   To bounce a message, select the message in the Mail program and click Message | Bounce to Sender. Click OK to the confirmation message that appears.

I need to receive copies of messages I send

Cause   Mail doesn't by default send you copies of the mail messages you send, but in some cases, you may want to receive a copy—basically CC'ing yourself. Before you configure this option, though, keep in mind that all mail messages you send are kept in the Sent folder, where you can browse them easily at any time. Still, if you want to be automatically CC'd on your messages, you can configure the option.

The Painkiller   To automatically CC yourself, follow these steps:

1.   Open Mail and click Mail | Preferences.

2.   In the Preferences window, click the Composing button.

3.   In the Composing window, shown in the following illustration, select the Always CC Myself check box.

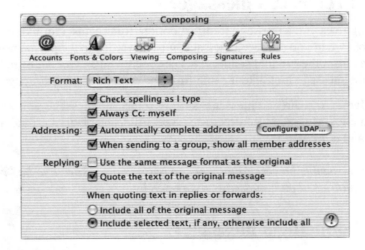

While you are at it, check out the other options here as well.

I don't know where to find the BCC (Blind Carbon Copy) option

Cause   By default, Mail gives you a To, CC, and Subject line when you type a message. However, you can also use a BCC field, which lets you copy other people in a blind fashion. In other words, when you BCC someone, users to whom the message is sent or CC'd can't see the recipients in the blind field. This option is great if you want to copy a message to someone without everyone else knowing. Most people don't use the BCC field that much, so it's not listed automatically. However, you can easily add it to a particular message.

The Painkiller   To add the BCC field, follow these steps:

1. Open a new mail message.

2. Click Edit | Add BCC Header.

3. The BCC field now appears at the top of your message, shown in the following illustration. Add the desired e-mail addresses to the To, CC, and BCC fields as desired.

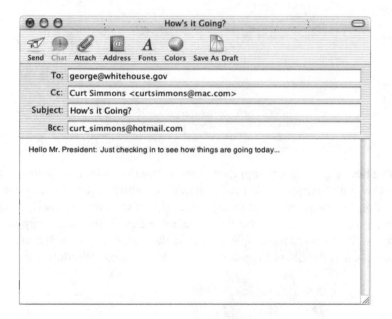

 # I don't know how to use a signature

Cause   A signature is a clipping of text that you can add to an outgoing message. This may include your name, your e-mail address, your phone number, a link to your web page, a quote or some other remark—basically anything. You can create multiple signatures and apply them to all outgoing mail messages, or you can apply different signatures in a message-by-message manner.

The Painkiller   To create a signature, follow these steps:

1. Open Mail and click Mail | Preferences.

2. Click the Signatures button in the toolbar. Then, click the Add Signatures button that appears.

3. In the Description dialog box, enter a name for the signature and type the signature as desired, shown in the following illustration You can use the Format menu to apply different fonts and colors as desired. Click OK when you're done.

4. The new signature now appears in the Signatures window, as shown in the following illustration. You can add new signatures at any time or use the Edit button to change an existing signature. If you want to use a certain signature in all messages, choose the signature in the Select Signature drop-down menu. If you want to be able to choose the signature for each message you type, select the Show Signature Menu On Compose Window check box.

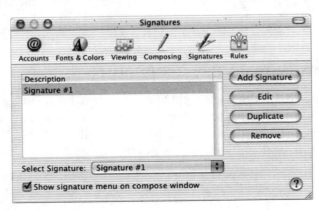

I can't open an attachment

Cause   If you receive an attachment, you double-click the attachment to open it or drag the attachment to your desktop, where you can open it later. But what if the attachment will not open? One of several issues may be at work.

The Painkiller   If an attachment will not open…

1. It may be compressed or encoded. Drag the attachment to StuffIt Expander (found in your Applications | Utilities folder) to see whether StuffIt can open the compressed file.

2. It may be corrupt. Sometimes, attachments get fouled up when users send them over the Internet. If you receive a picture or HTML file that will not open, ask the sender to resend it.

3. It may be a Windows application. If the file has an .exe extension, it is a Windows program—which Mac can't open.

4. It may require a program that you don't have. For example, if the file is a PowerPoint presentation, but you don't have PowerPoint or a related program that can open PowerPoint files, you will not be able to open the attachment.

Mailbox Headaches

Mail organizes your messages in a few default mailboxes:

- **In**   This mailbox contains messages you have received.

- **Out**   This mailbox contains messages that you have written but haven't sent.

- **Drafts**   This mailbox contains messages you are working on but have not yet sent (you can store a message you are working on by clicking Save As Draft on the message toolbar).

- **Sent**   This mailbox contains copies of the messages you have sent.

- **Trash**   This mailbox contains all the messages you have chosen to Delete.

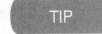

Trashed messages remain in the Trash for your records. However, if you don't want these messages taking up your hard disk space, click the Trash mailbox in the pull-out drawer, select the messages you want to permanently delete, and click Delete on the toolbar. If you want to delete them all, click Mailbox | Erase Deleted Messages.

Besides using these default mailboxes, you can create your own mailboxes to store mail messages. For example, when I am working on a book, I create a mailbox with the book's name. I store all mail messages concerning the book in that particular mailbox. When I'm done with the book, I simply drag the mailbox to another mailbox called Old Projects. That way, I can keep a record of the mail without the old project cluttering up my folder drawer, as you can see in the following illustration.

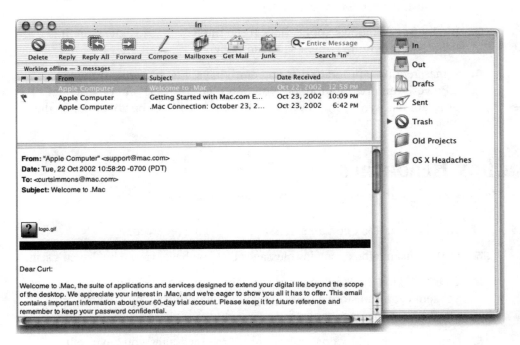

You can easily create mailboxes within mailboxes, and you can drag and drop mailboxes around as needed. To move mail messages around between mailboxes, again, just drag and drop. Overall, using mailboxes is so easy you aren't likely to run into many problems; however, you may encounter a few.

I can't create a mailbox

Cause   You can create as many mailboxes as you need to effectively organize your e-mail.

The Painkiller   To create a new box, click Mailbox | New Mailbox. In the New Mailbox window that appears, shown in the following illustration, enter the desired name of the new mailbox and click OK. Also note that you can create submailboxes by using a / between the mailbox names.

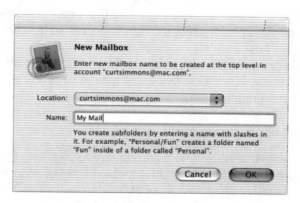

 # I can't create a submailbox

Cause   Mailboxes can contain submailboxes. For example, you might have a mailbox named Personal but have submailboxes with people's names with whom you communicate regularly, such as Uncle Bob or Aunt Ruth.

The Painkiller   To create a submailbox, first select the mailbox in the pull-out drawer that you want the new mailbox to reside under and click Mailbox | New Mailbox. In the New Mailbox window that appears, enter the desired name of the new mailbox and click OK. Mailboxes that have submailboxes appear with arrows next to them. Click the arrow to see the submailboxes.

 # I stored a message in a mailbox, but now I can't find it

Cause   If you get a lot of mail and you have several mailboxes, you may have trouble tracking messages down from time to time. That's no problem; Mail gives you a handy search feature.

The Painkiller   To find a message, select the desired mailbox and click the Search field on the main toolbar. Enter a search word and press Return. All matches appear.

Junk Mail Headaches

Junk e-mail, otherwise known as *spam,* is a constant problem with e-mail, and it is a problem that has grown a lot during the past few years. Depending on how much you use e-mail, you have likely been a victim of all kinds of junk mail advertising online stores, products, and possibly even pornography. Unfortunately, junk mail is just one of those things in life you have to contend with—there's no way to completely avoid it, but you can take a few actions.

- If you shop online, or do anything online that requires you to enter your e-mail address, consider using a different e-mail address for this purpose. For example, I use curt_simmons@hotmail.com as a "public" address. You can contact me there, and any time I do anything on the Internet, I use this address. I have to contend with a lot of junk mail at this address, but that's life. I also maintain a private address that I give out only to friends and family and the people I work with. This helps keep everything from the Internet out of my private mail.

- Use Mail's Bounce feature with all junk mail you receive in your In box. This returns the mail to the sender and creates the appearance that the message has failed to arrive because the address isn't valid. This is a cool little trick that will help you get off spammers' distribution lists. See the previous headache in this chapter called "What is bouncing a message?"

- Finally, Mail gives you some very helpful filtering options that you should use. Read on to learn more.

I don't know how to automatically sort my mail

Cause   Mail uses message rules to determine what to do with mail that it receives. Using the rules you configure, Mail checks messages that arrive and does whatever you say to do. For example, you might have a mailbox called Apple. You create a rule that says that any message that arrives from Apple should go in the Apple mailbox. You can browse through this mailbox once a week or so to review the messages. Or you might create a rule that sends messages with the subjects "sale," "XXX," "loan," and so on, to the Trash folder. These rules can help you manage all kinds of messages, especially spam.

The Painkiller   To create a message rule, just follow these steps:

1. Open Mail and click Mail | Preferences.

2. Click the Rules button on the toolbar. You see, as shown in the following illustration, that Mail already has a Junk rule and News From Apple rule. These rules display possible Junk mail in a different color that can help you to identify it. It does the same thing with news from Apple.

3. To create your own rule, click the Add Rule button.

4. In the dialog box that appears, enter a name for the rule and change the dialog boxes to create the rule. For example, in the following illustration, I am creating a rule that puts mail with certain spammer words directly into the Trash mailbox. Use the + and – symbols to create additional fields. Click OK when you're done.

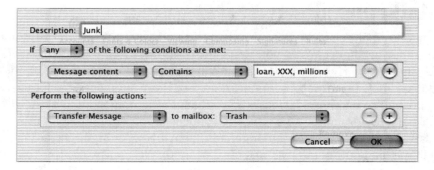

 ## But... I still get junk mail!

Cause   Even with message rules, you will still get junk mail in your In box from time to time. After all, nothing is foolproof. However, if you are having a lot of problems with junk mail, here's a few more tricks.

Message Rules...

If you play around with the Rule feature a little, you soon discover that this helpful Mail option does a lot of things. Besides managing junk mail, you can create all kinds of rules. For example, you can have certain messages displayed in different colors or configure a sound to play when you get a message from a certain person. If you are away from your computer, you can forward messages from certain people to another e-mail account—all kinds of things. Get to know message rules—they can do a lot for you!

The Painkiller   Try these additional options to help control junk mail.

- Many junk mail senders use the BCC field so you can't see whom the message was sent to. Consider creating a rule that puts all BCC field messages in a spam mailbox.

- When you get a message in your In mailbox that is junk mail, select it and click the Junk button on the toolbar. This tells Mail the message is junk, and Mail can help identify similar messages as junk in the future.

- ...and remember, use the Bounce feature with every e-mail you get that is junk mail.

If Mail runs slowly...

There's one final headache concerning mail that I want to mention, and that's sluggish performance. When you first start using Mail, you see that it works quickly and easily. However, keep in mind that your mail is stored in a number of database files. Over time, as you get more and more mail, delete mail, move it around, and so on, those databases can get a lot of junk in them that can slow down Mail's performance. This typically happens if you deal with a lot of e-mail on a daily basis. If so, you should highlight the mailbox (or highlight several at a time) in the mail pull-out drawer and click Mailbox | Rebuild Mailbox. Your Mac will work on the database and clean it up so that your Mail performance returns to normal.

 *If your e-mail will not open at all or you can't read it, try using the Rebuilt Mailbox command to solve this problem as well.*

Chapter 12

Networking Headaches

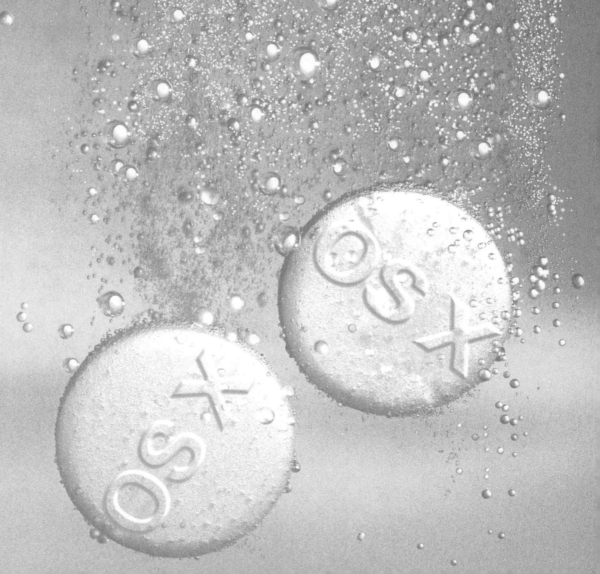

In this chapter, you'll cure...

- Problems using Ethernet and AirPort networks
- Difficulties connecting to Windows computers
- Aggravations with Internet sharing
- Troubles managing resource permissions

In the past, a network was something companies and medium-sized offices used. After all, the purpose of a network is to share resources, such as files, printers, and even Internet access. You, as a home user, don't need such a thing—right? Wrong, of course. Today, many, many home users now have home networks. After all, many of us have more than one computer. We use networks to share files, play games, use one Internet connection, share printers, and do a number of other "sharing" kinds of things. With a network, you can do much more than you can with a roomful of Macs that can't talk to each other.

The good news is that OS X Jaguar has more networking features than ever before, and networking is really easy. If you have wanted a network but were afraid to commit, or perhaps have tried networking and been left really frustrated, then this chapter is just for you. You can easily network your Macs together—in fact, you can even connect to Windows computers and share files without any additional software! You can share your Internet connection, your printer...and much more! This chapter explores those processes and shows you how to cure that headache pain quickly and easily.

Ethernet Networking Headaches

You can use two basic kinds of networks with your Mac OS X. The first is Ethernet networking, and the second is a wireless network called AirPort. Ethernet is a networking standard that basically all modern computers support. Your Mac comes equipped with a standard Ethernet card built right in. Ethernet networks work great with small networks for the home or the office, and they also work in large corporations.

When you use an Ethernet network, you connect an Ethernet cable to the back of your Mac and connect the other end to an Ethernet hub. The Ethernet cable has an RJ-45 connection on it, which looks like a big telephone cable connection (those are called RJ-11 connections, by the way). The Ethernet hub is a small box that has a row of ports. All computers on your network connect to the *hub*, which essentially manages the traffic between the computers. If you have only two computers on your network, you can bypass the need for a hub by simply using an Ethernet cross-over cable to connect the two computers directly to each other. You find these networking cables and hubs at any computer store, and, because they are so common, you can even sometimes find them at department stores. Hubs and cables are not specific to the Mac, so you can buy any brand you want—they are often called "switches," as well. You may even be able to find kits that include the wiring, a hub, and some extra Ethernet cards in case you happen to need one for another computer.

 # I don't know how to get my Mac to work on a network

Cause   Once your computers are connected together with a hub and Ethernet wires (or in the case of two Macs, with a cross-over cable), you can configure each computer to begin sharing on the network. To do so, you basically need to set up sharing. The painkiller shows you how.

The Painkiller   To turn on sharing, follow these steps:

1. Click the System Preferences icon on the Dock, or click Apple | System Preferences.

2. Click the Sharing icon.

3. On the Sharing window, give your computer a name to be used on the network. You can enter whatever you want, but the easier and shorter the name is, the easier other users will be able to connect to your computer and access resources.

4. On the Services tab, click Personal File Sharing to turn on file sharing. If you want to share a printer, turn that option on, as well. If you want to share with Windows computers, turn on Windows File Sharing, as shown in the following illustration.

5. Repeat these steps for each Mac OS X computer on your network. Note that each computer must have a different name.

I need to use a static IP address

Cause   Your Mac, like most other computers in the world, including all of the computers on the Internet, uses a network protocol standard called Transmission Control Protocol/Internet Protocol (TCP/IP). Although this sounds like a mouthful, TCP/IP is the de facto networking standard these days, and your Mac is built to fit right in.

To avoid requiring you to know anything about TCP/IP, OS X uses an automatic addressing scheme to ensure that each computer on your network has a valid IP address as well as a subnetting number called a subnet mask. However, for networking reasons you may need to assign a certain IP address or subnet mask to your computers. In this case, you can manually configure these properties.

 *Unless you have a specific reason for configuring a static IP address and subnet mask, don't. Your Mac can take care of this by itself without any intervention from you, so let it!*

The Painkiller   To configure a static IP address and subnet mask, follow these steps:

1. Click System Preferences on the Dock or click Apple | System Preferences.

2. Click the Network icon.

3. On the TCP/IP tab, choose Built-In Ethernet under Show.

4. On the TCP/IP tab, choose Configure: Manually, as shown in the following illustration. Enter the IP address and subnet mask you want to use. You should not need to enter a router value unless your network uses multiple subnets (which, if it is a home or small-office network, it doesn't).

5. Click Apply Now.

Be careful when manually assigning IP addresses and subnet masks. The computers on your network must use the same IP address range, such as 10.0.0.1, 10.0.0.2, 10.0.0.3, and so forth. The subnet mask value, such as 255.255.255.0, must be the same on the network as well.

I don't know how to access another computer on my network

Cause   Once all of the computers on your network are connected, you can begin accessing files and other shared items on other Macs. This, after all, is the reason you wanted a network in the first place. The good news is that connecting to other Macs on your network is easy; the painkiller shows you how to do it.

The Painkiller   To access another computer on the network, follow these steps:

1. Choose Go | Connect To Server.

2. In the Connect To Server box, shown in the following illustration, you may see a list of globe-like icons with names such as *, Local, Workgroup, or even MSHOME. These icons represent networks your Mac sees. To see the computers in the different networks, just click the globe icon. A list of computers appears in the right pane. (If you only have OS X computers on your network, you see only the names of those computers instead of the globe icons.) Here's what the icons mean:

   ■ *   This icon means that the Mac has detected another AppleTalk zone; this might happen if you are using Macs that came out before OS X.

   ■ **Local**   This icon appears to note all of the OS X computers on the network.

   ■ **MSHOME**   If there is a Windows network, you may see an MSHOME globe, or perhaps another name, depending on the name of the Microsoft workgroup. This chapter talks more about connecting with Windows computers in the "Connecting-to-Windows Headaches" section.

   ■ **Workgroup**   This name may appear if additional Windows workgroups exist.

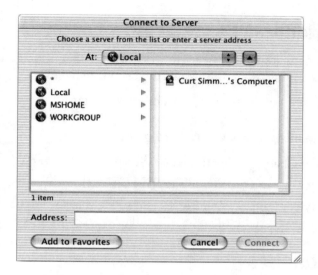

3. Double-click the name of the computer you want to access. A Connect To File Server box appears in which you can enter your username and password to access the shared files.

4. Click Connect and press RETURN or ENTER.

5. A volume containing the shared folders on the remote computer now appears on your desktop, as you can see here. Simply double-click them to open the folders and begin using them.

 # I can't access a certain Mac on my network

Cause If you should have problems accessing a particular Mac on your network, one of a few valid explanations usually fixes the problem.

The Painkiller To solve the access problem, consider these points:

- If the Mac doesn't appear at all in the Connect To Server box, the Mac you want to access is shut down, or some other problem on the Mac is preventing network access.

- The Mac you want to connect to has a manually configured IP address and/or subnet mask that is not correct for the network.

- The Mac you want to connect to has become unplugged from the network.

My network doesn't work at all!

Cause   If your network doesn't seem to work at all,—that is, no computers can access each other—one of the following suggestions may help.

The Painkiller   To fix the problem, consider these issues:

- The computers are not connected together with a hub.

- File sharing has not been turned on. See the "I don't know how to get my Mac to work on a network" headache previously in this chapter.

- Manually configured IP addresses and subnet masks are incorrect. See the "I need to use a static IP address" headache earlier in this chapter.

AirPort Headaches

The second type of network you may choose with OS X is a wireless network called AirPort. AirPort networks use AirPort cards, which look like thick credit cards, to communicate with other computers by way of radio waves. The Macs on your network all communicate with each other using an AirPort base station. The base station works much like a hub in an Ethernet network. As long as the Macs are within 150 feet of the base station, they can communicate, just as if they were connected with wires.

What Is Rendezvous?

If you bought OS X Jaguar, you probably heard a buzz about *rendezvous*, a networking technology that makes networking easier than ever. So, where is rendezvous and how do you use it? Actually, rendezvous is a collection of technology features that enables your Mac to discover other devices and Macs without you having to do anything. The idea is that you can plug your Mac into a network and automatically start working or playing.

Rendezvous is alive and well, but it is growing and will need to be adopted by other hardware manufacturers in order for it to work in more networking scenarios. The idea is that, as technology grows and develops, you will be able to automatically connect to and use network printers and will see some advantages when using instant messaging programs on your network. For now, rendezvous works with iChat and a new version of TiVo so you can share MP4s and pictures over the local area network. Other rendezvous features and options are in development and on the way.

The obvious benefit is that you can move around freely when you use a wireless network. If you have laptop computers, you can roam from room to room without ever losing network connectivity. The downside is that your Mac doesn't come equipped with the AirPort hardware you need. You need an AirPort card installed on each Mac and the base station, which costs about $200.

You can use a wireless router instead of a base station. The wireless router connects to an existing wired Ethernet network, so you can basically connect a wireless and a wired network together. The wireless router does the same thing as the base station. These kinds of routers usually carry the label 802.11b, which is the proper name for this kind of wireless network.

Once your AirPort hardware is installed, your network works in essentially the same way as a wired Ethernet network. See the previous section for headaches that may apply to you as well, but I've included a couple of issues that commonly arise.

 # I'm having problems setting up my AirPort network

Cause   If you are having problems setting up the AirPort network, make sure you follow the documentation that came with your AirPort cards and base station. Also, once you install the hardware on the computers, you can use AirPort Setup Assistant to help you.

The Painkiller   Verify that the AirPort card is correctly installed on your Mac. You may need to restart your Mac so that it detects the card. Once this is done, open Macintosh HD | Applications | Utilities | AirPort Setup Assistant. Follow the instructions that appear.

 *You cannot use the Mac OS 9 version of the AirPort Setup Assistant when you are in Classic. You must use the OS X version in the Utilities folder.*

 # I don't know how to join an AirPort network

Cause   If an AirPort network already exists and you have just installed an AirPort card in your Mac, you can easily locate and join the existing AirPort network.

The Painkiller   To join an AirPort network, open Macintosh HD | Applications | Utilities | Internet Connect. On the Configuration pop-up menu, choose AirPort. A list of available AirPort networks appears. Select the one you want to join and click Close. More easily, you can also click the AirPort icon that appears on the menu bar to join an AirPort network.

If you have trouble, make sure that you are in range of the base station and that the AirPort port is selected in Network, found under System Preferences.

There are multiple base stations on my network

Cause   If you need to connect to different base stations, you can use your Mac to specify which base station you need to use. OS X gives you a helpful utility for this purpose.

The Painkiller   Open Macintosh HD | Applications | Utilities | AirPort Admin Utility. Use the utility to search for and locate additional base stations that you need to connect to.

> **TIP**   *You can find a number of helpful documents about configuring and using AirPort networks at www.apple.com/support.*

Connecting-to-Windows Headaches

Let's face the facts—Windows computers are all over the place, and if you use your Mac on a network, the odds are good that you'll need to connect to one. In fact, you may even have a Windows computer at home along with your Mac.

The good news is that Mac OS X, particularly Mac OS X Jaguar, is very friendly with Windows computers. With OS X Jaguar, you can see and access Windows computers on your network, and they can see and access you without any additional software.

I don't know how to connect to a PC from a Mac

Cause   To connect to your PC from your Mac, just follow the steps in the painkiller.

The Painkiller   You connect to a Windows computer in basically the same way you connect to another Mac. Just follow these steps:

1. Choose Go | Connect To Server.

2. In the Connect To Server window, click the Windows workgroup name if necessary. The computers in the workgroup appear in the right column.

3. Double-click the name of the computer you want to connect to.

4. You may be prompted for your username and password, as shown in the following illustration. If you have a user account on the Windows PC, type that name and password. Depending on how the PC is configured, you may not need to enter a password.

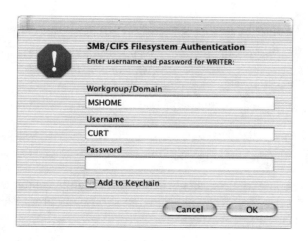

5. From the pop-up menu that appears, choose the shared resource you want to connect to and click OK, as shown in the following illustration.

6. The volume appears on your desktop. You can open it and use its contents. To stop using a volume, just drag it to the Trash.

 *If Windows XP Professional is used on the network, Windows users may have specific share access configured on different folders. This means that even if you can connect to a certain shared folder, you won't necessarily have permission to open the folder and use everything you see in it.*

 ## I don't know how to connect to a Mac from a PC

Cause   To connect to your Mac from a PC, you do things a little differently. First, you need to create an account on the Mac that is Windows-friendly.

The Painkiller   To connect to a Mac from the PC, just follow these steps:

1. Click System Preferences on the Dock or click Apple | System Preferences.

2. Click the Sharing icon.

3. Select the Windows File Sharing check box and return to System Preferences.

4. Click the Accounts icon.

5. Click the New User button.

6. On the Accounts window, shown in the following illustration, enter a name and password as desired. Click the Allow User To Log In From Windows check box. This is the account a Windows user will use to connect to the Mac.

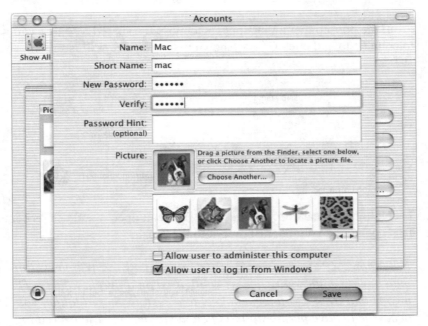

TIP   *If you don't want to create a new account, you can edit an existing one and select the Allow User To Log In From Windows check box.*

7. Click Save.

8. On the Windows computer, open My Network Places or Network Neighborhood.

9. Select Microsoft Windows Network and open the Workgroup icon.

10. Your Mac will appear there under the name "Samba," as shown in the following illustration. This name refers to the SMB protocol that is used for the connection.

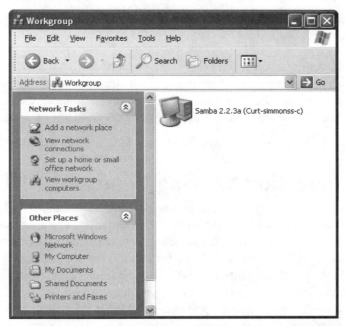

11. Double-click the icon to open the Mac. You see a dialog box prompting you to enter a username and password, as shown in the following illustration. Remember that you must enter the account's name and password that is configured to allow Windows users access.

12. Begin using the files as you like.

My PC still can't see the Mac

Cause   If you followed the steps in the previous headache and your PC still can't see your Mac, one of several explanations may apply.

The Painkiller   Consider these issues:

- Your PC and Mac computers each must be using an IP address from the same class and an appropriate subnet mask. Open Network Places on the Windows PC and check out the IP address and subnet mask. Compare these values to the Mac. The PC's IP address and subnet mask may need to be edited.

- Restart the PC. If you are using Windows Me, this may be all you need to do.

Internet-Connection Sharing Headaches

Let's say you have a network of three Macs, but only one Mac has an Internet connection. You would like all computers on the network to be able to access the Internet, but you don't want to configure a separate connection for each Mac. In another example, perhaps you are using a broadband connection that is available on only one Mac. What can you do? You simply share the single Internet connection, and your other Macs use it over your network.

In order to use the Internet Sharing feature, the Mac that you want to share from must be connected to both your network and the Internet. You can share an always-on broadband connection, such as cable or DSL. You can even share a dial-up connection. All Internet traffic comes through the sharing computer. Of course, for the other computers to use the Internet, the sharing computer must be turned on.

I don't know how to share an Internet connection

Cause   Sharing an Internet connection in OS X is easy; just follow the steps in the painkiller.

The Painkiller   To share an Internet connection, follow these steps:

1. On the Mac that has the Internet connection, click System Preferences on the Dock, or click Apple | System Preferences.

2. Click the Sharing icon.

3. On the Sharing window, click the Internet tab. Select the check box to Share The Connection With Other Computers On Ethernet/AirPort Network, as shown in the following illustration. Then click the Start button. Once the service starts, you are sharing the connection.

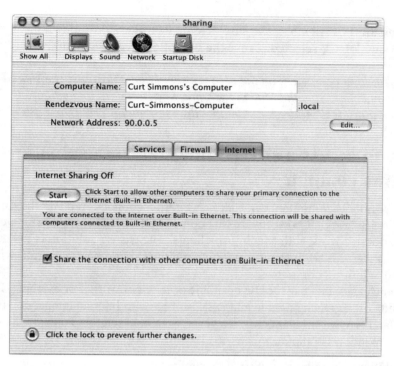

PREVENTION

If your Internet connection and your local area network use the same port (such as the Ethernet port), you may experience problems with sharing. In fact, the configuration can cause problems with other ISP users, causing your ISP to stop your service. Visit www.apple.com/support to learn more or check with your ISP for details.

The other computers on the network can't use the shared Internet connection

Cause You may need to make sure your other network clients are using a protocol called Dynamic Host Configuration Protocol (DHCP). You're probably using this feature anyway because it enables you to network without having to manually configure IP addresses. If you are not, you need to use it so that the other Macs on the network can use the shared Internet connection.

The Painkiller To make sure the client computers are using DHCP, follow these steps:

1. On the Mac that needs to access the shared connection, click System Preferences on the Dock, or click Apple | System Preferences.

2. Click the Network icon.

3. On the TCP/IP tab, make sure that the Configure drop-down menu has Using DHCP selected. Leave the other fields you see blank.

Windows computers on the network should be able to use the shared Internet connection from the Mac in the same way. You need to configure them to Obtain An IP Address Automatically. See Windows Help to learn more.

I need to access a shared Internet connection on a Windows computer

Cause   Windows computers can share an Internet connection using the Internet Connection Sharing (ICS) software that comes with Windows. Unfortunately, this software doesn't work with Macintosh clients. The easiest solution is to configure the Mac as the primary Internet computer and then share the connection with other Macs and Windows computers.

In some cases, this may not be desirable or may not work. For example, I live just outside of the reach of cable and DSL, so I have an Internet connection provided by StarBand (www.starband.com). However, StarBand satellite connections work only with Windows computers.

The Painkiller   Your best solution is to purchase some software called WinProxy (www.winproxy.com). You configure the Windows Internet computer with the WinProxy software and configure your other clients' browsers to access the Windows computer. Using this solution, you enable your Mac clients to access the Internet connection.

I don't know how to use the OS X Jaguar firewall

Cause   A firewall is a piece of hardware or software that protects a computer from outside threats, namely from the Internet. If you, like many people, use a broadband connection, your computer is basically connected to the Internet all of the time. This opens the computer to the possibility of a malicious attack from a hacker. Fortunately, OS X Jaguar gives you a built-in firewall so you can protect yourself against such threats. Basically, the firewall blocks all traffic coming to your computer except information you have requested or information from your local area network.

The Painkiller   To turn on the OS X Jaguar firewall, follow these steps:

1. Open System Preferences on the Dock or click Apple | System Preferences.

2. Click the Sharing button.

3. Click the Firewall tab.

4. On the Firewall tab, shown in the following illustration, you see services that are enabled to pass through the firewall. Notice that you can't enable or disable the services here. Rather, click the Services tab and make any desired changes.

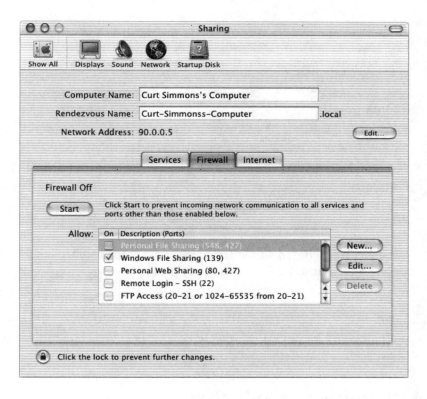

5. If a service you want to enable is not present, click the New button. From the drop-down menu that appears, locate the service you want to enable on the Port Name menu, shown next, and simply click OK.

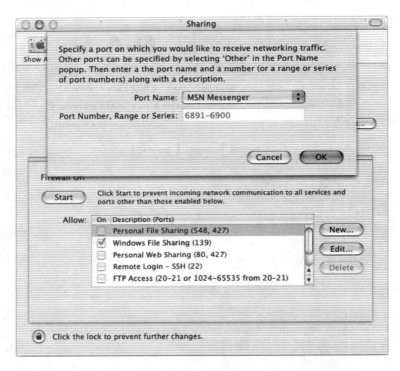

6. When you have chosen all the services you want to enable, click the Start button on the Firewall tab to start the firewall.

Keep in mind that any service you don't select on the Firewall tab will not be allowed, including local networking features and options. Also, you should not use the firewall if your Internet connection comes to you over a router or residential gateway.

Network Resource Headaches

If you have networked your computers together and started sharing resources, you have probably noticed that OS X has some fairly strict control over who can do what where. These controls protect your computer and are a great improvement over OS 9, which basically enables any network user to do whatever he or she wants with your Mac.

In OS X, what you can do when you are networked has a lot to do with your access permissions. Specifically it has to do with whether you are a guest, a Normal user, or an Administrator. If you are a guest, all you can really do is put stuff in someone's drop-box folder. When networked, OS X uses a drop-box folder so that a guest can drop documents and files off to you but can't actually see anything. However, you can open anything that people have put into their Public folders. Other than this, you can't do much else.

If you are a Normal account user, you can access your Mac over the network and use anything in your Home folder as if you were sitting there locally. If you are an Administrator, you can access most folders but can't access the System folder.

Of course, you can't see what is in someone else's Home folder, regardless of what account you are using. This keeps things in line with OS X's general security features.

This rigid system may cause you some headaches because it doesn't give you the flexibility you might need—at first glance, anyway. However, you can easily change the permissions on desired folders or files.

To do so, select the file or folder and CONTROL-click it. Then choose Get Info. Notice that if you expand the Ownership & Permissions triangle, as shown in the following illustration, you can change the Access option.

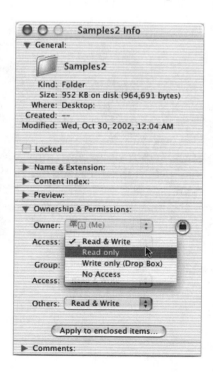

You have the following options:

- **Read & Write**   This option gives the users full access to the folder or file. They can open and read the items they see there and even delete them!

- **Read Only**   This option enables users to open the file or folder, open files, and copy files to their hard drives. However, users can't save any changes to the folder or copy anything to it. They also can't delete any files. As the permission says, they can read what's there, but that's all. This is a great way to make documents available on the network so people can view but can't change them.

- **Write Only (Drop Box)**   This permission, which works only with folders, enables people to see a folder but not open it. Users can drop documents and files into the folder, but they can't open the folder, see what's inside, or access any of the documents.

- **No Access**   This option makes the folder or file unavailable. The folder or file icon appears dimmed when viewed.

Watch Out for Parent Folders

When adjusting permissions, you need to keep parent folders in mind. Let's say you have a folder called "Docs." Inside the folder is a series of other folders that contain documents. If you configure a No Access permission on Docs, users will not be able to see the other folders in Docs—even if those folders have different permissions, such as Read. As you are working with folders, keep in mind how the permissions on the parent folder will affect folders or files inside them. As you can imagine, you run into fewer problems if you are as lenient as possible with your permissions.

Chapter 13

iPhoto Headaches

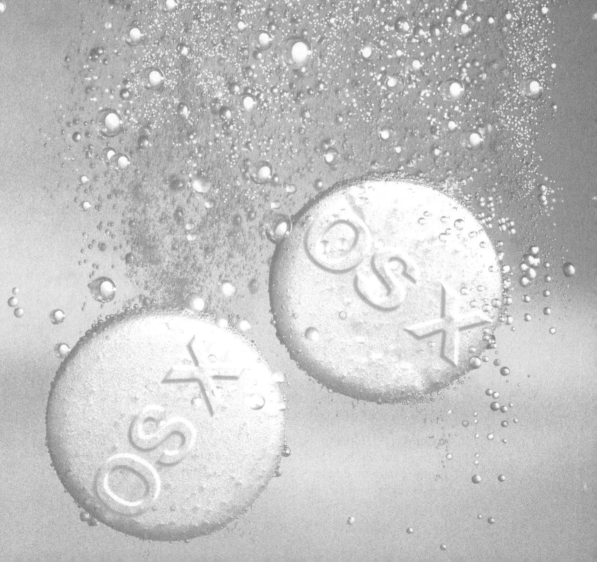

In this chapter, you'll cure...

- Import problems
- Headaches from managing albums
- Photo aggravations
- Headaches from books, slide shows, and sharing features

Digital Photography has become extremely popular in the past few years. In fact, with millions of digital cameras sold and popular photo-editing software topping the best-seller lists, we have become a world of people who love to take pictures. And why not? Photography is fun, creative, and entertaining, and it gives you a way to keep those memories you cherish. With digital photography, you can use memory to store images instead of using film. The shutterbug craze attacked many of us (me included). I can take as many pictures as I want, keep the ones I like, store them electronically without any trips to the film developing center, and even print them with great quality.

To address the growing demand for digital photography, Apple provides iPhoto, an application designed to help you store, edit, and share your digital photos. iPhoto is included in the OS X operating systems purchased after January 2002. These systems shipped with iPhoto 1.0. In April 2002, iPhoto 1.1.1 was released. If you don't have iPhoto on your Mac, or if you need to upgrade to the latest edition of iPhoto, don't worry; you can freely download it from www.apple.com/iphoto/.

NOTE   *The download is about 20 megabytes, so if you are using a modem, be prepared to wait for quite a while for the download to complete.*

So, what is iPhoto? iPhoto is an easy and cool application that helps you with your digital photography. Specifically, iPhoto does five major things:

- **Import**   You can connect your camera to your Mac and use iPhoto to import the pictures from the camera. You can also import existing pictures from a number of imaging file formats.

- **Organize**   Unlike in the real world, there's no need to have stacks of pictures stuffed here and there. iPhoto collects your pictures in the Photo Library, but you create Albums to organize them. You can even assign keywords so you can easily search for and locate the pictures you want.

- **Edit** Do your photos need a little help? That's no problem; iPhoto enables you to crop photos, adjust their size, fix brightness and contrast problems, fix red-eye, and even turn a color photo into a black-and-white photo.

- **Book** Organize a collection of photos and create your own electronic book. You can even send that book to an Apple-provided publisher to get a real book created!

- **Share** iPhoto helps you share your photos by printing them, presenting them in a slide show, e-mailing them, ordering prints, creating a home page, or exporting them to a different file format for use in other programs. You can also create a desktop picture and a custom screensaver.

Think of iPhoto as your one-stop solution for managing and working with digital photos on your Mac. The good news is that iPhoto is easy to use—the bad news is that it may throw a few headaches your way. In this chapter, I assume you are working with iPhoto (or have at least tried) and need some extra help. The following headache sections take a look at each feature of iPhoto and show you how to solve those aggravating problems.

NOTE *Let's get one nagging problem out of the way up front. iPhoto is a photo-management program—it is really not an image editor. While you can make some basic editing changes using iPhoto, such as cropping and adjusting brightness or contrast, it doesn't do a lot more. You can think of iPhoto as a tool to touch up photos before you use them; if you want to do more editing, you need some kind of photo-editing software, such as Photoshop Elements from Adobe (www.adobe.com).*

Import and Library Headaches

With iPhoto, your pictures are imported into your Photo Library when you connect your digital camera or directly import a file. If you open iPhoto, which you can find on the Dock or in your Applications folder, you see a left pane that contains your Photo Library, an option to see the Last Import, and any additional albums you might have created. The right pane shows you what is selected in the left pane (such as Photo Library, as shown in the following illustration). The bottom portion of the interface gives you button options so you choose the tasks you want. Of course, to do all of this, you need to import photos into iPhoto. If you are having problems or are not sure what you are doing, the following headaches and painkillers will help you out.

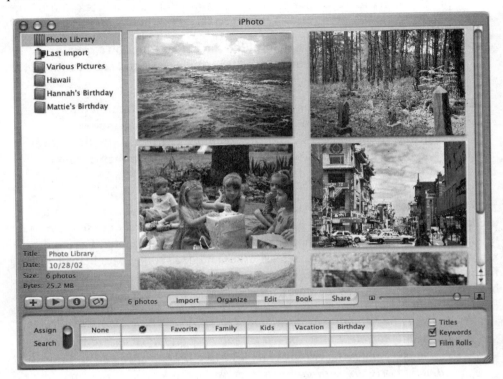

I don't know how to import pictures from my digital camera or memory card reader

Cause   Under most circumstances, importing pictures to iPhoto directly from your digital camera or memory card reader is very easy. Just see the painkiller for instructions.

The Painkiller   To import pictures from a digital camera or memory card to iPhoto, follow these steps:

1. Turn off your digital camera or memory card reader.

2. Using the USB cable provided with your digital camera or card reader, plug the USB cable into the camera and into an available USB port on your Mac.

3. Turn on your digital camera or card reader. iPhoto opens automatically. If this is the first time you have imported pictures from a digital camera or memory card, you'll probably see a message asking whether you want iPhoto to be the default program for importing pictures. Just click Yes.

4. In the iPhoto interface, shown in the following illustration, you see that the Import button option is highlighted. At the bottom of the window, you see your camera name and a button to import the pictures. Notice that you can also erase the pictures off the camera or memory card after transfer is complete. Select the check box option if you want to use this feature. Just click Import to start the transfer. The pictures are imported to your Photo Library.

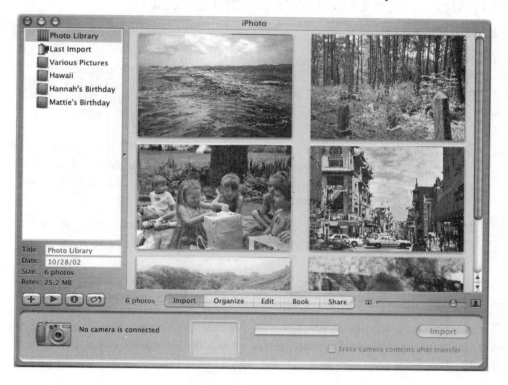

5. When you're done, turn off your digital camera or memory card reader and unmount it before disconnecting it. If you don't turn off the camera or memory card reader first, you see a message saying, The Storage Device That You Just Removed Was Not Properly Put Away…. Just click OK.

Should you have iPhoto erase your pictures from the memory card when the transfer is complete? That all depends. In one way, this feature saves you the time of having to manually delete the pictures from the memory card. On the other hand, if you are working with very important pictures, you may consider using them in iPhoto and also storing them on a CD-ROM or some other location. The iPhoto transfer and delete operation is safe, but of course nothing is 100 percent foolproof. So, if you have any worries at all about losing pictures, transfer them first and then delete them from the camera or memory card at a later time.

My Mac doesn't seem to see my camera or memory card

Cause   Most modern cameras use a USB port to connect with the computer. Sometimes, however, your Mac may not be able to detect your camera or may have trouble seeing when the camera or memory card reader is connected.

The Painkiller   You can try a few things in order to solve this problem:

1. You may have plugged the camera into the USB port when the camera was turned on. Turn the camera off and turn it back on. Your Mac will usually be able to detect the camera at this point. If you are using a memory card reader, remove the card and insert it again.

2. If you have a bunch of USB devices using a hub, try unplugging some of those devices. Then plug your camera or memory card reader in again and turn it on.

3. Restart the Mac. A system glitch may be keeping the Mac from seeing your camera. Restarting will clear the board and probably fix the problem.

4. If you are still having problems, see your camera manual or the manufacturer's web site for help. If you have technical support with your camera, don't hesitate to call.

My camera doesn't use a USB port

Cause   If you are using an older camera, it may have a serial port connection designed for the PC. Or you may be using a Sony brand that doesn't physically connect to the computer but stores images on a 3.5-inch floppy disk or a mini CD-R or CD-RW disk. In these cases, you can use a few possible solutions.

The Painkiller Consider these options:

1. If the camera uses a serial port, you may have to use a PC to transfer the images and then move them to iPhoto on a CD or over a network (you could even e-mail them yourself). Of course, you may consider the fact that it is time for a new digital camera if your budget allows. Or, if you are willing to part with around $50, you can buy a mass-storage compliant card reader that will read all types of media.

2. If your camera uses a floppy disk to store images, just put the floppy disk into the Mac's floppy drive and follow the next headache for importing steps. If your Mac doesn't have a floppy disk drive, you can buy an external one that plugs into a USB port for around $60 (see www.macwarehouse.com for examples). If you don't want to buy a floppy drive, you need to have someone who has a floppy drive pull the pictures off the disk and either burn them onto a CD or e-mail them to you.

 # I need to get photos I already have into iPhoto

Cause If you have a bunch of existing pictures that you want to move to iPhoto, you can easily do so. These pictures are simply imported into the iPhoto Photo Library from their source location, such as your computer, a CD, or some other disk, just as they are when you import them from your camera.

The Painkiller To import existing pictures, follow these steps:

1. Open iPhoto and select File | Import.

2. An import photo window appears. Browse for the desired photos and click Import. You can import several photos at the same time by holding down COMMAND and selecting them. When you're done, the imported photos appear in the Photo Library.

 If you don't want to hassle with the Import command, you can just open iPhoto and drag and drop pictures into the picture area. They will be automatically added to the Photo Library.

 # iPhoto will not import a certain file type

Cause iPhoto can read and import most major picture file types. Specifically, you can import JPEG, TIFF, BMP, GIF, MacPaint, PICT, PNG, Photoshop, SGI, Targa, and FlashPix. However, iPhoto cannot import photos saved in other image-editing software program file types or in certain other file types that might be available.

The Painkiller   If you have a file type that you can't import, you need to use some image-editing program that can read it. Choose the Save As option and choose a file type that is supported.

NOTE   *By the way, although you can import pictures from a number of picture formats, iPhoto automatically resaves pictures that you edit as JPEG pictures. Even rotating a picture causes iPhoto to save it as a JPEG; if you create a book, the files are saved as JPEGs, as well. As you can see, JPEG is the file format of choice, and JPEG is generally the default choice for most digital cameras.*

The Photo Library displays pictures in a very big format, and I have to scroll around a lot to see them

Cause   iPhoto keeps all pictures in the Photo Library. The Library can display pictures in the viewing window so that each picture takes up the entire window, or it can display the pictures as small thumbnails. You can change the magnification of the pictures at any time in order to see more or less of them.

The Painkiller   To change the magnification of the pictures in the Photo Library, first select Photo Library in the left pane and then use the magnification slider bar found to the right, under the viewer area of iPhoto to change the magnification, as shown in the following illustration. You can perform this same action within albums, as well.

PREVENTION   *Your Photo Library is stored in your Pictures folder, found in your Home folder. This enables different people to use the Mac with their own accounts. Each person can have his or her own Photo Library without mixing all of the photos together. If you look in the folder, you see a bunch of subfolders named by creation dates. Don't mess with these folders or rename them—doing so can hopelessly confuse iPhoto and even cause it to crash!*

The Case of the Sluggish and Slow iPhoto

So you're running iPhoto and you seem to be spending quite a bit of time tapping your fingers on the table as you wait... If this is you, there's probably a good reason. Like all image-editing and image-management programs, iPhoto uses a lot of RAM. In fact, displaying pictures, editing them, and managing them takes a lot of RAM, and iPhoto is no exception to this rule. If your Mac is a little behind the times in the RAM department, this may be an ongoing problem for you. iPhoto will work, but it may be slower than you want. You can help this problem by quitting all other programs when you are using iPhoto and, of course, considering a RAM upgrade for your Mac.

Organize Headaches

Once you import pictures into iPhoto, your next trick is to keep them organized. iPhoto makes organizing photos really easy, but a few headaches and aggravations can come your way. Read on...

I don't know how to use an album

Cause   The Photo Library holds all of your pictures, but let's face it—if you have 300 pictures in the Photo Library, finding what you want can be a real pain. To help you stay organized, iPhoto gives you the option of organizing pictures into albums. An album is really just a folder for storing pictures under a certain category. For example, you might create albums for birthday pictures, vacation pictures, Christmas pictures, and so forth. You can even be very specific and store pictures by months and dates, such as Christmas 2002. You can create as many as you need, and the albums all appear in the list in the left pane of iPhoto.

The Painkiller   To create an album, follow these steps:

1. Open iPhoto. In the left iPhoto pane, click + or select File | New Album.

2. A New Album dialog box appears. Enter a name for the album and click OK. The new album appears in the left console pane.

3. To put pictures in an album, click the Photo Library and simply drag the pictures you want into the album, as you can see in the following illustration. You can drag multiple pictures at the same time by holding down COMMAND

and selecting them. If your Photo Library is organized by film rolls, you can drag and drop an entire film roll.

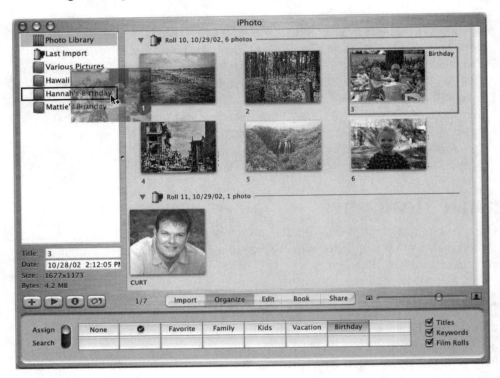

 *Remember that albums are provided to help you stay organized. Try to keep your album titles meaningful and descriptive so you can more easily find what you are looking for.*

I deleted pictures from an album or deleted an entire album, but the pictures still show up in the Photo Library

Cause   You can easily delete pictures from an album by selecting the picture and selecting Edit | Delete. You can also select an entire album and delete it in the same way. However, albums are managed separately from the Photo Library, so even if you delete an item or an entire album, it appears in the Photo Library.

The Painkiller   If you really want to get rid of a picture permanently, select Photo Library and the picture and select Edit | Delete. You see a confirmation message asking whether you really want to delete the picture permanently.

I don't know how to use film rolls

Cause   iPhoto contains a feature called film rolls. In a nutshell, the *film roll* is just another organizational method. To organize your photos into film rolls, select the Photo Library or any album and click the Film Rolls check box at the bottom right of the iPhoto interface. Film rolls are collected by the date you imported the pictures. For example, if you import ten pictures from your digital camera, those ten pictures become part of a film roll defined by the date you imported them.

The Painkiller   To use the film roll feature, follow these steps:

1. Open iPhoto. Select the Photo Library or the desired album.

2. Make sure the Organize button is selected in the lower portion of the interface and click Film Rolls, as shown in the following illustration.

3. The items in the display area now appear organized by film rolls, as shown in the following illustration. Click the arrow next to the film roll to see its contents.

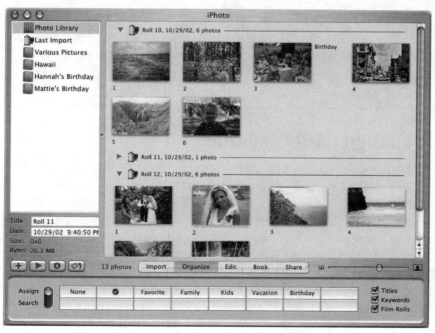

4. As I mentioned, film rolls are organized by the date you imported the pictures to iPhoto. That organization may not work best. In many cases, you would rather have the film roll organized by when the pictures were taken. So, you can easily change the name and date. Just select the roll in the viewing area and change the title and date in the Title and Date boxes found in the lower left portion of the iPhoto interface, as you can see in the following illustration.

 ## I can't assign labels and titles

Cause   iPhoto gives you the chance to create a picture, change the title of a picture, and assign keywords, or labels, to photos. The reason, you may wonder? It's all about finding photos. Let's say you have 1000 photos stored in iPhoto. You want to quickly find all photos of your children's birthday parties, but your pictures are stored in a monthly album format. The only way to find your pictures is to browse through the albums and locate them, right? Wrong! Using iPhoto, you can simply search for the pictures and find them all—provided you used keyword assignments and/or titles. You can do a few different things with titles and labels, and the following painkiller gets you up to speed.

The Painkiller   To use titles and labels, follow these steps:

1. Every photo imported into iPhoto has a title. The title may be a title you previously assigned, or it may be a title your camera has created for the file, such as WPS004876.JPG. That means a lot, right? Well, you can retitle your pictures quickly and easily and, if you are careful in titling them, easily find them with a search. To retitle a picture, go to Organize mode and select the picture. In the Title dialog box in the lower-left portion of the interface, just type a new title. You can even give multiple photos the same name if you want. For example, all of the photos of my wedding are titled "wedding," so all I have to do is search for "wedding" to find them all.

2. iPhoto gives you a few default keywords you can also apply to photos, such as Favorite, Family, Kids, Vacation, and Birthday. If you give all of your birthday pictures the keyword of "birthday," then you can easily find them in a search. To assign a default keyword, just go to Organize Mode, select the picture, and click the desired keyword, as shown in the following illustration. The new keyword appears with the picture. You can assign multiple keywords if you wish.

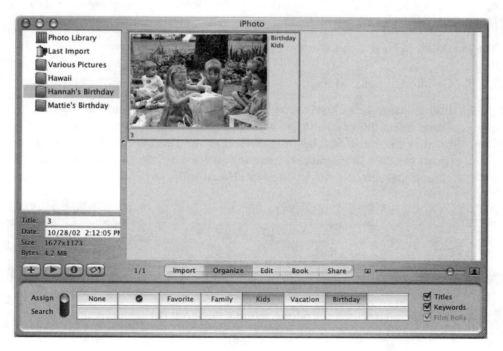

3. You can use the default keywords, change them, or create nine additional keywords. Just go into Organize Mode and select Edit | Keywords. You can change the existing keywords and add your own in the keyword dialog boxes provided, as shown in the following illustration. When you are finished, just click Done.

TIP *You can also add comments to a picture that can help you when searching. Just select the picture and click Show Information in the lower-left portion of the interface (it looks like an i).*

I don't know how to search for a picture

Cause   If you have used titles, keywords, and comments, you can easily search for pictures in your Photo Library.

The Painkiller   To search for a photo, just follow these steps:

1. Go into Organize Mode.

2. In the Assign/Search selection slider, move the slider option to search. Then, select the keyword you want (make sure the title and keywords check boxes are selected, as shown in the following illustration). iPhoto will bring up all matches in the display area. If you want to search on a particular album, just select it and try the search again.

3. You can also search for photos using a keyword that you type in. For example, if I wanted to find all of my wedding photos, which I titled

"wedding" but did not assign keywords for, I can search by entering my own keyword. To do this, click iPhoto | Preferences. In the Assign/Searches option, choose the Comments radio button, shown in the following illustration.

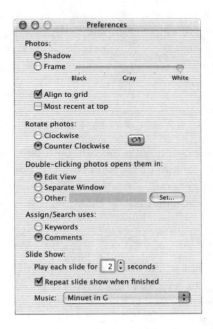

4. As you can see in the following illustration, you now have a search field instead of keywords. Type the word or words for your search (make sure the Titles and Keywords check boxes are selected on the right side of the interface).

TIP   *Just change the preferences back to the original setting when you're done to get your keywords back.*

The Check Mark

You may have noticed that one of the keyword buttons is a check mark. You can't edit the check mark button either. The check mark is simply a little organizational tool that you can use. When you select a photo and click the check mark button, a check appears in the right corner of the photo. This feature is helpful if you are working with a lot of photos and you want to keep track of which photos you have worked with and which ones you have not.

Edit Headaches

You can go into Edit mode by clicking the Edit button in the lower portion of the iPhoto interface. The edit feature gives you just a few options to edit and clean up your photos, and they are generally easy to use. The following headaches show you how to get over any pain you may be experiencing.

I can't crop a photo

Cause   When you take photos, they can often use a little cropping. Essentially, when you crop a photo, you remove portions of the photo that you don't want. Cropping can be a really great way to make a good photo much, much better. When you crop a photo, you decide what areas you want to keep and what areas of the photo you want to throw away.

The Painkiller   To crop a photo, just follow these steps:

1. In Organize Mode, locate the picture that you want to edit and click Edit Mode.

2. The picture that you want to edit now appears in the display area.

3. Move your mouse onto the picture. You see that your mouse appears as a +. Choose the desired location for the new corner of the picture and, holding down your mouse button, drag over the desired area to create a selection. The area you have selected is the area you will *keep*, as noted by the grayed-out appearance of the remaining areas. Drag the selection area around to change it, if necessary.

4. When you are happy with the selection area, click the Crop button in the lower toolbar. The cropped picture now appears in the display area. If you have made a mistake, just click Edit | Undo Crop Photo to return to the original.

 *Is the picture upside down or sideways as imported from your camera? That's no problem. Double-click the picture to open it in Edit Mode and use the Rotate button on the left side of the interface to change the orientation of the picture.*

I can't make a photo a standard size

Cause When you crop a photo, you are basically doing so freehand, which means you can select the size and square or rectangle shape that you want. However, if

A Different View...

By default, pictures you are editing appear in the display window. However, you can change this behavior so that each picture opens in a separate window in which you can apply the editing tools as desired. Just select iPhoto | Preferences. In the Preferences window, under Double-Clicking Photos Opens Them In:, choose the Separate Window option. Close the Preferences dialog box and double-click a photo. You see that it opens in a separate window, as shown in the following illustration, with the editing toolbar at the top. From here, you can work directly with the photo as desired.

you are going to print the photo (or order prints), you probably want it to appear in a standard size, such as 4×3, 4×6, 5×7, and so on. To make sure this happens, use the constrain feature.

The Painkiller   To use the constrain feature, just follow these steps:

1. In Organize Mode, locate the picture that you want to edit and click Edit Mode.

2. The picture that you want to edit now appears in the display area.

3. Click the Constrain drop-down menu and select the desired size.

4. Go to the picture and drag over the area for cropping. Notice that the crop shape is "constrained" to the size you selected. Adjust as necessary and click the Crop button. Now you have a cropped photo that will print in a standard photo format size.

A picture is too bright or too dark

Cause   Due to lighting conditions, some pictures are too light or too dark. The good news is that iPhoto gives you an easy way to adjust the brightness and contrast of a picture to clean it up.

The Painkiller   To adjust the brightness or contrast, just follow these steps:

1. In Organize Mode, locate the picture that you want to edit and click Edit Mode.

2. The picture that you want to edit now appears in the display area.

3. Use the Brightness/Contrast slider bars to adjust the picture quality. You may have to play around with these settings a bit to find the best look. Also, hold down CONTROL to toggle between the edited photo and the original. This will help you see the difference between the two.

Don't like the changes you made? Just use Edit | Undo to go back to the previous version. Already left Edit mode? It's not too late—just select File | Revert to Original. This removes all editing changes you have made.

Some of my pictures have red-eye

Cause   Red-eye is the very common and awful condition that makes the subjects in your pictures look like vampires. Red-eye normally occurs when the photographer uses a flash indoors, typically in poor light. The flash passes through the eye, bounces off the subject's retina (which is full of blood), and goes back to the camera, creating red eyes. Some newer and admittedly more expensive digital cameras have a red-eye reduction mode to help solve this problem, but iPhoto can solve it for you too. Here's how.

The Painkiller   To fix red-eye, just follow these steps:

1. In Organize Mode, locate the picture that you want to edit and click Edit Mode.

2. The picture now appears in the display area.

3. Use the magnification slider bar to make the picture bigger so you can easily see and work with the eyes.

4. Place your mouse in the picture and drag to create a small box around the eye, as shown in the following illustration. Click the Red-Eye button to remove the red from the selection. Repeat this process on the other eye.

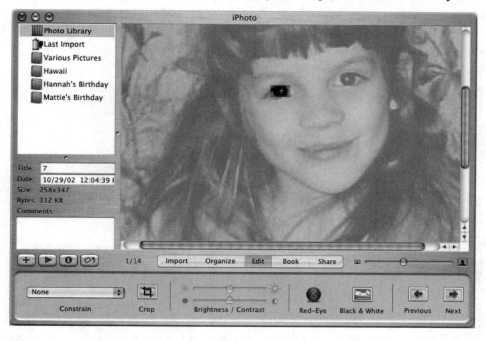

NOTE   *You can also convert images to black and white by simply clicking the Black and White button. You can then use the Brightness/Contrast controls to adjust the black-and-white photo as necessary.*

Book and Slide Show Headaches

iPhoto gives you a cool feature that enables you to create your own book from the electronic photos. You can organize and arrange your book, add text to it, and make it basically look how you want using a few provided themes. You can upload your files and have your book bound, printed, and mailed to you for around $30 (that's for a ten-page book—more pages cost extra). You can also create slide shows quickly and easily that you can view on your Mac or save and e-mail to friends.

For the most part, creating your book or slide show is easy. There are just a few headaches that we should address, but let me point out that the iPhoto help files can give you basic tutorial information about creating your book or slide show. I won't go into that here—I'm assuming you are already trying these tasks and are frustrated.

Concerning the book, you need to organize the photos you want in the book into an album. Select the album and click the Book Mode button. As you can see in the following illustration, iPhoto gives you a title slide and a suggested order. You can drag pictures around to change the order and use the Theme drop-down menu to try different themes. The important point to remember is that the layout and text you enter look exactly the way they will when you get the book, so it's important to spend some time on the book and check your spelling. When you are happy and ready to place your order, go to Share Mode and click Order Book. You need a connection to the Internet to place the order. Now, onto a few headaches you might encounter…

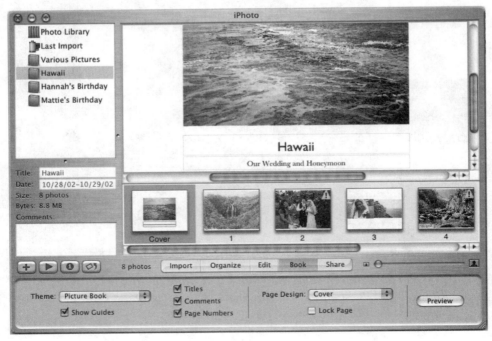

Some pages of my book display two or more pictures on a page—I don't want this

Cause   The book feature will try to organize pictures by how they fit on the book pages and according to their resolution. If the book has automatically placed two more pictures on the same page, you can easily change it.

The Painkiller   To change the pages of pictures, just follow these steps:

1. In Book Mode, select the page that you want to change. You may want two pictures on a page instead of one, or one picture instead of two.

2. In the toolbar area at the bottom of the page, click the Page Design drop-down menu and change the page design to whatever you want.

 *If your book is longer than ten pages, you must pay $3 for each additional page—combining photos on a single page can save you money!*

 ## I don't like the fonts that appear in the text

Cause   The book uses a default font for your text, but you can easily change it.

The Painkiller   Hidden away on the Edit menu is a font option that enables you to change the font, bold the font, use italics, and so forth. Just use these items as needed. Also notice the spell check feature—take advantage of it!

 You can CONTROL-click any text and get to the fonts and spelling that way. Also, you can choose Speech and have your Mac read the text to you as an extra error-checking step!

 ## Some of my book photos have yellow exclamation points over them

Cause   If one of your photos has a yellow exclamation point over it, the book feature is telling you that the photo's resolution is not high enough when it is printed. When you are working with files electronically, the resolution isn't that big of a deal. However, when you print a file with low resolution, you get a grainy look.

The Painkiller   A couple of options exist, although they might not be what you want to hear:

- You need to use higher-resolution photographs. Remove the offending photographs from the book (go back to Organize mode) and choose some different photographs.

- Export the offending image, print it, and scan it using a scanner. Scan the image as a high-resolution photo (300 dpi or more will usually do the trick). Import the photo back into iPhoto. Note that this trick may not give you the best-looking photo, however.

- Change the layout of the book to put two or three pictures on each page. Making the image smaller on the page reduces the amount of resolution needed. The yellow exclamation point will disappear when your photos are in the clear.

Now, concerning the slide show feature, you can watch a slide show of an album at any time by simply clicking the Play button in iPhoto. You aren't likely to experience any headaches, but while we are on the subject, I'll point out two cool options:

- Click iPhoto | Preferences. In the Preferences window, notice the Slide Show category. Use this section to determine how long each slide should be displayed. Notice that you can also use some canned music iPhoto gives you. However, you can also use any MP3 file for the music, as well. Click the Music drop-down menu and select Other to browse for the MP3 file. You can download a ton of MP3 files from the Internet, or you can make your own using iTunes 3. See Chapter 15 for details.

- Want to share your slide show with friends and family? That's no problem—you can save it as a QuickTime movie and e-mail it to them. To save it as a QuickTime movie, choose File | Export. Click the QuickTime movie tab and review the options. Then click the Export button.

TIP   *Windows computers can also view QuickTime movies, with the appropriate download, so you have no worries there.*

About Share Mode

When you click Share Mode, you see a number of different options, most of which are self-explanatory. You can print your photos, view a slide show, e-mail a photo, order prints of your photos, order your book, create a home page at www.mac.com, set a picture as your desktop picture, use an album of pictures for a screensaver, and export pictures so you can do other things with them. If you play around with these features, you'll see they are all rather easy. Enjoy!

Why Printed Pictures Look Bad

As I mentioned, pictures may look great when you view them on the monitor but look not so great when printed. Why? It's all about resolution. In order to print larger photos, such as 5×7 or 8×10, you must have a picture with a high enough resolution to print without graininess or distortion. Check your camera documentation for more details about printing and resolution.

Chapter 14

iMovie Headaches

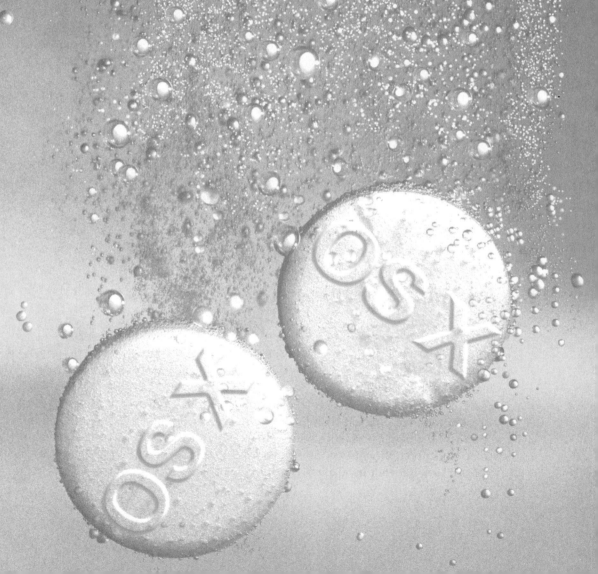

In this chapter, you'll cure...

- Problems with importing video and pictures

- Aggravations with movie assembly

- Difficulties with titles, effects, audio, and more

OS X includes a really cool movie-editing application called iMovie 2. Using iMovie 2, you can import video from your digital camcorder or even import existing QuickTime movies and still shots. Then, you can edit those movies, clips, and pictures together to create your own polished movie, complete with a title page, transitions, and even music! Across the board, iMovie 2 is easy to use, once you get the hang of how things work—and the great news is that iMovie 2 is very powerful, providing you with plenty of functions and features that enable you to create the movies you really want. Of course, with any application like iMovie 2, you are likely to run into a few snags here and there. In this chapter, we take a look at the headaches and painkillers you will most likely need!

People have written entire books about iMovie 2 because the application does so much. If you are just now getting your feet wet with iMovie 2, you might want to invest in one of these books, such as How to Do Everything with iMovie 2 *(Reveaux, McGraw-Hill/Osborne, 2002), which can give you tutorials and other usage tips outside of troubleshooting.*

Digital Video and Importing Headaches

iMovie 2 can record movies directly from your digital camcorder, or you can import movies and even pictures directly into iMovie 2. For the most part, getting movies and pictures into iMovie 2 is rather easy, but you may run into a few headaches along the way. The following headaches and painkillers guide you on your way.

Before we get into digital video and importing files, however, it is a good idea to first familiarize yourself with the iMovie 2 interface. The following illustration shows you the major portions of the iMovie 2 interface. You may want to refer back to this illustration as we move forward; I refer to different portions of it as we work to solve your headaches.

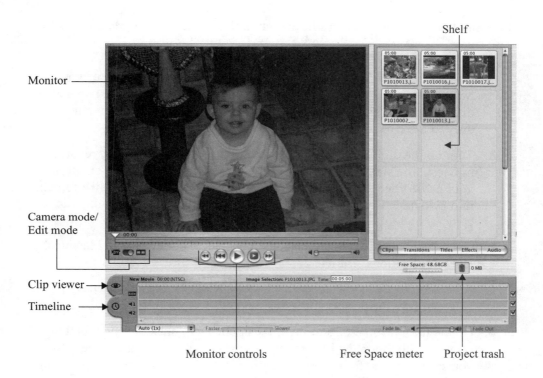

Shelf

Monitor

Camera mode/
Edit mode

Clip viewer

Timeline

Monitor controls   Free Space meter   Project trash

I don't know how to get movies from my digital camcorder to iMovie 2

Cause: First things first: you must be using a digital camcorder that can connect with your Mac. Read it again: iMovie 2 only works with digital camcorders, not with analog camcorders that use VHS tapes or 8mm analog videotapes. In order to directly run movies through iMovie 2, you must be using a digital camcorder.

Once you are sure you are using a digital camcorder, make sure your camcorder provides a FireWire port so you can connect the camcorder to the FireWire port on your Mac. The FireWire port on your camcorder may be called an IEEE 1394, DV Terminal, DV In/Out, or i.Link, but it is still a FireWire port and can connect with your Mac. Most digital camcorders provide this port, so you are probably in good shape.

Once you are sure you have a digital camcorder and a FireWire port, you are ready to get connected.

The Painkiller: To move movies from your digital camcorder to iMovie 2, follow these steps:

1. Connect the FireWire cable to the FireWire port on the back of your Mac and to your digital camcorder. Note that the ends of the cable are different—one end connects only to the Mac, and the other connects only to the camcorder.

2. Turn on the digital camcorder. If you want to move previously recorded movies into iMovie, insert the correct tape in your camcorder and turn your camcorder to VCR or VTR mode. If you want to record live footage into iMovie 2 as you shoot it with your camcorder, turn the camcorder to camera mode.

3. Open iMovie 2 by clicking its icon on the Dock, or navigate to Macintosh HD | Applications | iMovie 2.

4. A New Project window appears. Choose a name for the new project, decide where to save the project, and click Save.

5. On the iMovie monitor portion of the application, click the slider button, shown in the following illustration, so that the DV option is selected. Now you see the movie from your camcorder in the Monitor window (assuming you have pressed Play on your digital camcorder).

6. To begin recording the movie, press the Import button that appears on the toolbar below the monitor. You see a new movie clip appear in the Shelf, and iMovie 2 records your movie.

TIP   *iMovie 2 can record clips that are 2GB in length, which equals about nine minutes and twenty-eight seconds of footage. If you exceed this length, iMovie 2 simply creates a new clip and continues recording. As you are recording, be sure to watch the Free Space meter, shown here,*

Free Space: 48.68GB   *so you know how much disk space your movie is consuming (and they consume a lot!).*

iMovie doesn't seem to recognize my digital camcorder

Cause: Most of the time, iMovie can easily see your digital camcorder, but some problems could come your way. Before proceeding, check the previous headache and make sure you have your camcorder correctly connected to your Mac through the FireWire port. If you seem to have the camcorder connected properly, see the painkiller for additional help.

The Painkiller: Try these solutions to get your camera working:

- First, make sure you are using a digital camcorder. iMovie 2 cannot work with analog camcorders.

- Unplug any other FireWire devices.

- Quit iMovie, unplug your digital camcorder, plug it back in, and start iMovie again.

- Some JVC camcorders do not work with Mac's FireWire port. You may need to use a different camera.

- You need to be running the Mac FireWire software version 2.5 or later. You can download and install the latest FireWire software from www.info.apple.com/support/downloads.html.

- If you see a Navigation Services Not Installed message or you have previously installed a professional digital video-editing program, such as EditDV, you need to turn on the QuickTime FireWire extension in Extensions Manager.

I need to import analog video

Cause: Digital video is the wave of the future, but if you are like me, you have tons of older VHS and even 8-mm analog videotapes around your house. iMovie 2 only works with digital video, so what can you do? There are a few solutions to importing analog video, which are described in the painkiller.

The Painkiller: Try these solutions for importing analog video:

- Some camcorders, such as the Sony Digital8, can play both analog and digital video. The material becomes digitized when sent over the FireWire cable to your Mac, and iMovie doesn't know the difference. Try to get your hands on one of these camcorders if possible.

■ You can use the video and audio jacks on your old camcorder to connect to your digital camcorder. Insert a blank tape into the digital camcorder and simply record the analog video coming from the old camcorder. You can then import the new digital movie into iMovie. See your camcorder's documentation for more information about recording from another camcorder.

■ You can purchase a converter box for around $300 that sits between your Mac and the analog camcorder. The box converts the analog video stream to a digital stream before sending it on to your Mac. You can find a converter box at your favorite electronics store.

I can't import a QuickTime movie

Cause:　iMovie 2 can import QuickTime movies that you create with another application, such as iPhoto, or ones that you download from the Internet. As long as you don't sell your movie, you can use any movie from the Internet without worrying about copyright infringement. However, if you have ever tried to click File | Import, you probably noticed that all QuickTime movies are grayed out. What's the problem? Here's the answer: iMovie 2 can't directly import a QuickTime movie, but it *can* import a QuickTime movie saved as a Digital Video Stream. In order to convert a QuickTime movie to a Digital Video Stream, upgrade your QuickTime Player to QuickTime Player Pro. You can do this over the Internet, and it costs you $30.

The Painkiller:　To import a Digital Video Stream, follow these steps:

1. First, open QuickTime Player found in Macintosh HD | Applications. Each time you open QuickTime Player, you see a box option to Upgrade to QuickTime Pro. Click the Upgrade Now option. You need Internet access to upgrade the player and pay your $30 upgrade fee.

2. Once you have upgraded, open the desired movie in QuickTime Player Pro.

3. Click File | Export.

4. In the Export window, choose the Movie To DV Stream option, enter a name, choose the desired location to save the clip, and click Save.

5. Open the desired iMovie 2 project.

6. Choose File | Import, select Navigate To The DV Stream, and click Open.

7. The DV Stream file now appears as a clip on the Shelf in iMovie 2.

I don't know how to import a photo

Cause: iMovie 2 enables you to mix movies and photos. With this feature you can create very interesting movies containing mixes of photos and video clips. You can also use this feature to import a more customized title page that you have created with another application. iMovie 2 can read most common graphics files (anything QuickTime can read), such as JPEG, TIFF, PICT, and even GIF files. Your best bet is to use a JPEG or PICT file format.

The Painkiller: To import a picture into iMovie, follow these steps:

1. Open the desired project and click File | Import.

2. Navigate to the desired picture file and click Open.

3. The picture file appears on the Shelf, shown in the following illustration, in the same way a movie clip appears on the Shelf.

NOTE   *In fact, you can use iMovie 2 simply to work with photo files. Why? The answer is simple: iMovie 2 gives you more control when creating slide shows, including transition options and title page options that other applications, such as iPhoto and iDVD, do not give you.*

Imported pictures appear with black borders around them in the monitor

Cause: If you select a photo you have imported on the Shelf, you can see the photo in the iMovie monitor. However, if you notice that the picture has a black border around the sides or top (or both), like the example shown in the following illustration, then you know that the photo was cropped to a size that is outside of iMovie's parameters. If you want your photos to fill the screen area, then they need to be 640×480 pixels in size.

The Painkiller: To fix this problem, you need to remove the photo from iMovie and open the original file in a program that can adjust the size for you, such as iPhoto, PhotoShop Elements, or some other graphics program. Then change the size to 640×480 and import the photo again into iMovie.

Movie Assembly Headaches

Once you import the desired movie clips or photos into iMovie, you are ready to begin assembling your movie. You assemble the movie by editing any clips as necessary and then assembling the movie clips and photos in the movie Timeline. The good news here is that iMovie is really easy to use, so you'll be creating your movie in no time. However, the following headaches and painkillers show you how to solve a few aggravating problems you may run across.

I need to break apart an existing clip

Cause: When you import video into iMovie, that video may not be exactly what you want when you create the actual movie. The clip you imported may be too long or may contain boring video that you want to get rid of, or you may want to break the clip into smaller clips so you can organize your movie differently. Regardless of the task at hand, iMovie 2 gives you total control over the clips on the Shelf so you can edit them as needed.

The Painkiller: To break a clip apart (split the clip), follow these steps:

1. To split a clip so that it becomes two clips, select the clip on the Shelf.

2. Press the Play button on the Monitor control bar, shown in the following illustration. When the clip reaches the place that you want to split, press the Play button again to pause it.

 *When you select a clip on the Shelf, the Monitor should move to Edit mode. If it doesn't, just click the slider button on the bottom left of the Monitor control window so that it moves to Edit mode.*

3. Click Edit | Split Video Clip At Playhead, or just press COMMAND-T. The video clip is split, and the new clip appears on the Shelf.

 # I need to cut or crop a portion of video from a clip

Cause: Let's face it, sometimes portions of clips are boring or the video shot simply isn't good. Perhaps you are waiting for your dog to do some trick or you accidentally film the back of someone's head. Regardless of the problem, iMovie gives you the control to crop portions of video from any clip.

The Painkiller: To crop a clip, follow these steps:

1. Select the clip that you want to crop so that it appears in the monitor.

2. At the point where you want to create the crop area, position your mouse cursor under the tick marks (the small lines) under the scrubber bar, as shown in the following illustration. A pale triangle appears.

3. Using your mouse, drag the triangle. The triangle splits into two and creates a yellow highlight over the area on the scrubber bar. Drag the triangles around as desired—this highlights the section of the movie you want to keep, which is the area between the two triangles.

4. Choose Edit | Cut or Edit | Crop. This action removes all video outside of the selected areas you chose in Step 3.

PREVENTION   *As you are working with the cut or crop features, make sure you keep in mind that Edit | Cut or Edit | Crop, affects two different things. Cutting removes what you have selected, and cropping removes everything except what you have selected. The good news is that if you make a mistake, you can simply click Edit | Undo to fix the last change you made. You can do this for up to ten previous actions.*

Cutting and Cropping

When you make a selection on the scrubber bar, you can choose to either cut or crop all of the video outside of the selected area. When you crop the clip, the excess portions are trimmed away and put in the iMovie trash. When you cut a portion of a clip away, the cut clip is taken out of the original clip, but the cut section now appears as a new clip on the Shelf. You can then use the cut material and paste it in another clip using the Edit | Paste command.

I don't know how to assemble my movie clips

Cause: You use the Shelf area to work on your clips, cropping, cutting, and pasting as needed. You can have the clips in the Shelf area in any order, but when you are ready to begin assembling your movie in order, you need to place the clips on the Storyboard.

The Painkiller: To assemble the clips on the Storyboard, follow these steps:

1. Select the Storyboard tab on the bottom portion of the iMovie interface, shown in the following illustration (the tab has an "eye" icon on it).

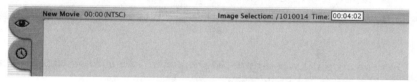

2. Drag the movie clips or photos from the Shelf to the Storyboard portion at the bottom of the iMovie interface. Place them in the order that you want them to appear in your movie, as you can see in the following illustration. Note that you can drag clips back to the Shelf or around on the Storyboard as needed until you get the desired order.

Reversing Clips, Speeding Them Up, and Slowing Them Down

If you want to add a comical element to a movie clip, such as showing someone jumping out of the water instead of into the water, or you simply want to reverse the action of a clip for some other artistic reason, you can easily do so in iMovie. Simply select the movie clip and click Advanced | Reverse Clip Direction. Now, the clip plays in reverse! You can also speed a clip up or slow a clip down from its normal speed. Just select the clip in either the Shelf or Timeline viewer and move the Faster/Slower slider bar that appears at the bottom of the Timeline viewer.

 TIP   *You can drag several clips at the same time. Just hold down* SHIFT *and select them on the Shelf. Then simply drag the selection.*

Transitions, Titles, and Effects Headaches

One of the great things about iMovie is that it enables you to assemble clips of movies and pictures and manage the transitions between clips. The transitions give your movies a polished, professional look, and you can even add a title page and a few specialized effects to your movies as well. The following headaches and painkillers show you how to use these features and cure common ailments.

I don't know how to create a title page

Cause: iMovie allows you great flexibility in designing your interactive title page. This title page gives your movie the polish and shine that you want, and it gives you a lot of flexibility. For example, you can create end credits for your movie that look just like those in a real movie, and you can even superimpose text, such as you might see on a music video. You simply make the title you want and drag your creation to the Timeline; the painkiller shows you how.

The Painkiller: To create a title page, follow these steps:

1. At the bottom of the Shelf, click the Titles button, shown in the following illustration.

2. The Shelf changes to a window in which you can create your title page. As you can see in the following illustration, you basically use a few different controls to create the title page. The following steps walk you through the controls.

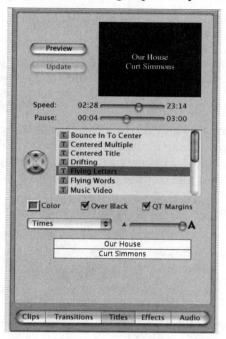

3. The Speed and Pause slider bars affect how fast the text is displayed on the title page and how long the text remains before it fades away. For example, you could choose to have the text letters fly onto the page and pause for five seconds before fading. You need to play around with these settings to get the effect you want as you create the title page.

4. In the center of the window, select the effect you want to use. When you select an effect, it plays for you in the small preview window at the top of the page. Depending on your selection, the round arrow selector will be available so you control how the text enters the screen, such as from top to bottom, side to side, and so on. The selector is only available if the text effect you have chosen works with text that moves onto the screen.

5. Use the Color button to choose a color for the text.

6. If you click the Over Black check box, the text appears on a black background. Otherwise, it is displayed at the beginning of your first clip or photo. Choosing Over Black essentially creates a new clip.

7. If you select QT Margins, the title slide keeps the text within the safe margins for QuickTime movies. Select this option if you plan to export your movie to a QuickTime format.

8. Use the font selection drop-down menu to choose a font for your title and use the size slider bar to choose a size.

9. Finally, enter the text for your movie title in the provided text box. The box options change, depending on the title file you have selected.

10. When you're done, click the Preview button to see your title page in action.

11. When you are happy with your Title page, simply drag the title file from the title selection box to your Timeline, as shown in the following illustration. You can place the title anywhere on the Timeline that you want, and you can even create multiple title pages if you want to break your movie into sections.

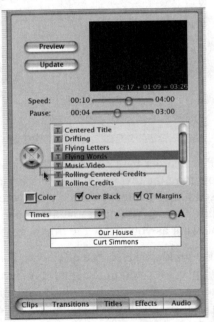

I don't know how to use transitions

Cause: Transitions give you a sleek way to move from one video clip to the next or from clip to photo, photo to photo, and so on. iMovie gives you several transition effects that you can readily add to your Storyboard. You can also adjust the speed at which the transitions take effect.

The Painkiller: To use transitions, follow these steps:

1. At the bottom of the Shelf, click the Transitions button.

2. The Shelf area now displays the transitions available to you, shown in the following illustration.

3. Click the desired transition to see a preview in the preview window. You can adjust the speed of the transition using the provided slider bar.

4. When you have made your selection, simply drag the transition from the transition box to the desired location on your Storyboard. The Storyboard displays the transition, as shown in the following illustration.

I don't know how to use effects

Cause: iMovie 2 gives you a few effects you can apply to clips. A few enable you to fix problems with a clip or photo, such as adjusting the colors, sharpening the picture, and so forth. In the effects department, you can convert a clip to black-and-white, apply sepia tones or a soft focus, or use a water ripple effect.

The Painkiller: To use an effect, follow these steps:

1. At the bottom of the Shelf, click the Effects button.

2. The Shelf area displays the effects available to you, shown in the following illustration.

3. Select the clip that you want to apply the effect to.

4. Choose the desired effect. Depending on the effect you choose, you may see additional controls appear. For example, if you choose Adjust Colors, you see slider bars where you can adjust the hue, color, and lightness of the clip or photo.

5. Click the Preview button to see the effect. Adjust the Effect In and Effect Out time as necessary.

6. When you are done, click Apply to apply the effect to the clip. If you are unhappy with the change, simply click the Restore Clip button to return the clip to its previous state.

NOTE *Some transitions do not work with some effects, so you may see a message stating such. Also, if you apply an effect to a photo, iMovie needs to render the photo as a clip in order to apply the effect. Simply click OK to the message that appears and iMovie takes care of the rendering process for you.*

TIP *Do you want more effects? No problem—you can download the iMovie 2 plug-in pack, found at www.apple.com.imovie. The plug-in pack gives you more cool effects, and it's free.*

Audio Headaches

What would a movie be without sound? The good news is that iMovie can readily use the sound from your digital camera that you imported—and you can also add your own sound effects, music, and narration! These features can really make your movie or slide show shine, and they are generally easy to use. The following headaches and painkillers show you how to quickly use these audio features.

Before we jump into solving audio problems, let's first turn our attention to the Timeline portion of the Storyboard, which you can access by clicking the clock tab, shown in the following illustration. As you can see, you have a movie track, but iMovie gives you two additional tracks for adding music, narration, and sound effects to your movie. So, what kind of sound can you use in your movies? The following list outlines them for you:

- **Camcorder audio** You can use the audio portion of your camcorder, of course, but you can also manipulate it with iMovie.

- **MP3 and AIFF files** You can use MP3 music in your movie, and you can also record directly from a CD (AIFF files).

- **Narration** You can record narration directly into iMovie.

- **Sound Effects** iMovie offers some fun sound effects as well.

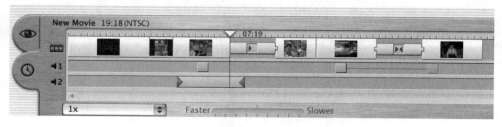

I don't know how to record narration

Cause: Assuming your Mac has either a built-in microphone or an external one that you have added, you can record narration for your movie directly into iMovie. The good news is that recording narration is really easy. The bad news is that you need to practice first and even prepare a script that goes along with your movie so you know what you want to say.

The Painkiller: To record narration, follow these steps:

1. Click the Audio button that appears at the bottom of the Shelf. This opens the audio window. You see a button there titled Record Voice, as shown in the following illustration.

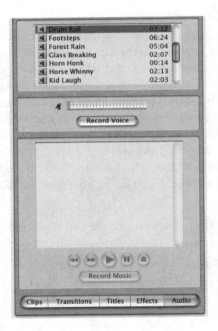

2. Click anywhere on the iMovie interface to make sure that no clip is selected.

3. When you are ready to begin recording your narration, click the Play button in the Monitor window and click the Record Voice button. You can now record your narration as you watch the movie. When you are done, click Stop. Your voice track appears on one of the audio tracks in orange.

 *You probably noticed those little sound effect options in the Audio window, such as drum roll, footsteps, forest rain, and so on. If you want to use one of these, just drag the sound file to the desired location on the audio track.*

 ## How do I use music on a CD?

Cause: You can directly record music from any music CD and create a sound track for your movie. This is a cool feature of iMovie because you don't have to use another program to record the music you want first.

The Painkiller: To record music from a music CD, follow these steps:

1. Insert the music CD into your Mac.

2. Click the Audio button. The Audio CD window is now populated with the music tracks, shown in the following illustration. Locate the desired track and listen to it using the Play button.

3. When you are ready to record the music, press the Record Music button and press Play to play the track. The music is recorded on your movie, and the music track appears in purple.

Do you have an existing MP3 or AIFF file you want to use? No problem. Just click File | Import File and browse to the desired MP3 or AIFF file. Then click Open to import it.

I can't manipulate the location of sound tracks

Cause: Once you record or import any sound track or effect, you can move it around on the Timeline so that the sounds or music occur just when you want them to. This, of course, takes a little tinkering on your part to get everything just right.

The Painkiller: To manipulate the location of sound tracks, simply select the audio track on the Timeline and drag it around to wherever you want. Then, use the arrow that appears on the Timeline bar, shown in the following illustration, to finely control the beginning and ending of the track. This fine level of movement is a little tricky and takes a little practice, but the results are well worth it!

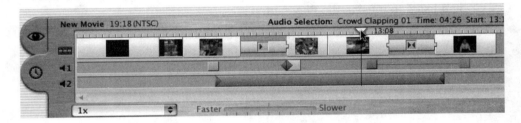

Exporting Your Movie

Once you have finished with your movie, you are ready to export it and use it in whatever way you wish. iMovie enables you to export your movie back to your digital camera, where you can record it onto a videocassette. You can also export the movie as a QuickTime movie or export it so it is ready for iDVD. To export, simply click File | Export Movie. Select the export method you want from the drop-down menu and click Export. As you think about exporting, keep the following points in mind.

- If you are exporting to your camera. Get your tape ready in the camera, then edit the wait time and number of black seconds on the export window, as shown in the illustration. The default is five seconds of wait time (which is the amount of time iMovie waits for the camera to start recording) and one second of black space before the movie begins. However, note that some cameras need a few more seconds than five to get going, so you may need to raise the five-second default value. Experiment with your camera to see what works for you.

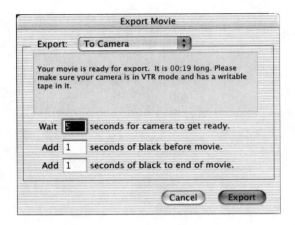

If you live in Europe, there is a good chance that your camera will not record digital video due to copyright laws. See your camera documentation for more info.

- If you are exporting to QuickTime. Use the Formats drop-down menu to select the format you want. For example, if you want a lower quality movie that can be e-mailed, choose the Email Movie, Small option.

- If you are exporting for use in iDVD burning. iMovie formats everything; for you. All you have to do is export your movie and import it into iDVD; then you're ready to go!

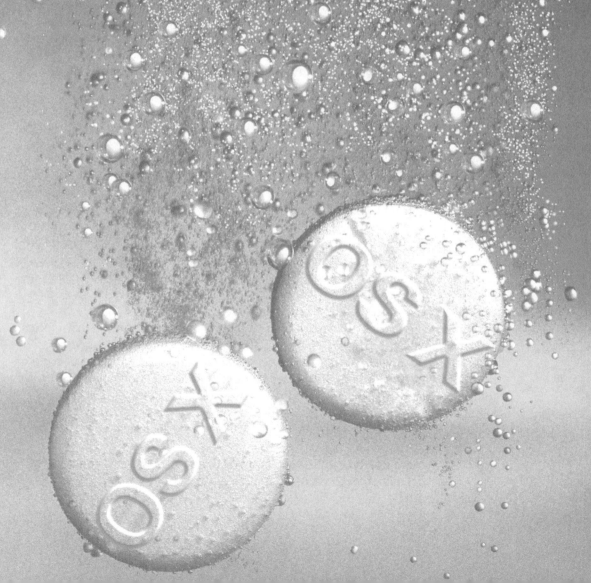

Chapter 15

iTunes Headaches

In this chapter, you'll cure...

- ■ Music headaches
- ■ Preference problems
- ■ CD-burning headaches

Want to use your Mac to listen to CDs or Internet music? Want to copy songs from a CD and keep them on your hard drive or iPod so you can listen to them at any time? Are you a music fan who needs a way to manage a lot of music in an easy and customizable way? iTunes 3, the digital music-management center from Apple, does all this and more. The good news is that iTunes 3 does a lot of cool stuff; the bad news is that although the interface is easy, it may give you a few headaches along the way as you learn to use it.

Getting to Know iTunes 3

iTunes is the Mac's song-management tool. Using iTunes 3, you can listen to CD music, listen to Internet radio, rip (that means copy) songs to your hard drive, manage the songs with your own custom playlists, and much more. You can copy songs directly from CDs using the CD's native AIFF format. Using iTunes 3, you can also burn MP3 music CDs (which can hold a lot more songs then a standard AIFF format—although the quality suffers somewhat). You can even manage the sound quality of playback using a graphic equalizer. If you are using OS X Jaguar, iTunes 3 was installed when you installed Jaguar. If not, you can download iTunes 3 from Apple's web site at www.apple.com. This is a good idea because version 3 contains more features than the previous version.

When you first click iTunes 3 to open it, you see a license agreement that appears. This message basically asks you to agree not to steal anything or do anything otherwise illegal with iTunes. Click Accept to continue. You may also see a dialog box telling you that iTunes has detected an existing iTunes folder in your Documents folder, especially if you have downloaded and installed iTunes 2. This does not affect the playback of music in the folder; therefore, you should click Yes. Finally, you see an iTunes Setup Assistant, which walks you through these steps:

1. A Welcome screen appears, telling you that iTunes will ask you a few questions in order to set itself up. Click Next.

2. The Internet audio page appears. If you want to use iTunes to use Internet audio, click Yes. iTunes configures itself as the default application for Internet audio. The window also asks whether iTunes can automatically connect to the Internet from time to time to update information about CDs and streaming broadcasts. If you want iTunes to automatically connect, click Yes; otherwise, choose No. Make your selections and click Next.

3. A Music Library window appears telling you that iTunes will automatically copy music to your iTunes folder when you add songs to your library. This is just an FYI screen, so click Next.

4. The final window tells you that iTunes can keep your music organized for you. If you want iTunes to manage the organization of your music, click Yes. If you want to change file and folder names yourself when necessary, click No. Click Done.

5. The iTunes interface appears finally, as you can see in the following illustration.

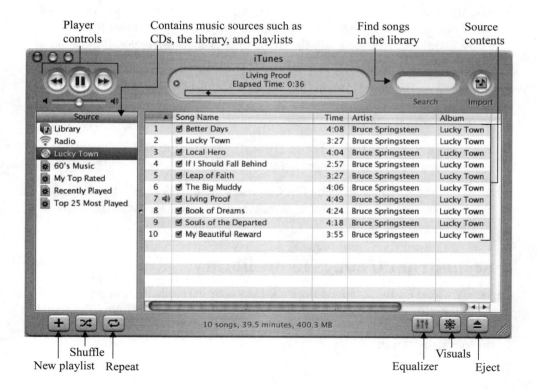

Music and Ripping Headaches

iTunes 3 lets you listen to CDs and Internet radio, along with any information stored in your music library, MP3 files from the Internet, and so forth. iTunes 3 is very versatile, and it will play just about any music file you want to hear. With just a little experimentation, you can do all kinds of things with iTunes 3, so it's important to play around with the interface and get used to how things work.

To listen to a music CD, simply open iTunes 3 and insert the music CD in your CD drive. iTunes 3 displays the contents of the CD and starts playing the songs for you. If you are connected to the Internet, you can click the Radio feature in the left pane and browse for an Internet radio station. You can listen to music and rip it to your hard drive so you can listen to it whenever you want. You can also copy the music you rip to your iPod to listen on the go.

iTunes 3 doesn't see the names of the songs on a CD

Cause   When you insert a music CD, iTunes 3 reads the tracks on the CD and displays the track numbers in the iTunes 3 interface. To see the names of the tracks, you must connect to the Internet so that iTunes can get the song titles for the CD. This way, should you decide to rip the songs to your hard drive, you'll have the correct names instead of Track 1, Track 2, and so forth.

The Painkiller   To get the correct info for your CD, follow these steps:

1. Connect to the Internet.

2. Insert the desired CD and open iTunes 3. If the name of the album and the track names do not appear, go to Step 3.

3. Click the Advanced menu | Get CD Track Names. iTunes 3 queries an Internet server for the names and automatically replaces track names with the correct names.

How do I rip CD songs to my library?

Cause   You can easily rip songs from a CD to your hard disk. These songs are stored in your library, where you can listen to them at any time without the actual CD, create playlists with them, or copy them to your iPod for listening on the go. To rip songs, see the Painkiller.

The Painkiller   To rip songs from a CD, follow these steps:

1. Insert the desired CD and open iTunes 3.

2. In the Song name column, remove the check from each song that you do not want to rip to your library.

3. Click the Import button in the upper-right corner of the iTunes 3 interface.

4. iTunes 3 begins copying the desired songs. You can see the status as the copying occurs, shown in the following illustration.

 # I don't know how to use the library

Cause   The music library, which is found in the Source column of iTunes, is the storage location for all of your music. You can easily open the library and locate songs that you want to play.

The Painkiller   If you click the library to open it, the contents of the library are displayed in the right pane of iTunes. Just select an album and click Play to start playing it. As you can see in the following illustration, the library contents display the artist's name, the album, and the songs. Also, keep in mind that you can use the Browse button in the upper-right corner to locate songs that you want to hear.

You can easily remove a song from the library (or multiple songs, or even albums) by simply dragging the item or items to the Trash. This deletes the item or items from your iTunes folder.

I don't know how to use the Radio feature

Cause   The iTunes 3 radio feature enables you to listen to Internet radio. You can easily do this with an Internet connection, using the iTunes interface.

The Painkiller   If you click the Radio icon in the Source pane, you see a listing of different music categories. You can browse the radio stations in the list. Just double-click the one you want to start listening to. If you know the web address of a particular radio station that you want to listen to, just click Advanced | Open Stream. Type the web address of the radio station you want to hear and press RETURN.

Internet radio plays intermittently

Cause   Internet radio works by streaming media to your Mac. iTunes interprets the streaming data so that you can listen to the Internet radio station. However, getting a solid stream that is free of problems requires a fast Internet connection.

The Painkiller   If you are using a modem, you probably experience interruptions when you listen to the Internet radio. If your modem connection is very slow, you likely hear a lot of interruptions. There is no direct solution for this problem—except to upgrade your Internet account to a broadband account (if available), of course.

I don't know how to use a playlist

Cause   Let's say you have ten different albums stored in your library. Within those albums, you may have a few favorite songs. With iTunes, you can organize all of your favorite songs on a single playlist. Then, you can simply play the playlist whenever you want, without having to wade through the albums to find the songs that you really like.

The Painkiller   To create a playlist, follow these steps:

1. Click File | New Playlist.

2. The new playlist appears in the Source section of iTunes. Give the playlist a name and open the library. Browse and locate the songs you want on the playlist and simply drag those songs to the playlist.

3. When you're done, just select your playlist and click Play to begin playing it.

I don't know how to use a smart playlist

Cause   iTunes 3 has the ability to create a smart playlist for you. A *smart playlist* works like a regular playlist, but iTunes uses information that you enter to retrieve matching songs and creates the playlist for you. For example, you could automatically have iTunes create a smart playlist based on types of songs: songs with high ratings, songs by artist or even genre, and so on. When you create the smart playlist, iTunes scans your music library to find songs that match your requirements.

Helpful Playlist Tips

The playlist is a powerful feature of iTunes 3. Here are a few additional things you can do.

- You can create as many different playlists as you want—the number of songs on each playlist and the number of playlists you use are entirely up to you.

- You can delete a playlist or delete songs from a playlist at any time—this does not delete the songs from your library. A playlist is really just links to the songs that you want, so only the links disappear, not the songs.

- You can add new songs at any time to a playlist.

- You can change the order of a playlist. Just select it and drag the songs around in the right pane to change the order.

- You can import a playlist from another Mac. Use the File menu to import and export items.

- You can burn a playlist to a CD, creating your own customized CD. Just select the playlist, insert a CD-R or CD-RW disk, and click the Burn CD button in the upper right corner of iTunes 3.

The Painkiller   To create a smart playlist, follow these steps:

1. Click File | New Smart Playlist.

2. On the Simple tab, you can create a playlist based on artist, composer, or genre and enter the information in the contents box. You can also place restrictions on the number of songs and their selection order if you like. Click OK when you're done, and iTunes creates the playlist for you.

3. You can also click the Advanced tab and create a more customized search option based on conditions that you enter.

When I play music in iTunes 3, the music output doesn't sound very good

Cause   Music is all about quality, of course, and in iTunes 3, you should get great music playback, assuming the speakers you are using with your Mac are good speakers (which they probably are). If you are having trouble with music quality or good playback sound, you should check your speaker settings on your Mac. You can use the graphical equalizer in iTunes 3, shown in the following illustration, to adjust the quality, as well. Also, you can check your Sound Enhancement setting.

The Painkiller   To check the Sound Enhancement setting, follow these steps:

1. Choose iTunes | Preferences.

2. Click the Effects icon.

3. Make sure the Sound Enhancer is selected and that the setting is more toward the High range. Click OK.

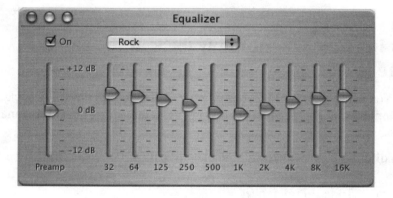

PREVENTION   *If you need a certain song to use a certain equalizer setting, such as Rock or whatever, you can fix the setting for that particular song. Locate the song in the library and CONTROL-click it. Select the Get Info option. On the Options tab, use the Equalizer Preset option to select an equalizer setting, as you can see in the following illustration. Also, I should note here that these settings carry over to your iPod as well.*

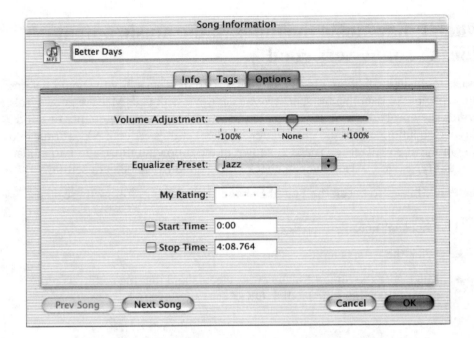

Songs in iTunes do not play back at the same volume level

Cause You can normalize all songs in your library so that they play back at the same volume level. This prevents you from having to adjust the volume manually for each song.

The Painkiller To normalize volume playback for all songs, follow these steps:

1. Select iTunes | Preferences.
2. Click the Effects button.
3. In the Effects window, select the Sound Check check box. Click OK.

iPod and iTunes always synchronize when I connect iPod, but I want to manually control what is on the iPod

Cause   By default, iPod and iTunes always synchronize when you connect iPod to the Mac. Basically, the synchronization keeps everything in your library on the iPod so that the two are the same. The idea is that you can access music in your library on the Mac when you are at home or on the iPod when you are mobile, without any additional configuration. However, what if you don't want the iPod to have the same songs, or what if you want a specific playlist on the iPod that is not in iTunes? In this case, you can stop the automatic synchronization feature. However, keep in mind that data flow from iTunes to the iPod is one-way—you can copy data to the iPod easily, but getting the songs from the iPod to iTunes can be a little more challenging.

The Painkiller   To stop automatic synchronization with iTunes and iPod, follow these steps:

1. Connect iPod. Open iTunes. You'll see the iPod appear in the Source pane of iTunes.

2. Select iPod and click the iPod button that appears at the bottom edge of the iTunes screen.

3. In the iPod preferences dialog box that appears, click Manually Manage Songs And Playlists. Click OK.

4. You can now select iPod in the Source list and create a new playlist for the iPod as desired.

I can't convert songs to MP3 format

Cause   The MP3 format, which is widely used on the Internet today as a way to listen to music, is supported in iTunes. In fact, you can copy songs from a regular old CD and convert them to MP3 format for use on the iPod, and you can also use the MP3 files to burn an MP3 music CD. Why, you might ask? The answer is simple— megabytes. The MP3 format uses much less storage space than the typical AIFF format used when ripping music from CDs. The end result is that you can put more songs on the iPod and burn more songs onto a single CD (in fact, you can put about 130 MP3 files on a single CD!). This saves you tons of storage space, but there is one caveat if you are burning CDs—not all CD players can play MP3s. In fact, many typical home CD players won't play the MP3 format. Before you burn away, think carefully about compatibility. If you purchased an MP3 CD player, you're in good shape, though.

The Painkiller   To convert songs to the MP3 format, follow these steps:

1. To convert a song to the MP3 format, locate the song in your library and select it. If you want to convert several songs at one time, hold down COMMAND and click the songs.

2. Click Advanced | Convert Selection To MP3.

3. iTunes begins the conversion to MP3. Once you have completed the conversion, you'll see your original file and the MP3 file in your library.

TIP   *If you want to quickly see what songs are MP3 files, AIFF files, or whatever, select the album in the library and click File | Show Song File (or press COMMAND-R.)*

PREVENTION   *Keep one issue in mind before converting a song to MP3. Make sure the song is not already an MP3. If it is, iTunes will not tell you, and it will compress the song again, resulting in much lower music quality. How can you tell if the song is already an MP3? The best way is to CONTROL-click the file and choose Get Info.*

I want iTunes 3 to run in the background and play CD music automatically, or I want iTunes to start playing whenever I start my Mac

Cause   iTunes 3 is a program just like any other, so you can configure it to start when the Mac starts and run in the background. You can also configure it to start playing music CDs when you insert them.

The Painkiller   To have iTunes 3 start playing automatically when a CD is inserted, see the "My CDs do not automatically play" headache in the next section. To configure iTunes 3 to start when the Mac starts, see Chapter 8.

Preferences Headaches

Like most programs, iTunes 3 has a few settings that determine how it behaves by default. As a general rule, the default settings are all you need, but a few behaviors may drive you batty. No problem. You can easily change these preference settings; the following headaches and painkillers show you how.

My CDs do not automatically play

Cause   By default, iTunes 2 shows you the songs on a CD when you insert it. "Great," you may think, "I want to hear the songs, not see them." This preference setting enables you to do whatever you want; if you want iTunes 2 to start playing the CD when you insert it into the CD drive, you can change this setting easily.

The Painkiller   To change the default CD insert behavior, follow these steps:

1. Open iTunes 3 and click iTunes | Preferences.

2. Click General. On the On CD Insert drop-down menu, choose the Begin Playing option, as shown in the following illustration. Click OK.

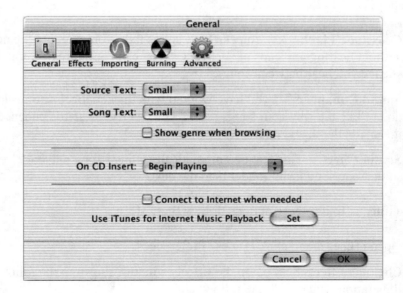

I want iTunes 3 to connect to the Internet automatically when it needs to, or I want to use iTunes 3 for all Internet music playback

Cause   iTunes 3 can be configured to automatically connect to the Internet when it needs information, and it can be configured to play all music on the Internet. You can easily configure both of these options.

The Painkiller   To change the default Internet behavior, follow these steps:

1. Open iTunes 3 and click iTunes | Preferences.

2. Click General. If you want iTunes 3 to connect to the Internet automatically when needed, click the check box options. To have iTunes play all Internet music, click Set.

I can't control the amount of space between songs during playback

Cause   You can use iTunes to configure a couple of "effects" options that you might enjoy:

- **Crossfade Playback**   You can have songs fade from one into the next without hearing any gaps of silence. Or, you can configure how much silence you hear between songs.

- **Sound Enhancer**   If you have worked with the equalizer settings and still do not like the way your songs sound, you can try the sound enhancer tool; it can add depth and quality to playback music.

- **Sound Check**   This feature automatically adjusts song playback volume so that one song is not louder than the next.

The Painkiller   To use these options, follow these steps:

1. Open iTunes 3 and click iTunes | Preferences.

2. Click the Effects button. On the Effects window, shown in the following illustration, you can do the following:

- **Crossfade Playback** Move the slider bar to the desired level. A setting of 0 places no silence between songs.

- **Sound Enhancer** The medium setting is the default, but you can try moving the slider bar to adjust quality.

- **Sound Check** Click the check box option to turn on the feature.

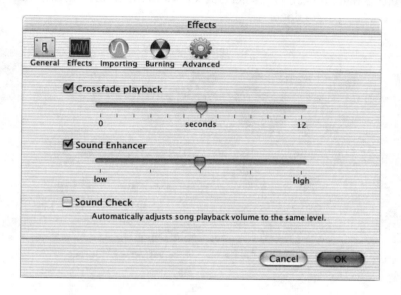

Songs do not import in the right format, or the quality of imported songs is not good

Cause iTunes 3 uses various encoders when importing music. In other words, encoders determine the format at which the music is saved. For example, iTunes 2 can use an MP3 encoder or an AIFF encoder. You can also choose the quality configuration when importing songs. Keep in mind that AIFF gives you CD quality, while MP3 does not provide as high a level of quality as MP3. However, you save a lot of disk space using MP3 rather than AIFF. The choice is yours, and you can select the default format you want to use.

The Painkiller   To choose the format option, follow these steps:

1. Open iTunes 3 and click iTunes | Preferences.

2. Click Importing. On the Import Using drop-down menu, select the format you want to use (MP3, AIFF, WAV). If you choose MP3, note the quality setting that you can also select, as shown in the following illustration. Click OK when you're done.

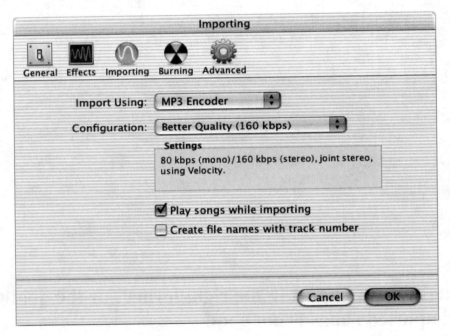

I need to change the default location of the iTunes Music folder

Cause   By default, the iTunes music folder is stored in Macintosh HD/Users/ *username*/Music/iTunes/iTunes Music. However, you can store the iTunes folder in a different location if you want.

The Painkiller   To select a different storage location, follow these steps:

1.   Open iTunes 3 and click iTunes | Preferences.

2.   Click Advanced. As you can see in the following illustration, the default
     storage location is listed. To change the location, click Change and browse
     to the new location. When you're done, click OK.

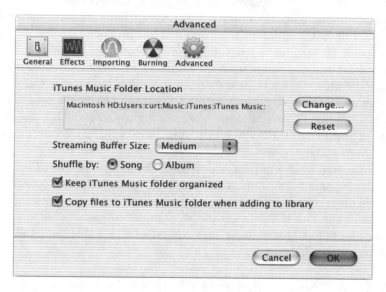

About Those Visuals...

You probably noticed that iTunes 3 can entertain you with some visual effects
as you are listening to music. These effects are purely to entertain—they don't
do anything else (except possibly hypnotize you). If you want to see the visual
effects, just click Visual in the lower-right portion of the iTunes interface or
select Visuals | Turn Visuals On. Notice also on the Visuals menu that you can
see Small, Medium, or Large screen effects. You can even choose a full-screen
mode. One other thing you can do is press ? on your keyboard when the visual
is active. This gives you a quick help list of keyboard keys you can use for
various items, such as displaying the song name, title, and so on. Check it out!

CD-Burning Headaches

In addition to organizing songs into playlists and listening to those songs on your computer or iPod whenever you want, you can burn playlists onto CDs. You can listen to these CDs on any CD player. Basically, this puts you in charge of your music because you burn any combination of songs from different sources onto one CD. For example, I have a favorite music group that has produced seven albums. The problem, though, is that I like a few songs of each album the most. So, using iTunes, I simply copy all of those songs from the various CDs, create my own playlist of the songs in the order I want to hear them, and, voilà, I burn a new CD containing all of my favorite songs. No more juggling CDs around to hear what I want!

Keep in mind that iTunes can burn a regular audio CD (which is the default), or it can burn an MP3 CD. However, you must have an MP3 player in order to listen to an MP3 CD.

You can use two basic kinds of read/write CDs—CD-RW and CD-R. CD-RW disks are best for data because most CD players in your home stereo or car can't read CD-RW disks. CD-R disks are best for playback purposes and usually work in any stereo or car. Use these for creating CD music to ensure compatibility (plus, they are cheaper than CD-RW disks anyway). Most CD-R disks can hold about 70–75 minutes of music.

I don't like iTunes' default CD-burning settings

Cause   iTunes 3 gives you a few default CD burn settings, which you can change if you want. If you haven't thought about the default CD-burning settings, you should take a look at them. You might want to make a couple of changes.

The Painkiller   To change the CD settings, follow these steps:

1. Open iTunes 3 and click iTunes | Preferences.

2. Click Burning. In the Burning window that appears, shown in the following illustration, you see the CD burner that is available and the preferred speed. The Maximum Possible setting is usually best. Notice that you can choose the disk format that you want—Audio or MP3. If you choose MP3, make sure you have an MP3 player that can actually play the CD you create. If you choose the Audio CD option, notice that you can adjust the gap between songs. Two seconds is about right, but if you like more or less, you can change this value. Click OK when you're done.

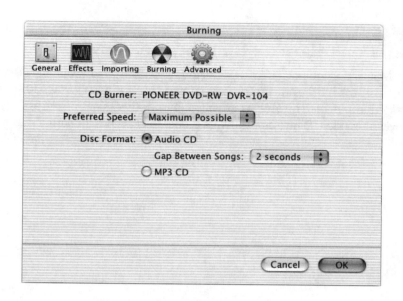

 ## I don't know how to burn a CD

Cause   You can easily burn a CD whenever you are ready. To do so, see the Painkiller.

The Painkiller   To burn a CD, follow these steps:

1. Open iTunes 3.

2. Create a playlist with the songs you want. Then, select the playlist in the source window.

3. In the song list (right pane), drag the songs around to get the order that you want.

4. When you are happy with your playlist, click the Burn CD button in the upper-left corner of iTunes.

5. Insert a burnable CD and click Burn again. Depending on how many songs you are burning, the process may take some time. You can move on and do other tasks while you are waiting, though.

If You Don't Have a CD Burner

If your Mac is not equipped with a CD burner, you can buy an external CD burner that plugs into a USB port. Check www.apple.com for a list of compatible CD burners. You may also be able to use a CD burner that is not on Apple's list, but you have to use the CD burner's software, rather than iTunes, to burn a music CD.

Chapter 16

iDVD Headaches

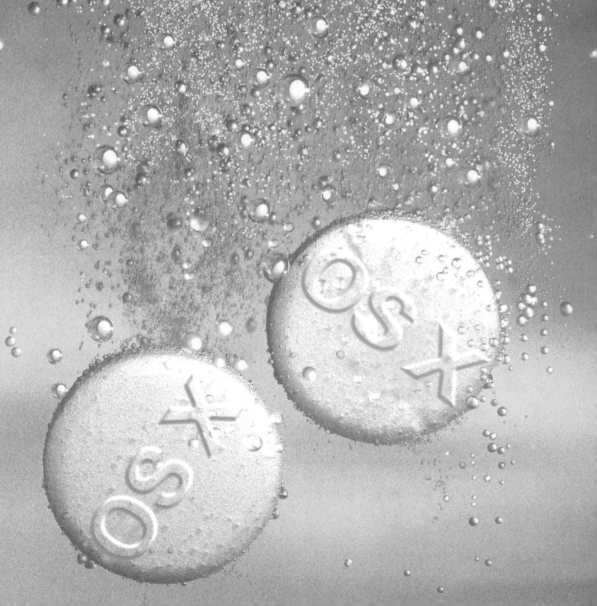

In this chapter, you'll cure…

■ Problems with creating your own DVDs

■ Issues with burning DVDs

You want to be in the movies? Don't we all! In Chapters 13, 14, 15, we took a look at headaches concerning iPhoto, iMovie, and iTunes. These applications, sometimes called the "digital hub" of the Mac, all enable you to produce great pictures, movies, slide shows, and music. Using iDVD, another piece of Apple's digital pie in the sky, you can take your digital playground one step further by burning your own DVD. That's right, using iDVD you can create a themed menu, complete with music, and burn your movies, photos, and slide shows onto a DVD-R disk. Once you're done, you can play that DVD on any standard DVD player. Pretty cool, huh?

Aside from being fun, iDVD is a great way to catalog your life that can be viewed in the comfort of your living room, and it is a great way to make cool gifts for family and friends. The bad news—well, there isn't much. DVD-R disks cost around $5 each, and once you burn one, it's a done deal (you can't erase what you have done and burn again), and you need a DVD burner in order to make one (no, you can't use your CD burner). If your Mac has a SuperDrive, you're all set. The SuperDrive is a CD/DVD player, but it is also a CD/DVD burner. If your Mac doesn't have a SuperDrive, you can consider purchasing a DVD burner as an add-on component. See www.apple.com to learn more.

Understanding iDVD

iDVD is simply a Mac utility that enables you to burn DVD disks. iDVD 2, the current version at the time of this writing, enables you to burn movie files onto a DVD and create a title page that has buttons you can select with any standard DVD remote control. In other words, when you get finished burning your DVD, it looks just like any DVD you might play in your DVD player.

The iDVD 2 interface, as shown in the following illustration, seems simple enough to use. However, as you might imagine, things that appear simple often are not. iDVD is a powerful application, and you'll probably run into a few snags along the way. We solve those snags in this chapter, of course.

So, what exactly can you create with iDVD? You can use iDVD to burn DVDs of movies and slide shows that you create with iPhoto or iMovie 2. Additionally, you can configure your own background music directly from iTunes. You need to use the correct file formats in order to create a DVD, but this should be no problem using iPhoto, iMovie, and iTunes. Your slide shows and movies must be saved in the QuickTime format. Once you dump your movie into iDVD, the application automatically converts it for you into the MPEG 2 format—a universally accepted DVD format that all DVD players can read. For your music, it has to be saved in an AIFF or AC3 format. AIFF is the standard CD format, so you can simply rip songs you want to play into iTunes and use them in iDVD—no problem. See Chapters 13, 14, and 15 for more information about these file formats when using your digital applications.

So, how do you create a DVD? You should follow a few basic steps to keep on track:

1. Play your DVD. It is always best to start with pencil and paper and plan the DVD before you create your movie files and burn the DVD. Burning

your DVD is a one-way process: once you burn, the movie is a done deal, so plan before you waste DVD-R media.

2. Create your files. Use iPhoto, iMovie 2, and iTunes 2 to create the files that you want to use on your DVD.

3. Use iDVD to assemble your files and create the title page, along with navigational buttons.

4. Burn the DVD.

Now that you've looked at the five-minute overview, let's get your hands dirty and look at some problems you might run across along the way.

 You can use iDVD to assemble a slide show of JPEG photos, just as you can use iPhoto (or even iMovie) to create the slide show. There's really no difference, it is just a matter of which application you want to use. If you use iPhoto or iMovie to create the slide show, just remember to export the slide show in the QuickTime format, and you're all set.

Data Headaches

Once you have decided what data you want to use for your movie, gather all of your files together; you're ready to dump them into iDVD.

 ## I don't know how to get my movies and pictures into iDVD

Cause   You can get your movie files and/or pictures into iDVD just like most Apple applications. You can either use the import menu feature or, better yet, just drag and drop the files to the iDVD interface.

The Painkiller   To import files into iDVD, do this:

1. Click File | Import and select Video, Audio, Image, or Background Video. You see the typical browse window. Make your selection and click Open. (Or, drag and drop the files you want to use onto the iDVD interface.)

2. The movies you have imported now appear in the iDVD interface, as you can see in the following illustration.

I don't understand how to use a background movie

Cause   A background movie is simply a movie that you choose to run in the background on the title screen, also known as the selection screen. In other words, when you burn the DVD disk, this little movie plays behind the selection screen. You can use any movie you want for the background movie, or you don't have to use one at all.

The Painkiller   To use a background movie, do this:

1. Click File | Import | Background Video.

 *You can't drag and drop a background video—you must use the Import command.*

2. The background movie now appears in the iDVD interface and plays. If it is not playing, click the Motion button.

3. You can now drag and drop your movies to the interface as well, as shown in the following illustration.

How do I use iDVD to create a slide show?

Cause   You can create a slide show in iPhoto or iMovie and import it to iDVD as a QuickTime movie. You can also just create the slide show directly within iDVD. The Painkiller shows you how to do this.

The Painkiller   To create a slide show, use these steps:

1. In iDVD, click the Slideshow button. A slide show box now appears in the iDVD viewing area, as shown in the following illustration. Click the slide show text to change it to whatever you want.

2. Double-click the Slideshow icon on the interface. This opens a slide show window.

3. Drag the picture files you want to use in the slide show to the interface. You can see the picture files displayed in the following illustration.

4. If you want to use music in your slide show, drag the audio file to the Audio well on the interface, shown in the following illustration. You can also use File | Import if you like.

5. Use the Slide Duration drop-down menu to determine how long each picture should appear. You also may choose the Fit To Audio selection in the drop-down menu in order to make iDVD have the slides fit to the length of the audio segment you have selected.

6. If you want control arrows displayed during the slide show, click that option, too. This enables you to skip forward and back using a standard DVD remote.

7. When you're done, click the Preview button to see how everything looks.

How do I use a folder?

Cause You can drag and drop your movie files directly to the iDVD interface and play them with any standard DVD remote. However, what if your movie is not one continuous movie but rather a bunch of smaller movies? In this case, you can click the Folder option on the iDVD toolbar and place a folder icon on the iDVD interface. That enables you to organize movie clips by folders so you can easily find and play them.

The Painkiller To use a folder, just click the option on the toolbar. Then double-click the folder icon that appears in the iDVD interface. You can drag and drop movie files into that folder.

 *Although you can use as many folders as you want, try to keep things as simple as possible. It's easier to find what you want without having to use your DVD remote to wade through some ridiculous folder structure. So, plan carefully and keep it simple.*

Getting DVD-R Media

If you have an Internet connection, you can buy DVD-R media directly from within iDVD by clicking File | Buy DVD Media. This takes you to Apple's web site, where you can buy a five-disk pack for about $24 (at the time of this writing). However, you can also buy DVD-R media from other vendors and from other manufacturers. In fact, at the time I checked, you could get a ten-DVD-R Memorex pack from www.amazon.com for $29, so it certainly pays to shop around.

Theme Headaches

iDVD gives you 14 cool themes you can use for your DVD. These themes affect the title page appearance but not your actual movies or slide shows. In essence, they are provided for looks and nothing more. You can use the predefined themes as they are, and you can even customize them a bit. The following headaches and painkillers show you how to cure common aggravations.

How do I apply a theme?

Cause   When you first open iDVD and start a project, you see a default theme (usually a chalkboard). However, you can select a different theme, which affects the appearance and fonts of the title page.

The Painkiller   To use a theme, follow these steps:

1. Open iDVD. You can drag and organize your media at this time if you wish.

2. Click the Theme button. A Theme drawer slides out, as shown in the following illustration. Scroll through the themes and select the one you want. It appears in the iDVD interface. To choose a different theme, just click a new one.

3. Once you have applied the theme, just click the text to change it to whatever you want.

Some themes use music, some don't. Just play around with them to find what you like.

I can't customize a theme

Cause If you don't like the appearance of a theme, you can simply try a different one. However, what if you like the theme but want to change some parts of it? No problem—you can do that, too.

The Painkiller To change a theme, select it in the Theme pull-out drawer and click the Customize tab. The following steps show you an example of how I have customized a theme.

1. First of all, I selected a theme that I liked. In this example, I'm using the Family theme, as shown in the following illustration. I like the fonts and content boxes but want to make some changes.

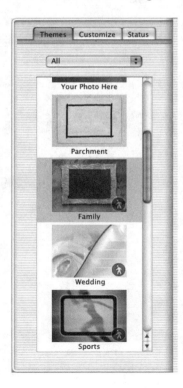

2. I click the Customize menu. Notice there are two wells in the Background column, shown in the following illustration. I want to change the background image to one of my own, so I simply drag and drop the image I want into the well. The same is true with the music—I just drag and drop the file I want to use.

3. Now, as you can see in the following illustration, my new image appears (along with the new music).

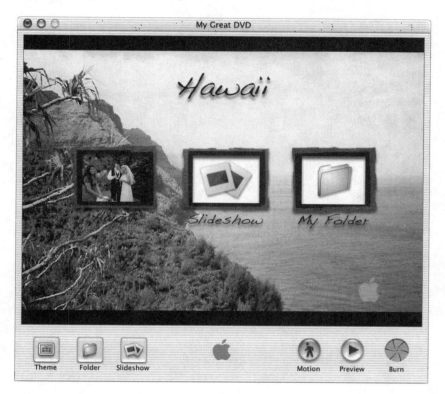

4. Back in the Customize pane, I can also change the Title position, font, color, and size. You can change the font characteristics such as color and size—for example, I increased the size of the font.

5. Next, under the Button category, I can change the name of the buttons and change the location to Free Position so I can move them around where I want. I can also change the font and size.

6. Now I'm done, as you can see in the following illustration. I've just created my own customized theme!

 ## I see an Apple symbol at the bottom corner of each theme, and I want to get rid of it

Cause   This Apple symbol, called a watermark, appears at the bottom of each theme. Basically, the watermark is just an advertisement for Apple, but you can easily get rid of it.

The Painkiller   To lose the watermark from your theme, click iDVD | Preferences. In the iDVD Preferences window, clear the Show Watermark check box, as shown in the following illustration. Click OK.

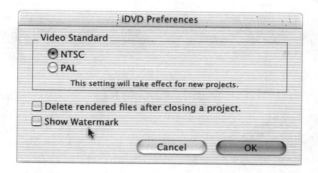

DVD-Burning Headaches

Okay, you've done all your work, and you are ready to burn your DVD, right? After you make sure everything is the way you want it, all you have to do is click the Burn button to burn the DVD. The Burn button pulsates, letting you know it is ready; click it again to continue. However, before doing so, read these two headaches for important painkillers.

I previously burned a DVD, but parts of the title page run off the screen

Cause This problem, which can be really aggravating because you've just wasted a $5 DVD-R disk, occurs when text and buttons are not within the TV viewing area. Some televisions can't display everything on the DVD screen, so in order to make sure this doesn't happen, you can use a little, not-well-documented trick.

The Painkiller In iDVD, click Advanced | Show TV Safe Area. A box appears on the title page showing you the area that will appear on all televisions. As you can see in the following illustration, part of my button would be off the screen. I can see the TV-safe area, so I can just rearrange my title slide to make sure everything will appear on screen.

 ## When I started to burn a DVD, a message appeared telling me that motion menus are turned off

Cause   If you have used motion menus, such as motion on your slide show button or background picture, you need to turn those on before burning—otherwise, the motion menus do not work when you burn the DVD.

The Painkiller   Just cancel out, turn on the motion menus, and click Burn again.

> **TIP**   *Burning a DVD can take a while—even hours, depending on the length of your movie. Be patient, though; you'll be a star in no time.*

Chapter 17

Multimedia Headaches

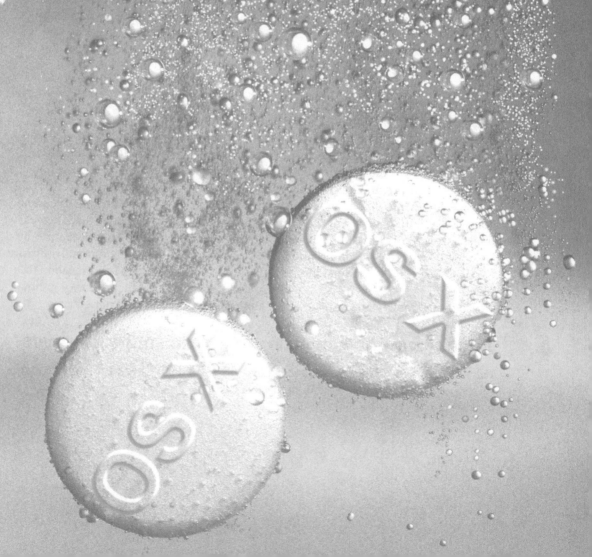

In this chapter, you'll cure...

- Problems with speed
- Sound headaches
- QuickTime problems
- Font aggravations

Mac OS X, being the full-featured operating system that it is, offers some built-in multimedia features. I use the term *multimedia* in this chapter loosely—referring specifically to OS X's speech capabilities, sound and recording features, QuickTime, and even fonts. The good news is that these features are easy and fun to use. However, I'll show you some common headaches you may experience, along with the quick painkillers for those headaches, of course.

Speech Headaches

OS X comes with some cool speech technologies. First, you can have OS X read items to you using a pleasant computerized voice. The read-aloud feature is very good—the voice recognizes commas and periods and actually sounds like someone reading something (rather than a monotone robot). The other feature is voice command. OS X has the capability to listen to you and respond to certain commands from voice instead of from the keyboard or mouse. Understand, however, that this feature is limited to OS commands; it is not a speech-to-text feature in which you can have the program type while you talk. You need additional software for that. However, it can read things back to you (text-to-speech) and respond to certain voice commands. The following headaches and painkillers show you how to use these features and quickly solve any problems you may experience.

I don't know how to make OS X read stuff back to me

Cause   The text-to-speech feature to have OS X read stuff back to you is probably already enabled. All you have to do is start it.

The Painkiller   To have OS X read a document back to you, use the following steps:

1. Open the document.

2. Choose Edit | Speech | Start Speaking. Or, just CONTROL-click the text you want read and choose Speech | Start Speaking, as shown in the following illustration. If you don't see the Speech option on the Edit menu, try selecting Applications | Services | Speech.

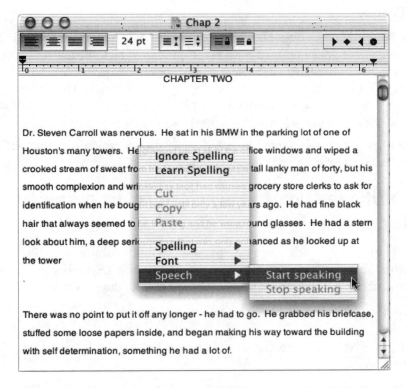

3. To stop OS X from speaking, just choose Edit | Speech | Stop Speaking or CONTROL-click the text and choose Speech | Stop Speaking.

You may wonder if there is really a point to using text-to-speech. In many cases, the feature is simply fun. However, consider using the feature for proofreading. Let's say you write a letter or paper. Have the text-to-speech feature read it aloud to you so you can more easily catch mistakes you might have made when typing.

Text-to-speech will not read to me from certain programs

Cause   The good news is that OS X's text-to-speech feature is really cool. The bad news is that it does not work with all programs. In fact, the text-to-speech feature is rather limited. You can use it in such programs as AppleWorks, Mail, TextEdit, and a few other programs that display text. However, the text-to-speech feature does not work in web browsers, like Internet Explorer, or in a number of other third-party programs you might choose to install.

The Painkiller   The only thing you can do here is open your document with a program that supports the text-to-speech feature.

I don't like the text-to-speech voice, or the voice is too fast or too slow

Cause   The text-to-speech voice gives you some fun flexibility, so if you are not happy with the default voice or speed, you can change it. (Even if you are happy, you should check out the other options for their entertainment value.)

The Painkiller   To change the voice, follow these steps:

1. Click System Preferences on the Dock, or select Apple | System Preferences.

2. In System Preferences, click the Speech icon found under the System category.

3. Click the Default Voice tab, shown in the following illustration. Here you see the default voice and speed used (probably Victoria using a Normal rate setting). You can click around through these and try different voices and speeds.

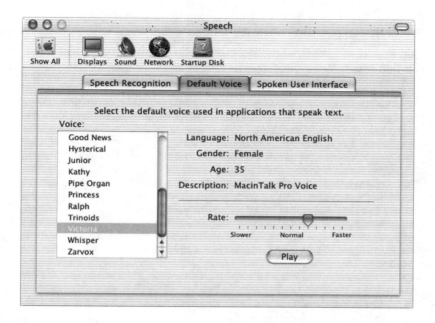

TIP   *For pure entertainment value, try the Bad News, Bells, Cellos, Good News, and Pipe Organ voices—these sing instead of talk.*

I want OS X to automatically read alerts and other prompts out loud

Cause   Aside from reading text that you select, OS X can read a few other items to you automatically. This feature is a great way for the computer to get your attention when alerts appear, along with some other items you can choose.

The Painkiller   To configure alert reading and other spoken items, follow these steps:

1. Click System Preferences on the Dock, or select Apple | System Preferences.

2. In System Preferences, click the Speech icon found under the System category.

3. Click the Spoken User Interface tab, shown in the following illustration. Turn on Speak The Phrase and Speak The Alert Text to have the alert read

aloud. If you just want a vocal attention-getter to go with the alert, select Speak The Phrase and choose something from the drop-down list (such as Pardon Me!).

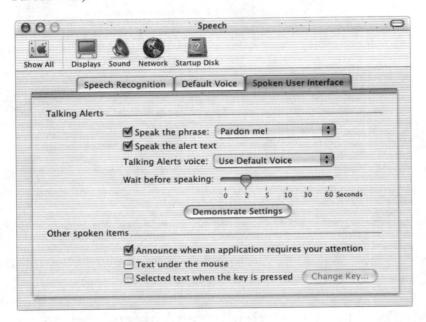

4. You can have a few other items automatically spoken, as well. Click the provided check boxes to do the following:

- Announce when an application requires your attention.

- Read the text under the mouse. If you select this option, you also must turn on assistive features found in Universal Access in System Preferences. See Chapter 5 to learn more.

- Select a keyboard key you can press to read any text that you highlight.

I don't know how to use voice commands with OS X

Cause   Aside from having OS X read text-to-speech, you can have OS X respond to your voice using a series of commands. For example, you can say "Get My

Mail," and OS X opens the Mail application and check mail for you. In order to use speech recognition, you must turn it on and configure it.

The Painkiller   To turn on and configure Speech Recognition, follow these steps:

1. Click System Preferences on the Dock, or select Apple | System Preferences.

2. In System Preferences, click the Speech icon found under the System category.

3. On the Speech Recognition tab, shown in the following illustration, click the On radio button to turn on speech recognition. A window appears giving you instructions for speaking to your Mac. Notice that you can start speakable items at logon and have the computer play a sound when it recognizes a command. You can even have it read the command back to you and answer when appropriate.

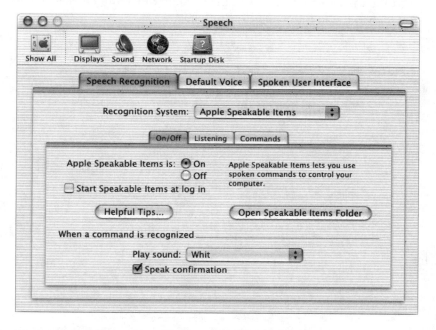

4. Notice that when speech is turned on, you see a hovering button on your desktop, shown in the following illustration. By default, when you want the Mac to listen to you, you can press ESC and say what you want to say.

If you have turned on speak confirmation, the Mac repeats what you say and carries out your request.

TIP *The Mac doesn't listen to you unless you have ESC pressed when you talk.*

5. If you want to change the key that you use to tell the Mac to listen to you, click the Listening tab and click the Change Key button to select a different key, shown in the following illustration.

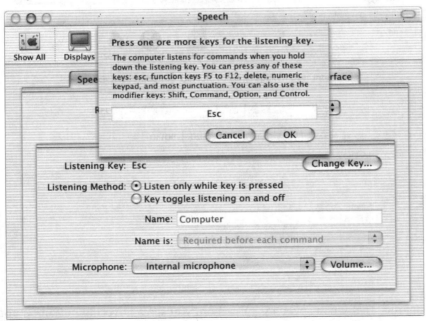

TIP *Don't want to hold down the key while you speak? You can select the Key Toggles radio button on the Listening tab—just remember to press the key again to turn off speech once you finish. Otherwise, your Mac keeps listening to you and tries to do whatever you say (which might not be such a good thing).*

I don't know what voice commands to use

Cause   Once you have turned on speech recognition (see the previous headache), you can use a number of voice commands to tell OS X what you want to do. OS X only understands certain voice commands, which change according to the application that you are using at the moment.

The Painkiller   To see a list of commands you can use, do the following:

1. Click System Preferences on the Dock, or select Apple | System Preferences.

2. In System Preferences, click the Speech icon found under the System category.

3. Select the On/Off tab and then click the Open Speakable Items folder, shown in the following illustration. You can also open this folder by speaking the command. Then, review all of the available commands.

4. Also, click the Commands tab in the Speech window, shown in the following illustration. Notice that you can turn on general and application-specific commands, application-switching commands, front window commands, and menu bar commands as well.

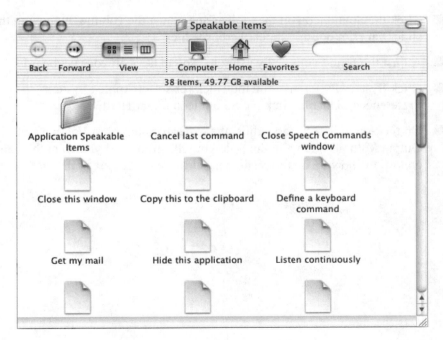

You can also quickly get to the speech commands window by clicking the down arrow on the speech recognition icon (the floating button) and clicking the Open Speech Commands window.

By default, the Require Exact Wording Of Speakable Item Command Names check box is selected. This requires you to say the exact wording. However, if you clear this check box, you can use variations that OS X can understand. Try deselecting this check box for more flexibility.

Sound Headaches

Your Mac is equipped to play a number of sounds that alert you to things. The following sections take a look at some sound headaches you might run into.

 ## The sound is not loud enough or is too loud

Cause   You can adjust the sound volume on your Mac at any time, quickly and easily. See the painkiller for the steps.

The Painkiller   To adjust the sound, try the following methods:

- Click the Sound icon on the toolbar and adjust the volume by moving the slider bar (if it doesn't appear here, see Step 3).

- Adjust the sound volume by using the sound keys on your keyboard.

- Click System Preferences on the Dock (or select Apple | System Preferences). Double-click the Sound icon under Hardware.

- On the Sound Effects tab, adjust the slider bars for Alert Volume and Output Volume, shown in the following illustration. If you want the volume control to show up on the menu bar, click the check box at the bottom.

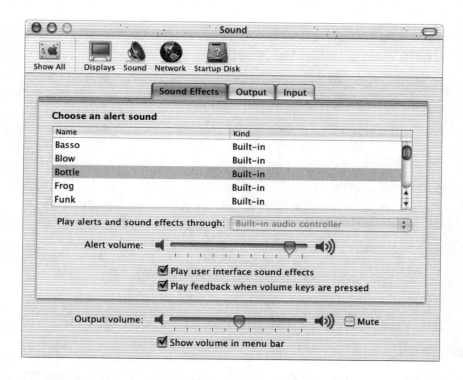

 ## I don't like the alert sound that plays

Cause   If you don't like the default alert sound that plays when an alert occurs, you can easily select a different sound.

The Painkiller   To adjust the alert selection, use these steps:

1. Open System Preferences on the Dock (or select Apple | System Preferences). Double-click the Sound icon under Hardware.

2. On the Sound Effects tab, choose a different alert sound.

Adding Your Own Alert Sounds

If you don't like any of the alert sounds and you want to use something of your own, you can do so, with a few caveats:

- Put the sound files in your Home Folder | Library | Sounds Folder. Or, if you are an Administrator and you want the new alert sounds available to everyone, put them in the Library | Sounds Folder.

- The sound files you want to use must be the AIFF format, and they must have the AIFF extension (not just AIF), or System Preferences won't recognize them.

- Quit System Preferences and reopen it to see the new sounds available in the Alert Sound list.

My internal or external microphone doesn't hear me very well

Cause   Some Macs have a built-in internal microphone, while others require an external microphone. Regardless of what you have, you can adjust the input level of the microphone so that the Mac can hear you well. Of course, you also need to make sure you are close enough to the microphone.

The Painkiller   To adjust the microphone volume, follow these steps:

1. Open System Preferences on the Dock (or select Apple | System Preferences). Double-click the Sound icon under Hardware.

2. Click the Input tab, shown in the following illustration. Adjust the input volume slider to the desired level.

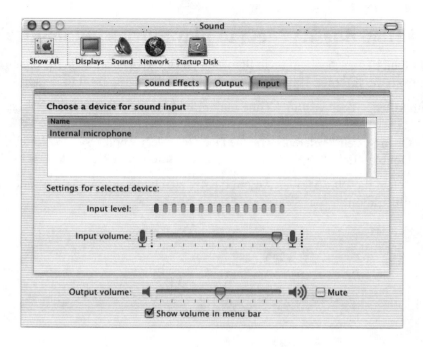

QuickTime Headaches

OS X includes a QuickTime Player, shown in the following illustration. It is your
default program for playing QuickTime movies and streaming media from the
Internet. The good news is that QuickTime Player is a simple tool, and the odds
are good it will never give you any trouble. However a few settings and options
might not be readily apparent, and I point those out in the next few sections.

 *QuickTime Player jumps to life when you need it. However, if want to
open it manually, you can find it in Macintosh HD | Applications. It also
appears on the Dock by default (it looks like a blue Q).*

QuickTime doesn't seem to play movies automatically

Cause   QuickTime should jump to life when you try to open a movie file or streaming media from the Internet. If it doesn't, you can easily configure it to do so.

The Painkiller   To have QuickTime play movies automatically, follow these steps:

1. Open System Preferences on the Dock (or select Apple | System Preferences). Double-click the QuickTime icon under Internet & Network.

2. Select the Play Movies Automatically check box, shown in the following illustration.

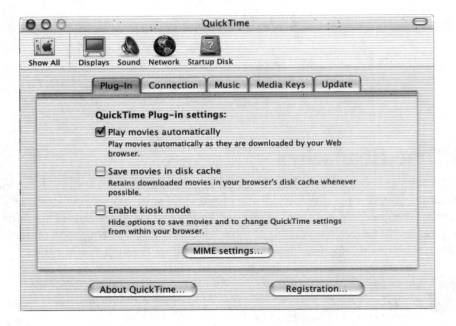

QuickTime movies are choppy when played from the Internet

Cause   QuickTime uses your Internet settings to determine what speed you have. The software uses this speed to determine how best to play movies back to you. Understand that with a modem connection, you may see delays. You can help QuickTime with this problem by making sure it has the correct connection speed configured.

The Painkiller   To adjust QuickTime's connection speed, follow these steps:

1. Open System Preferences on the Dock (or select Apple | System Preferences). Double-click the QuickTime icon under Internet & Network.

2. Click the Connection tab, shown in the following illustration. Choose your connection speed from the drop-down menu. Notice also that you can choose to allow multiple, simultaneous streams. This option is enabled automatically if you are using a broadband connection (such as cable or DSL), but not if you are using a modem. If you enable this option when using a modem, however, you will probably see a decline in performance due to the lower bandwidth available over the modem connection.

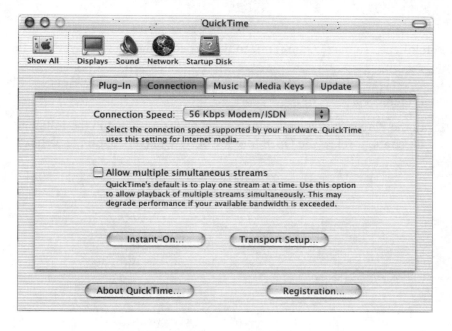

When I use QuickTime player, movies always open in the same window

Cause   When you try to watch several QuickTime movies at the same time, each should open in its own QuickTime Player. However, if this doesn't happen, you can easily fix it.

QuickTime Options

Aside from managing the Plug-in and Connection settings, also keep in mind that you can…

- Click the music tab and select a different program for default music and MIDI (electronic music) file playback.

- Click the Media Keys tab and enter any media keys you may be using to access secure content.

- Check the QuickTime web site for updates using the Update tab.

The Painkiller   To make QuickTime movies open in their own players, do this:

1. Open QuickTime Player and click QuickTime Player | Preferences | Player Preferences.

2. In the Player Preferences window that appears, shown in the following illustration, select the Open Movies In New Players option and click OK.

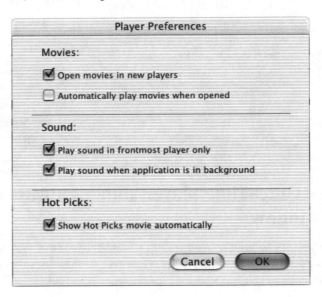

The QuickTime movies I watch don't look very good

Cause   If you are streaming media over the Internet, you'll probably suffer from some performance problems, which seem to be the nature of the beast. However, what if you notice that all of your movies tend to look bad? You might need to take advantage of two cool controls that enable you to adjust the quality of your movies.

The Painkiller   When you're using QuickTime Player to watch a movie, click the Movie menu. You see options to Show Sound Controls and Show Movie Controls. You see control options on the player to adjust the video brightness and audio playback (including bass, treble, and so forth).

Font Headaches

Fonts enable you to use different kinds of type, both on your screen and when you print a document. In the past, fonts could be a real headache. You might create some type that looks great on the screen but comes out jagged when you print the document. Due to different font technology used in the Mac these days, you don't have to worry about using fonts and printing them. The smooth fonts you see on the screen are what you get when you print them.

If you are used to working with fonts in OS 9, you're probably turning to this section to answer one crazy question, "Where is the Fonts folder?" Things work differently in OS X concerning fonts (as they do with most things), and you no longer have one single folder for fonts on your OS. Instead, you have five. Don't worry, though; things are not as crazy as they first appear. As far as your work is concerned, you can simply use the fonts without worrying about where they are stored. But in case you're wondering...

- **Home Folder | Library | Fonts**   This folder resides in your Home folder and contains all of the fonts you add. The reason? It is designed so you can add or remove as many fonts as you want without interfering with anyone else's fonts. If that sounds confusing, check out Chapter 3 to learn how OS X manages users.

- **Library | Fonts**   This global library contains all of the fonts you'll probably use, available to everyone who uses the computer. This is basically what you think of when you say "Fonts folder." However, you can't make any changes to the fonts or add new ones here unless you are an Administrator.

- ■ **Network | Library | Fonts**   If you are on a network, this folder enables you to share fonts across the network.

- ■ **System | Library | Fonts**   This folder has the fonts that OS X uses in your menus, dialog boxes, and other system components.

- ■ …and, of course, if you are using OS, the Fonts folder still exists under that operating system, and OS 9 can use those fonts as well.

I don't know how to add a font

Cause   If you want to add new fonts, you can do so easily in your Home Folder | Library | Fonts, or, if you are an Administrator, you can make the fonts you add available to everyone by putting them in the Library | Fonts folder. If you check out the Fonts folder in the Library, you see over 50 fonts already in place, giving you a lot of flexibility. However, if you want to use some of your own or some that you have downloaded from the Web, see the painkiller.

The Painkiller   The great news is that there is no limit to the amount of fonts you can install, and all you have to do is drag them to the appropriate folder. These folders include the Fonts folder in your Home folder library, or in the main library Fonts folder (Administrator permission required), shown in the following illustration.

Some of my fonts look fuzzy on the screen

Cause   OS X uses a font technology called antialiasing to make fonts look smooth on the screen. Sometimes this feature, also called the text smoothing feature, can make smaller fonts look a little fuzzy. You could print this font without the fuzzy result, but if viewing it is giving you a headache (literally), you can use a quick feature to fix the fuzziness of the font.

The Painkiller   To fix font fuzziness, follow these steps:

1. Click System Preferences on the Dock, or select Apple | System Preferences.

2. Click the General icon.

3. At the very bottom of the window, shown in the following illustration, you see an option for Turn Off Text Smoothing For Font Sizes X And Smaller. Choose a higher number. You may have to experiment with a few different settings here to find the one that works best for your font.

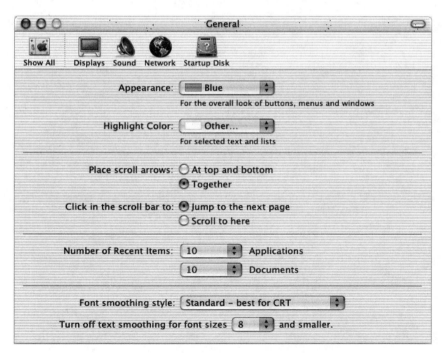

Chapter 18

OS X Migraine Headaches

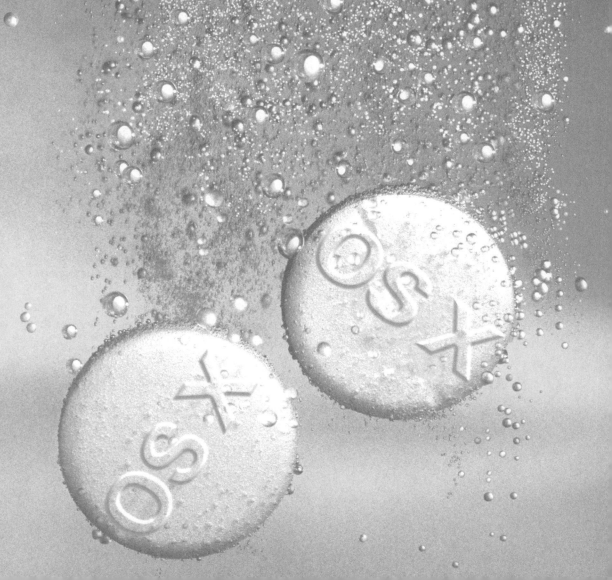

In this chapter, you'll cure…

- Application migraines
- OS X migraines

If you have ever experienced a real migraine headache, you know how terrible they can be—severe pain, sensitivity to sound and light, and a general feeling that you are slowly dying. That's right, migraine headaches are the most painful of all. I've lovingly named this chapter "OS X Migraine Headaches," and I bet you can guess why. The headaches we explore in this chapter are seriously painful headaches—big problems that are difficult to solve or that leave your Mac in shambles. The good news is that OS X is one of the most stable operating systems ever created, and the likelihood of you actually having an OS X migraine headache is pretty small. However, if a migraine strikes, you are in for some pain. Some of the migraines you can cure yourself, while others may require help from technical support. Either way, you can use this chapter to guide yourself though the haze of migraine pain and hopefully come out on the other side cured and happy!

Application Migraines

In many cases, applications are the cause of migraine headaches. An application simply refuses to work correctly, locks up and stops responding to your keyboard and mouse, or just acts crazy in general. The good news is that OS X handles applications effectively—each application that launches is held in its own memory container. If the application starts to go haywire, it doesn't crash other open applications or your entire Mac system.

Chapter 8 is devoted to application installation and usage problems, so be sure to check out that chapter for additional problems and solutions. However, for those really painful migraine headaches concerning applications, read on.

An application stops working or stops responding

Cause   If you are working with an application and it suddenly stops working or responding to keyboard and mouse input, something has happened to the program and caused it to lock up. This problem doesn't happen very often with OS X applications, but you may see it from time to time when you are using OS 9 applications. The only thing you can do is force the application to quit so you can get control again. Doing this causes you to lose any unsaved work within that application, though.

The Painkiller   To force an application to quit, try one of the following:

■ Click the Apple menu and select Force Quit.

■ You can also press COMMAND-OPTION-ESC at the same time or hold down OPTION and click the application's icon on the Dock. This opens a menu where you see a Force Quit option. Once you've forced an application to quit, you can simply start it again and go back to work.

An application doesn't work in OS X, but it worked before I upgraded to OS X from OS 9

Cause   OS 9 applications work differently because the OS 9 operating system was different from OS X. In order for an application to work with an operating system, that application must be designed to work with OS X. If it isn't, the application either will not work at all or will work intermittently. The good news is that OS X contains OS 9 for backward compatibility; all you have to do is run the application in the OS 9 environment.

The Painkiller   To have an application run under OS 9 instead of OS X, see Chapter 8.

   *You can configure OS 9 applications to always start the OS 9 environment when they are launched. See Chapter 8 for details.*

An application doesn't act the way it is supposed to

Cause   If you are using an application and it starts to act goofy, you can bet that something within the program has gone haywire. Sometimes this happens because of conflicting commands, or perhaps the programming gods are simply not smiling on you. In any case, the behavior is not your fault, but a program that doesn't act the way it is supposed to isn't much use.

The Painkiller   To fix this problem, try these tactics:

- Quit and restart the application. In most cases, simply reloading the application solves the problem.

- If the application acts goofy most of the time, there may be some compatibility problems—you may need to upgrade the application to a new version.

- If the application is OS X compatible and it still acts goofy, uninstall and reinstall it. Simply open the Applications folder and drag the icon to the Trash. Then, reinstall the application.

- If you continue to have problems, try the manufacturer's web site for technical support help or see your application's documentation for more info.

An application doesn't work well when I'm using it, but other users have no problems

Cause   Even with all of the grand changes OS X brought to us, programs still use *preference* files that are tied to your user account. Preference files are tiny files that hold preferences or configurations that you have made to a certain program. However, if a preference file becomes corrupted, it can utterly confuse the program. In this case, your corrupted preference file keeps the program from working correctly because the preference file is tied to you—the user. Other users have their own preference files, which explains why the program works for them.

The Painkiller   To fix a corrupted preference file, follow these steps:

1. Open Macintosh HD | Users | *Your account* | Library | Preferences.

2. The preferences files are named com.apple.*applicationname*.plist, for Apple applications For example, the Address Book's preferences file is called com.apple.AddressBook.plist, as you can see in the following illustration.

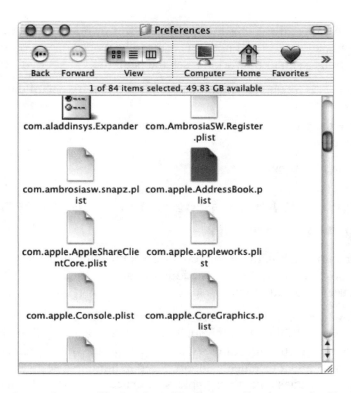

3. Drag the preference file for the offending application to the Trash, but don't delete it just yet. Close the Preferences folder.

4. Start the application. It should build a new preference file for you. If this solves the problem, you can delete the old one in the Trash.

 If all users are having problems, you can also try deleting the preferences file for all users found in Macintosh HD | Library | Preferences. You need to be logged on as the Administrator to perform this action.

 ## An application will not open

Cause If you try to open an application and nothing happens, there is usually a problem with the preference files for the application—or something in its program has become corrupted that keeps the application from working. First of all, make sure other applications work. If nothing seems to be working, restart OS X. If all other applications seem to be working, see the painkiller.

The Painkiller   To fix an application that will not open, try one of these options:

- ■ Delete the preference files. See the previous headache for more information.

- ■ Reinstall the program.

No matter what I try, a program still does not work or does not work correctly

Cause   Sometimes, no matter what you do, an application just doesn't work the way it is supposed to work. You've tried the troubleshooting steps in this chapter, and nothing seems to help. In this case…

The Painkiller   Make absolutely sure the program is designed for OS X. If it is, reinstall the program. If that doesn't help, it's time to get some help from the software manufacturer. See the manufacturer's web site or consult your documentation for more information about technical support. Keep in mind that software is usually developed by companies other than Apple, so you need to contact the manufacturer of the software—not Apple—to solve the problem.

OS X Migraines

OS X usually works great without any major problems, and the general problems you are likely to encounter involve different services and features explored throughout this book. However, what do you do if OS X stops working completely or will not even start? In this case, you get that sinking feeling and feel the migraine begin.

The good news is that, most of the time, you can even cure these dreadful migraines on your own. In some instances, however, you may need help from other people. Read on for more information…

When I start OS X, I see a bunch of gibberish on the screen

Cause   When OS X starts, it loads all of the operating system files and checks all of your system hardware. However, on rare occasions, something can go wrong.

Perhaps there is a problem with the motherboard, or perhaps another kind of hardware problem caused OS X to lose its mind. In this case, you may see a bunch of programming gibberish on your screen.

The Painkiller   To solve this problem, try the following:

1. Restart the Mac. This alone may solve the problem.

2. If restarting doesn't help, remove all extra devices you have added (USB hubs, and so on) and try to restart. If the Mac then starts correctly, one of your devices is acting goofy. In reality, you probably need to experiment by adding devices one at a time until you find the problem one. Then, you need to check the manufacturer's web site for support information and possibly a new driver.

When I start OS X, all I see is a screen; nothing else happens

Cause   The gray screen problem at startup can occur because of hardware problems, as described in the previous headache, or problems with firmware. Firmware is simply the drivers that make OS X work.

The Painkiller   To solve the problem, try the following:

1. Remove all extra hardware you have added and restart the Mac.

2. Check the Support page of Apple.com for firmware updates for your version of OS X.

3. Run Disk Utility (see Chapter 6 for details).

When I start OS X, all I see is a blue screen; nothing else happens

Cause   If a blue screen occurs when you start up, you can follow the troubleshooting steps in the previous two headaches. However, a blue screen at startup also can occur if you have a corrupted font in your OS 9 fonts folder or if some other application problem is keeping the Mac from moving forward.

The Painkiller   To fix the corrupted font, follow these steps:

1. Restart the Mac in OS 9.

2. Open the System Folder and drag the Fonts folder to the desktop.

3. Restart the Mac in OS X. If it starts correctly, then you have a corrupted OS 9 font.

 ## I still can't get OS X to start

Cause   If you have tried to get OS X to start using the previous troubleshooting steps but are still having no luck, then your best bet is to reinstall OS X. Fortunately, you can do this without losing any of your applications, files, or folders.

The Painkiller   To reinstall OS X, follow these steps:

1. Insert the OS X installation CD.

2. Restart OS X and hold down C on your keyboard. This starts the Mac from the CD.

3. Choose the option to Archive & Install OS X. OS X reinstalls any corrupted operating system files, which essentially fixes whatever was causing the problem.

4. If you have installed updates to the operating system, you need to reinstall those updates as well.

 ## I still can't get OS X to work—even after a reinstall!

Cause   In rare cases, your Mac may just go haywire. You may have a hardware problem, such as a failed disk or problems with the motherboard. There could also be an operating system problem that a reinstall just doesn't seem to fix. In this case, you need to get help from the professionals.

The Painkiller   Contact Apple support using the Apple web site, or contact AppleCare at (800) APLCARE (800-275-2273). Depending on your AppleCare agreement, you may have to pay for telephone technical support, so be sure to check out your Apple documentation for details.

Appendix A

Curt's Top 25 Mac OS X Headaches

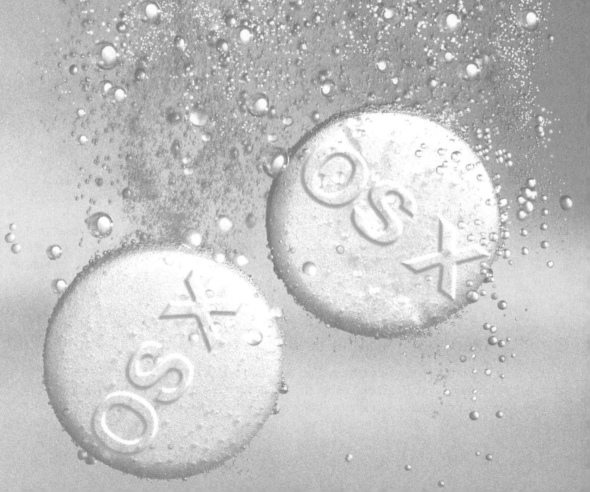

The chapters of this book explore a number of headaches and painkillers on a variety of topics. These are the headaches that have annoyed plenty of people—and if you peruse the headaches in this chapter, you may just come across a solution you need. All of the headaches found in this chapter are also explored in other places in the book, so I'll tell you where to go for more information on the subject at hand. All right, here we go—the top 25 (in my humble opinion) in chronological order:

25: I'm having problems working with Acrobat Reader

Cause   Documents that open in Acrobat Reader can be a little odd sometimes, mainly because they may be displayed at an unusual size or because you have problems getting around and seeing all of the document at first. That's no problem, though, because Acrobat Reader gives you easy controls along the toolbar. You can do a few cool things.

The Painkiller   To move around and change the document as you read, simply use the toolbar controls to move forward and back, zoom in on text, and change the overall size. For example, if the document is displayed at 150 percent, you probably need to reduce it a bit in order to see everything. If you are having problems reading the text, just increase the size. You can view a document in full-screen mode by choosing View | Full Screen, or pressing COMMAND-L. Just hit ESC to return to normal. You can also move from page to page in the document by pressing ENTER.

To use the Thumbnails view, just click the Thumbnails tab on the left side of the document. A list of thumbnails for the pages appears in a pane. Just click a page to go to it. You can also use the Document menu to move around through a PDF file and the View menu to choose a variety of viewing options.

To use the copy feature, click either the Copy Text or Copy Graphics button on the toolbar and then use your mouse to select the text or graphics (you can't do both at the same time). Click Edit | Copy and use the Edit | Paste command to paste the text or graphics into another program.

24: iPod and iTunes always synchronize when I connect iPod, but I want to manually control what is on the iPod

Cause   When you first use iPod, the Mac asks whether you want to use manual or auto sync. From that point, the Mac uses what you first chose. Basically, the synchronization keeps everything in your library on the iPod so that the two are the same. The idea is that you can access music in your library on the Mac, or on the iPod when you are mobile, without any additional configuration. However, what if you don't want the iPod to have the same songs, or what if you want a specific playlist on the iPod that is not in iTunes? In this case, you can stop the automatic synchronization feature. However, keep in mind that data flow from iTunes to the iPod is one-way—you can copy data to the iPod, but getting the songs from the iPod to iTunes is rather difficult.

The Painkiller   To stop automatic synchronization with iTunes and iPod, follow these steps:

1. Connect iPod. Open iTunes. You see the iPod appear in the Source pane of iTunes.

2. Select iPod and click the iPod button that appears at the bottom edge of the iTunes screen.

3. In the iPod preferences dialog box that appears, click Manually Manage Songs And Playlists. Click OK.

4. You can now select iPod in the Source list and create a new playlist for the iPod as desired.

TIP   *See Chapter 15 to learn more about iTunes.*

23: My CDs do not automatically play

Cause   By default, iTunes 3 shows you the songs on a CD when you insert it. "Great," you may think, "I want to hear the songs, not see them." This preference setting enables you to do whatever you want; if you primarily want iTunes 3 to start playing the CD when you insert it into the CD drive, you can change this setting easily.

The Painkiller   To change the default CD insert behavior, follow these steps:

1. Open iTunes 3, then click iTunes | Preferences.

2. Click the General button. In the On CD Insert drop-down menu, choose the Begin Playing option, as shown in the following illustration. Click OK.

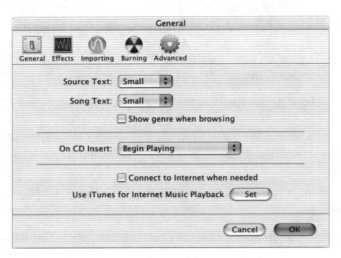

22: In iPhoto, I can't assign labels and titles

Cause   iPhoto gives you the chance to create a picture, change the title of a picture, and assign keywords, or labels, to photos. The reason, you may wonder? It's all about finding photos. Let's say you have a thousand photos stored in iPhoto. You want to quickly find all the photos of your children's birthday parties, but your pictures are stored in a monthly album format. The only way to find your pictures is to browse through the albums and locate them, right? Wrong! Using iPhoto, you can simply search for the pictures and find them all—provided you used keyword assignments and/or titles. You do a few different things with titles and labels, and the following painkiller gets you up to speed.

The Painkiller   To use titles and labels, follow these steps:

1. Every photo imported into iPhoto has a title. The title may be a title you previously assigned, or it may be a title your camera has created for the file, such as WPS004876.JPG. That means a lot, right? Well, you can retitle your pictures quickly and easily, and, if you are careful in titling them, easily find them with a search. To retitle a picture, go to Organize mode and select the picture. In the Title dialog box in the lower-left portion of the interface, just type a new title. You can even give multiple photos the same name if you want. For example, all of the photos of my wedding are titled "wedding," so all I have to do is search for "wedding" to find them all.

2. iPhoto gives you a few default keywords you can also apply to photos, such as Favorite, Family, Kids, Vacation, and Birthday. If you give all of your birthday pictures the keyword of "birthday," then you can easily find them in a search. To assign a default keyword, just go to Organize Mode, select the picture, and click the desired keyword from the available keywords, shown in the following illustration. The new keyword appears with the picture. You can assign multiple keywords, if you wish.

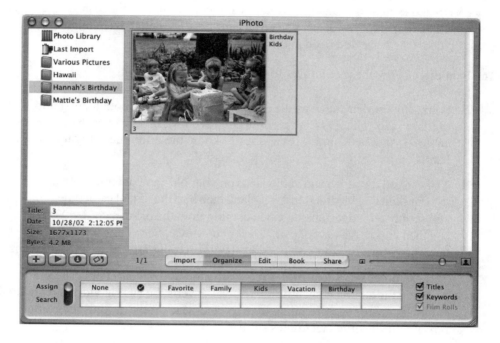

3. You can use the default keywords, change them, or create nine additional keywords. Just go into Organize Mode and select Edit | Keywords. You can now change the existing keywords and add your own in the keyword dialog boxes provided, as shown in the following illustration. When you are finished, just click Done.

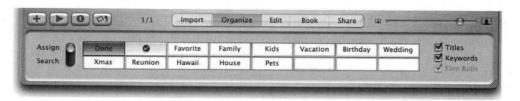

See Chapter 13 to learn more about iPhoto.

21: I need to import analog video in iMovie

Cause   Digital video is the wave of the future, but if you are like me, you have tons of older VHS and even 8-mm analog videotapes around your house. Since iMovie 2 only works with digital video, what can you do? There are a few solutions to importing analog video, which are described in the painkiller.

The Painkiller   Try these solutions for importing analog video:

- Some camcorders, such as the Sony Digital8, can play both analog and digital video. The material becomes digitized when sent over the FireWire cable to your Mac, and iMovie doesn't know the difference. Try to get your hands on one of these camcorders if possible.

- You can use the video and audio jacks on your old camcorder to connect to your digital camcorder. Insert a blank tape into the digital camcorder and simply record the analog video coming from the old camcorder. You can then import the new digital movie into iMovie. See your camcorder's documentation for more information about recording from another camcorder.

- You can purchase a converter box for around $300 that sits between your Mac and the analog camcorder. The box converts the analog video stream to a digital stream before sending it on to your Mac. You can find a converter box at your favorite electronics store.

- If you can connect an old camcorder to your new camcorder for play-through, you can also connect a standard VHS VCR to your camcorder and play through that way.

20: I can't import a QuickTime movie into iMovie

Cause   iMovie 2 can import QuickTime movies that you create with another application, such as iPhoto, or ones that you download from the Internet. As long as you don't sell your movie, you can use any movie from the Internet without worrying about copyright infringement. However, if you have ever tried to click File | Import, you probably noticed that all QuickTime movies are grayed out. What's the problem? Here's the answer: iMovie 2 can't directly import a QuickTime movie, but it can import a QuickTime movie saved as a Digital Video Stream (DV Stream). In order to convert a QuickTime movie to a digital video stream, upgrade your QuickTime Player to QuickTime Player Pro. You can do this over the Internet for $30.

The Painkiller   To import a DV Stream, follow these steps:

1. First, open QuickTime Player found in Macintosh HD | Applications. Each time you open QuickTime Player, you see a box option to Upgrade To QuickTime Pro. Click the Upgrade Now option. (You need Internet access to upgrade the player and pay your $30 upgrade fee.)

2. Once you have upgraded, open the desired movie in QuickTime Player Pro.

3. Click File | Export.

4. In the Export window, choose the Movie To DV Stream option, enter a name, choose the desired location to save the clip, and click Save.

5. Open the desired iMovie 2 project.

6. Choose File | Import, select Navigate To The DV Stream, and click Open.

7. The DV Stream file appears as a clip on the Shelf in iMovie 2.

TIP   *See Chapter 14 to learn more about iMovie.*

19: I can't customize a theme in iDVD

Cause   If you don't like the appearance of a theme, you can simply try a different one. However, what if you like the theme but want to change parts of it? No problem—you can do that, too.

The Painkiller   To change a theme, select it in the Theme pull-out drawer and click the Customize tab. The following steps show you an example of how I have customized a theme.

1. First of all, I selected a theme that I liked. In this example, I'm using the Sports theme, as shown in the following illustration. I like the fonts and content boxes but want to make some changes.

2. I click the Customize menu. Notice that you have two wells in the Background column, shown in the following illustration. I want to change the background image to one of my own, so I simply drag and drop the image I want into the well. The same is true with the music—I just drag and drop the file I want to use into the Audio well and the new image appears.

3. In the Customize pane, I can also change the Title position, font, color and size. You can change the font characteristics such as color and size—for example, here I changed the font size.

4. Under the Button category, I can change the name of the buttons and change the location to Free Position so I can move them around where I want. I could also change the font and size, too.

5. Now I'm done. I've just created my own customized theme!

See Chapter 16 to learn more about iDVD.

18: QuickTime movies are choppy when played from the Internet

Cause   QuickTime uses your Internet settings to determine what speed you have. The software uses this speed to determine how to best play back movies to you. Understand that with a modem connection, you may see delays. You can help QuickTime with this problem by making sure it has the correct connection speed configured.

The Painkiller   To adjust QuickTime's connection speed, follow these steps:

1. Open System Preferences on the Dock (or select Apple | System Preferences). Double-click the QuickTime icon under Internet & Network.

2. Click the Connection tab, shown in the following illustration. Choose your connection speed from the drop-down menu. Notice also that you can choose to allow multiple, simultaneous streams. This option is enabled automatically if you are using a broadband connection (such as cable or DSL), but not if you are using a modem. If you enable this option when using a modem, however, you will probably see a decline in performance due to the lower bandwidth available over the modem connection.

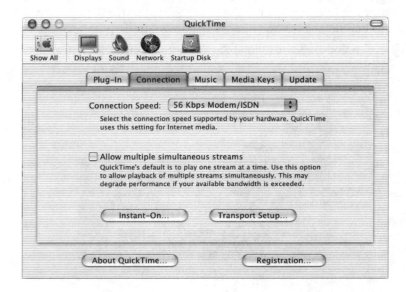

 *See Chapter 17 to learn more about QuickTime and other multimedia headaches.*

17: Icons in my windows are too big or too small

Cause   OS X gives you a default icon size in your windows, and it even gives you one on the desktop for that matter. However, the default size may not meet your needs. That's no problem, though—you can simply adjust it.

The Painkiller   To adjust icon size, follow these steps:

1. Click View | Show View Options.

2. In the View window that appears, shown in the following illustration, you can apply your changes to the current window you are using (This Window Only), or to all windows, by clicking the desired button. Then, simply move the slider bar to adjust the icon size as desired. You can also adjust the icon text size so that it is larger or smaller as well. When you're done, just close the box.

16: I can't drag a folder or file to a different location, or I can't move or copy a folder or file

Cause   As you are working with folders and files, it is important to remember that a few basic rules apply and that some of these rules are different from those in previous versions of Mac OS. So, if you are trying to move or copy a folder or file from one location to another, make sure you understand how Mac OS X handles these operations.

The Painkiller   These rules apply to moving and copying:

- Dragging a folder or file from one location to another on the same disk moves the folder.

- To copy a folder or file from one location to another on the same disk, hold down OPTION and drag the folder to the location where you want the copy made.

- Dragging a folder or file from one disk to another (such as from a CD to your hard drive) copies the folder to the new location.

- To move a folder or file from one disk to another, hold down COMMAND and drag the folder to the new disk. This moves the folder or file to the new disk and deletes it from the old disk.

15: Mail tries to check automatically for e-mail, but I use a dial-up connection

Cause   The Mail program tries to help you by checking the server for new mail every five minutes. However, if you are using a dial-up connection, you may not like Mail trying to dial out and check for you or you may want a longer interval between mail checks. That's no problem; you can easily change this behavior.

The Painkiller   To change how Mail checks for e-mail on the server, follow these steps:

1. Open Mail and select Mail Menu | Preferences.

2. In the Accounts window, you see the drop-down menu Check For New Mail. The default is every five minutes, but you can change this to a longer value. You can also choose Manually if you do not want the Mail program to check for you. Note that you can also choose to play a sound when new mail arrives.

14: I don't know how to set up my Internet connection

Cause   To set up an Internet connection, all you have to do is plug the information your ISP gives you into the correct place. I show you how in the painkiller.

The Painkiller   Make sure the documentation provided by your ISP is handy and follow these steps:

1. Click System Preferences on the Dock to open it.

2. In the Internet & Network category, click Network (not Internet).

3. In the Show drop-down menu, select Internal modem.

4. On the TCP/IP tab, shown in the following illustration, you can manually enter the Internet Protocol addresses of some servers your computer uses to communicate on the Internet. However, for most connections, you can accept the default of Using PPP instead of entering anything here. Check your ISP's instructions—if they don't tell you to do anything here, leave this tab alone.

5. Click the PPP tab. The PPP (Point to Point) tab is where you plug in the information provided by your ISP, as shown in the following illustration. Enter your ISP's name, your account name and password as provided to you by your ISP, and the phone number your Mac should call when connecting to the Internet. If your ISP provides optional numbers in the

event the first number is busy, enter the optional number as well. If you do not want to enter the ISP password every time you connect, click the Save Password option.

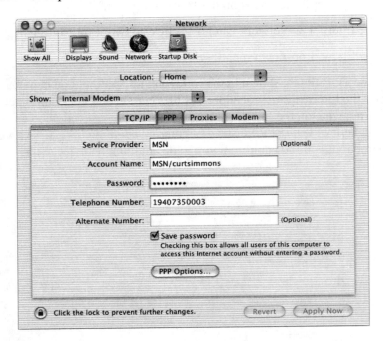

6. Click the Proxies tab, shown in the following illustration. The Proxies tab gives you a place to enter specific information about servers that provide the Internet services listed. You can enter the server address and TCP port—but the good news is that you probably don't have to do anything here. Check your ISP documentation. Unless it specifically tells you what to enter on this tab, don't do anything here.

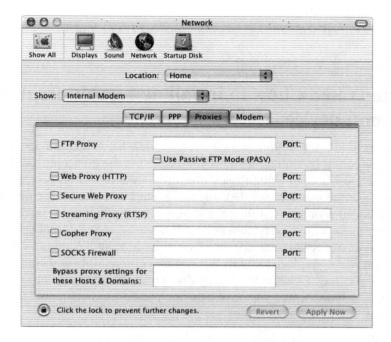

7. That's it! Click Apply Now.

13: My connection disconnects itself if I leave the computer idle

Cause   In order to keep you from forgetting about your connection and leaving your computer connected unnecessarily, OS X can automatically disconnect the connection for you after a certain amount of idle time has passed (the default is 15 minutes). However, you may find this behavior annoying. You can stop it if your Mac is the one disconnecting you. If your ISP is disconnecting you, you can't do much except complain.

The Painkiller   To stop the auto-disconnect feature, follow these steps:

1. Open System Preferences.

2. In the Internet & Network category, click Network.

3. Click the PPP tab.

4. Click the PPP Options button.

5. Uncheck the box that says Disconnect If Idle For X Minutes. Click OK and then click Apply Now.

See Chapter 9 to learn more about Internet connection headaches.

12: I don't know how to install new hardware or a new peripheral device

Cause   First of all, before you attempt to install new hardware or a new peripheral device, make sure it is compatible with your Mac. Let me give a personal example. I recently purchased an external floppy disk drive for an iMac. I know, I know, I really don't need to use a floppy disk any more, but I still like having one around. I first of all located an external floppy disk drive device that said "compatible with Mac." I then made sure the device was a USB device. Some external devices are sold as SCSI devices—an interface found on older Mac and Windows computers that has been widely replaced by FireWire. With compatibility and connection issues out of the way, I bought the floppy disk drive, which came to me with an installation CD-ROM. Once you have a device you know is compatible, what do you do next? The process is simple! See the painkiller.

The Painkiller   To install a new device, follow these steps:

1. Read the manufacturer's instructions, which usually tell you to attach the device to a USB or FireWire port as appropriate. Then turn on the device.

2. The odds are good that OS X will detect the new device and that it will appear on your desktop. For example, if you connect an external device, it appears as an item or drive on the desktop. If you connect a camera, you see a window asking what you want to do. If nothing seems to happen, you may need to install software that can use the device (as well as the device driver). Refer to the manufacturer's instructions for installing the software that came with your device.

11: My FireWire device doesn't work

Cause   In terms of connections and installation, FireWire devices are basically the same as USB devices. You should be able to connect to the FireWire port, turn on the device, and have the Mac see the new device. However, in some cases, you also need to install the device's software. See the manufacturer's instructions for more information and check the painkiller here for important tips.

The Painkiller   If you are still having problems with the FireWire device, consider this:

- Make sure the device is properly connected to the FireWire port.

- FireWire connections have a limited cable connection of 15 feet or less. Make sure your cable is not longer than 15 feet.

- Don't connect the FireWire device in two ways, such as to the FireWire port and the USB port (if the device also provides a USB connection).

TIP   *See Chapter 5 to learn more about hardware headaches.*

10: OS X will not let me install an application in the Applications folder

Cause   You're probably logged on with a Normal account. Normal account users can only install applications into their Home Applications folders—not into the systemwide Applications folder.

The Painkiller   In order to install an application in the systemwide Applications folder, you need to log in with an Administrator account. If you do not have an Administrator account, you need help from someone who does. See Chapter 3 to learn more about user headaches.

9: I need to make sure an application uses the Classic environment

Cause   OS X does a good job of deciding which applications should use the OS X environment and which applications need to use the Classic environment. However, in some cases you may want to make certain that an application opens in Classic so that helper applications or plug-ins can be used. In this case, you can configure the application to open in Classic.

The Painkiller   To make an application open in Classic, follow these steps:

1. Open Macintosh HD | Applications, or open your Home folder if the application is installed there.

2. CONTROL-click the application's icon and click Get Info. Or, select the application's icon and click File | Get Info.

3. In the Get Info window, select the check box to open the application in Classic. Close the Get Info window.

8: A file doesn't open with the right application

Cause   Files are created with applications, and when you double-click a file to open it, OS X uses the default application for that file. For example, if you open a JPEG picture file, the Preview application opens the file. However, what if you want a different application to open the file? For example, let's say you install Photoshop Elements and you want Photoshop Elements to open when you double-click a certain picture file. In this case, you can use Get Info to change the file's application association. This change tells OS X to open the file with the application you choose.

 *An application must be able to read the file type in order to open it. For example, you can't open a Quicken file using Photoshop Elements. Just keep in mind that applications can only open and read the types of files they were created to open and read.*

The Painkiller   To change a file's application association, follow these steps:

1. CONTROL-click the desired file and click Get Info, or select the file and click File | Get Info.

2. In the Get Info window, expand Open With and select the application you want to use to open the file, as shown in the following illustration.

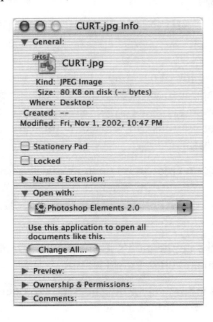

3. More easily, you can CONTROL-click the file's icon, point to Open With, and select the application you want to use. However, this option is a "once only" feature. The next time you open the file, it opens with the default application. To change the association permanently, use the Get Info option as described in Step 2.

TIP   *See Chapter 8 to learn more about problems with applications.*

7: I don't know how to get my Mac to work on a network

Cause   You can configure your computer to share on a network once you connect it with other computers. You can connect in several ways. You can use a hub and Ethernet cables. If you have two Macs, you can use a cross-over cable (newer Macs don't even need a cross-over cable). Or, you can connect wirelessly with AirPort. Once you do this, see the painkiller to learn how to set up sharing.

The Painkiller   To set up sharing, follow these steps:

1. Click the System Preferences icon on the Dock, or click Apple | System Preferences.

2. Click the Sharing icon.

3. On the Sharing window, give your computer a name to use on the network. You can enter whatever you want, but the easier (and shorter) the name is, the easier other users will be able to connect to your computer and access resources.

4. On the Services tab, click Personal File Sharing to turn on file sharing. If you want to share a printer, turn on that option as well. If you want to

share with Windows computers, turn on Windows File Sharing, as shown
in the following illustration.

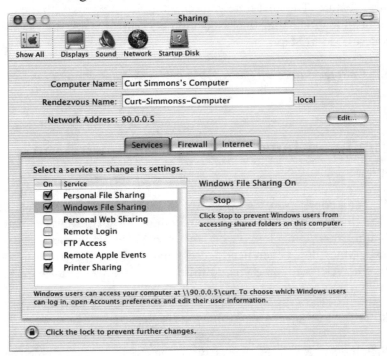

5. Repeat these steps for each Mac OS X computer on your network. Note that
   each computer must have a different name.

6: I don't know how to access another computer on my network

Cause   Once all of the computers on your network are connected, you can begin
accessing files and other shared items on other Macs. This, after all, is the reason
you wanted a network in the first place. The good news is that connecting to other
Macs on your network is easy, and the painkiller shows you how to do it.

The Painkiller   To access another computer on the network, follow these steps:

1. Choose Go | Connect to Server.

2. In the Connect To Server box, you may see a list of globe-like icons with
   names such as *, Local, Workgroup, or even MSHOME. These icons represent
   networks your Mac sees. To see the computers in the different networks,

just click the globe icon. A list of computers appears in the right pane. If you have only OS X computers on your network, you see only the names of those computers instead of the globe icons. But here's what the globe icons mean:

- ■   *   This icon means the Mac has detected another AppleTalk zone; this might happen if you are using Macs that came out before OS X.

- ■   **Local**   This icon appears to note all of the OS X computers on the network.

- ■   **MSHOME**   If there is a Windows network, you may see an MSHOME globe, or perhaps another name, depending on the name of the Microsoft workgroup.

- ■   **Workgroup**   This name may appear if there are additional Windows workgroups.

3. Double-click the name of the computer you want to access. A Connect To File Server box appears in which you can enter your username and password to access the shared files.

4. Click Connect and press RETURN or ENTER.

5. The disk or folders available on that computer now appear. Simply double-click them to open and begin using them.

> **TIP**   *See Chapter 12 to learn more about networking headaches.*

5: My existing printer doesn't work with OS X

Cause   Let's say you have a printer that worked fine under OS 9. You upgraded to OS X and now the printer does not work. Or, perhaps you bought a used printer that is supposed to work with OS X and it doesn't work either. Why? The issue comes back to the driver. OS X is a new operating system, completely different from OS 9. The problem with new operating systems is that software and hardware manufacturers have to play catch-up. The printer that worked fine under OS 9 may not work at all under OS X because the driver software is not compatible with OS X. So, what can you do?

The Painkiller   There is really only one way to solve this problem: you must have an updated driver. Start at the computer manufacturer's web site. Often, manufacturers develop new drivers that you can download and install. Once you do, the printer will start working. What if the manufacturer has not developed a new driver for your printer? In this case, I'm afraid you are out of luck. It's time to buy a new printer.

Are you dying to use your old ImageWriter, StyleWriter, or LaserWriter models? Sorry, those printers all use Apple's QuickDraw technology, which is no longer supported under OS X.

4: I can't manage how a file is printed

Cause   When you print a file, you can manipulate some options that determine how the file prints. They are readily available to you when you click File | Print from any application. The following painkiller shows what you can do.

The Painkiller   To manage a print file, follow these steps:

1. Open the file and click File | Print.

2. The standard print window appears, shown in the following illustration. By default, the Copies & Pages option is selected. You can determine how many copies you want to print and whether or not to print all pages of the file.

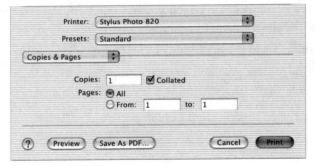

3. If you choose Layout from the drop-down menu, you determine the layout direction of the print job, as you can see in the following illustration. Also notice here that you can add a border to the printed page, if you like.

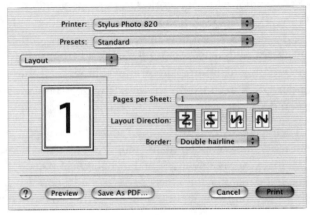

4. If you select Output Options from the drop-down menu, you can choose to save the print job as a file in the PDF format.

NOTE *Steps 5 and 6 may not appear as options, depending on the kind of printer you use. They typically appear for inkjet printers, but not all manufacturers provide these setting options.*

5. If you choose the Print Settings option in the drop-down menu, you can choose the kind of paper you use, choose between color ink and black ink, and choose a setting to determine the resolution of the printed file.

TIP *You normally don't need to change these settings unless you are trying to print high-quality photos on photo-quality paper.*

6. If you click the Color Management option in the drop-down menu, you can adjust the color used when printing. These settings may be helpful to you when printing photographs.

7. Finally, you can also select a Summary option where you can see a listing of the setting you have chosen on each option.

8. When you are done, you can save your settings or just click Print to print the file.

TIP *See Chapter 7 to learn more about printer headaches.*

3: An application doesn't act the way it is supposed to

Cause If you are using an application and it starts to act goofy, you can bet that something within the program has gone haywire. Sometimes this happens because of conflicting commands or because the programming gods are simply not smiling on you. In any case, the behavior is not your fault, but a program that doesn't act the way it should isn't much use.

The Painkiller To fix this problem, try these tactics:

■ Quit and restart the application. In most cases, simply reloading the application will solve the problem.

■ If the application acts goofy most of the time, check to make sure it is compatible with OS X—you may need to upgrade the application to a new version.

■ If the application is compatible with OS X and still acts goofy, uninstall and re-install it. Simply open the Applications folder and drag the icon to the Trash. Then, re-install the application.

■ If you continue to have problems, try the manufacturer's web site for technical support help or see your application's documentation for more info.

2: When I start OS X, all I see is a screen; nothing else happens

Cause   The gray screen problem at startup can occur because of hardware problems, as described in the previous headache, or problems with firmware. Firmware are simply the drivers that make OS X work.

The Painkiller   To solve the problem, try the following:

1. Remove all extra hardware you have added and restart the Mac.

2. Check the Support page of apple.com for firmware updates for your version of OS X.

3. Run Disk Utility (see Chapter 6 for details).

See Chapter 18 to learn more about problems starting your Mac.

1: I can't create a new user

Cause   When you are ready to begin using the multi-user environment by creating a new account or two, use the Accounts option under System in System Preferences. The painkiller steps show you how to create a new user; however, if you are having access problems, you are probably using a Normal account. In order to create new accounts, you need to log out and log back in using an Administrator account. If you do not have an Administrator account—that is, someone else is the Administrator— you can't create a new user. Only the Administrator has this power.

The Painkiller   To create a new user, follow these steps:

1. Log in with an Administrator account.

2. Open System Preferences. In the System section, click Accounts.

3. In the Accounts window on the Users tab, click the New User button.

4. In the New User window, enter the name, short name, password, password verification, and optional password hint. You can also select a picture, if you like. Notice that you have two additional options:

- **Allow User To Administer This Computer** If you check this option, the user becomes an Administrator, with the same power you have.

- **Allow User To Log In From Windows** If your Mac resides on a network with Windows computers, you can allow a network user to log in to the Mac from a Windows computer over the network.

5. Click OK when you are done. The new account is created and appears on the Users tab. When you log off or restart, the option to log on with this new account will appear on the login page.

Appendix B

Installation Headaches

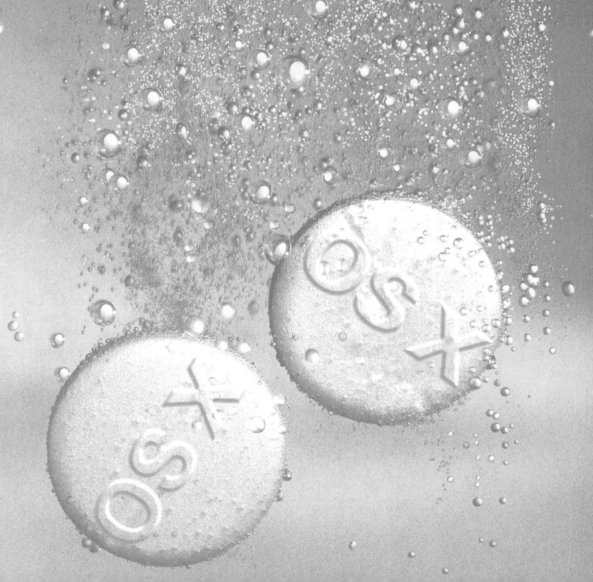

Do you like holding your breath? Probably not. Yet whenever you upgrade an operating system, you always feel like holding your breath. After all, will the upgrade work? Will the new operating system be all that it is supposed to be? These are important questions you must think about before performing an upgrade to OS X.

If you have bought a new Mac with OS X pre-installed, you have nothing to worry about. You know the Mac was designed to handle the needs of OS X. If you want to upgrade to OS X Jaguar, the process is rather easy because, once again, you know the Mac is ready to handle the demands of the operating system.

However, what if you are using an older Mac with OS 9? Can you upgrade to OS X? Probably…maybe…but you need to check a few things first to make sure you are ready. This appendix explores the installation process and addresses concerns and headaches you may have. The good news is that Mac upgrades are easy, so you are not likely to face a lot of problems.

I don't know if my Mac can be upgraded

Cause   Let's face the facts: things change. Hardware gets old, and operating systems become more complex and more demanding with each new release. Operating systems like OS X do more than ever before, but doing more requires more power. Your Mac must be able to handle the demands of OS X. Before you install OS X on your Mac, see the painkiller and make sure your Mac meets requirements.

The Painkiller   In order to handle OS X, your Mac must…

- Have a G3 or G4 processor. This includes PowerMac G3, PowerMac G4, iMac, PowerBook G3, PowerBook G4, or iBook. If you upgraded your Mac to a G3 or G4 with an upgrade card, it is not eligible for an upgrade to OS X. Also, pre–Wall Street PowerBook G3s are not eligible for an upgrade to OS X.

- Have at least 128MB of RAM. In truth, though, you need at least 256MB of RAM to see the performance you want. RAM is not too terribly expensive these days, so you may consider a RAM upgrade if necessary.

- Have at least 1.5GB of free hard disk space.

■ Mac OS 9.2.1. OS 9 and OS X can coexist on the same computer, but you should have the latest version of OS 9 before installing OS X, which is 9.2.1.

You also need to consider some other issues. For example, will your printer and/or scanner work with OS X? What about your applications? Will OS X meet your needs, or should you stay with OS 9 for the time being? Only you can answer these questions, but you might want to spend some reading and researching at www.apple.com before running the upgrade.

I don't know how to upgrade to OS X

Cause   Before you decide to upgrade to OS X, read the previous headache and make sure your computer can handle its demands. Once you are sure your computer is ready to go, just follow the steps in the following painkiller.

The Painkiller   To upgrade to OS X, follow these steps:

1. First, back up all of your data. This includes copying files to a CD-ROM or a Zip disk. If you are on a network, consider storing your important files on another network computer. Ask yourself, "If things completely fall apart during the upgrade, which files can I absolutely not live without?" Then, back up those files.

2. Insert the OS X installation CD-ROM. You see a Welcome window and access to a ReadMe document, which you should read.

3. Double-click the Install Mac OS X icon. You see a Restart button. Click it.

4. The Mac restarts from the installation CD-ROM, and you see an Installer screen. If you are upgrading from OS X to any newer version of X, such as Jaguar, you must enter your Administrator account and password.

5. Several screens appear that ask you to select a language, read important information, and accept the software license agreement. Read and follow the instructions on these screens.

6. Next, you see a destination screen. Choose the disk or partition you want to use for the OS X installation. Click Continue Installation.

TIP   *Before you complete Step 6, you have a last chance to exit the installation without actually installing OS X. If you decide you want to exit, click Installer | Quit.*

7. The Installation Type screen appears. You can simply click Continue to move forward with the installation. However, if you want to customize the installation, click the Customize button. A window appears where you can deselect certain OS X programs that you don't want to install. When you are done, click Continue.

8. OS X copies files to the Mac, which may take 20 minutes or more. Once the file copy process is complete, the Installer restarts the Mac and almost brings you to the desktop. However, you must complete a few more steps.

9. After the restart, you see some visual effects and hear some music; then, a setup assistant appears. The setup assistant asks you to enter your area of the country and choose a keyboard layout. At this point, you can then complete the registration form. You may also see a few other questions asking how you use your Mac.

10. Next, you are asked to create the Administrator account and password. See Chapter 3 to learn more about user headaches in OS X.

11. You see an option to enter your ISP information to set up an Internet account, if you like. Follow the instructions that appear.

12. Finally, you set the time zone and date. Click Continue, and you arrive at the OS X desktop for the first time.

I want to partition my hard disk before upgrading

Cause   Your Mac sees the hard disk as one big storage area. However, you can partition the hard disk so that the Mac sees it as two or more separate hard drives (a drive icon for each will appear on the desktop). Why would you do this, you might ask? One reason for partitioning is to keep OS 9 in one partition and OS X in another. Basically, you keep the two installations separate from each other. When you start your Mac, you can choose which operating system you want to boot into. This process, which is also called dual booting, enables you to keep OS 9 just as you like it while also having OS X available. The bad news, though, is that you have to completely erase your hard drive in order to partition it. You have to completely re-install OS 9 in one partition and OS X in another partition. Think carefully about partitioning before doing it and determine whether having the two operating systems on different partitions is really something you need to do. You can also visit www.apple.com to learn more about the ups and downs of partitioning.

Before you partition, keep in mind that you can install a second hard drive and have the two operating systems reside on two different physical disks. Of course, this method will cost you a second hard drive, and partitioning doesn't cost anything.

The Painkiller   If you decide to partition your disk, follow these steps:

1. You have to completely erase your hard disk, so you must back up everything that you want to keep. This means all files, including your e-mail. You can back up the data to a CD, a removable disk of some kind, or another computer on the network. Once you re-install OS 9, you can put all of your data back. Keep in mind that you also have to re-install any applications that you previously installed as well.

2. Insert the OS X CD. Click the Install Mac OS X button. Click Restart to restart the Mac.

3. When the Installer screen appears, click Installer | Open Disk Utility.

4. Click the Partition tab. In the Volume Scheme portion of the window, use the drop-down menu and choose the number of partitions that you want to create (you need at least two in order to make multiple partitions). Then determine the size for each partition.

5. Click OK. In the warning box that appears, click Partition. The Disk Utility erases your hard drive and partitions it as you have specified. When the partitioning is done, click Installer | Quit Disk Utility. This takes you back to the OS X installer screen. You are now ready to install OS X and then re-install OS 9 on the second partition.

TIP   *How big should you make each partition? If you think you'll use OS 9 and OS X evenly, just split the disk size in half and make the two partitions the same size. If not, try to give more space to the partition you expect to use the most.*

I want to perform a clean install

Cause   A clean install occurs when the OS X installer erases everything on your hard disk. OS X and OS 9 are then re-installed. Why would you want to do this? For some people, it's a great time to clean up the disk and get rid of all the stuff from OS 9 they don't want. Of course, this also includes all of your data and programs, so you should do a backup of all data you want to keep before choosing the clean install option.

The Painkiller   To perform a clean install, follow these steps:

1. First, back up all of your data. This includes copying files to a CD-ROM or a Zip disk. If you are on a network, consider storing your important files on another network computer. Ask yourself again, "If things completely fall apart during the upgrade, which files can I absolutely not live without?" Then, back up those files.

2. Insert the OS X installation CD-ROM. You see a Welcome window and access to a ReadMe document, which you should read.

3. Double-click the Install Mac OS X icon. A Restart button appears. Click it.

4. The Mac restarts from the installation CD-ROM, and you see an Installer screen. If you are upgrading from OS X to any newer version of X, such as Jaguar, you must enter your Administrator account and password.

5. Several screens appear that ask you to select a language, read important information, and accept the software license agreement. Read and follow the instructions on these screens.

6. Next, you see a destination screen. Choose the disk or partition you want to use for the OS X installation. To perform the clean installation, click the Erase Destination check box. This erases all old data on the disk. Click Continue Installation. At this point, installation continues as normal. See the "I Don't Know How To Upgrade To OS X" headache earlier for the remainder of the installation steps.

 # I want to go back to OS 9

Cause   If you installed OS 9 and OS X on different partitions, you can simply erase the OS X partition (provided that you back up any data you want to keep) to get rid of OS X. If you didn't, there is no easy way of removing OS X and getting back to OS 9. I didn't say it was impossible, but it is not easy. So many different OS X files are at work on the Mac that removing them and going back to OS 9 is rather complicated.

The Painkiller   The most practical way to get rid of OS X and go back to OS 9 is to back up all of the data you want to keep. Then, use the Drive Setup program on your OS 9 CD and erase the disk. Then, re-install OS 9 and return your data from backup.

Appendix C

A Quick Introduction to UNIX via Terminal

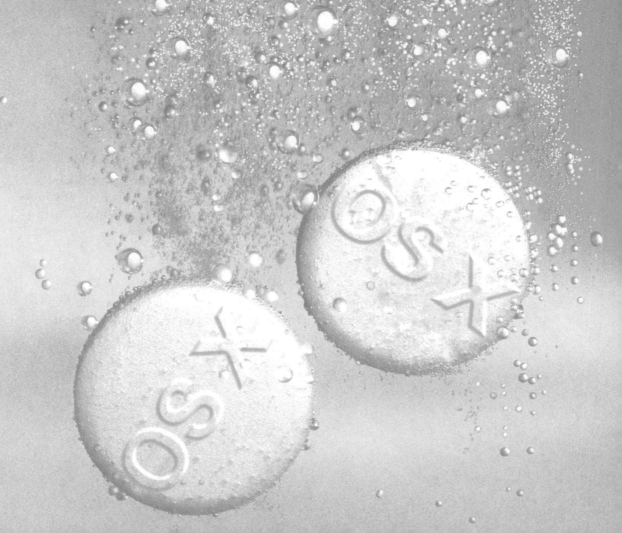

As I've mentioned a few times here and there, Mac OS X is built on the UNIX operating system. UNIX is a very old operating system—it was first built way back in the late 1960s—and it has been revamped, added to, and reworked over the years, bringing it to its current place. Why did Apple build the Mac on such an old system? The answer is really simple—UNIX is a very good operating system. It's stable, flexible, and used today by major corporations and even the government. In short, UNIX makes a rock-hard underpinning for the Mac, giving you the flexibility and stability you want in an operating system.

The good news is that OS X sits on top of UNIX, basically keeping it completely hidden from your view. You can use your Mac and do everything you might want to do without having to go into UNIX land and without really even being aware that it exists. However, OS X gives you a little window into the world of UNIX beneath your Mac through a program called *Terminal*. With Terminal, you can work at the UNIX level, running commands and doing whatever your heart desires.

So, why would you want to? For many people who know UNIX, working with the command line is the fastest way to use the Mac. You can get more done quickly and easily, and you have more flexibility while you work. If you don't know UNIX (and most of you don't), you don't ever have to use Terminal; if you're not interested, you can stop reading this appendix now.

However, if you want to look around a bit in the UNIX world, this appendix gives you a quick look and tells you a few of the major commands. Entire books are devoted to UNIX, of course, so this appendix just functions as a teaser—if you decide you like working in Terminal, you need a few other books to help you learn all about the commands and functions available in the UNIX world.

Opening Terminal

If you navigate to Macintosh HD | Applications | Utilities, you find the little program called Terminal. Double-click to open it, and you see a window appear, similar to the one in the following illustration.

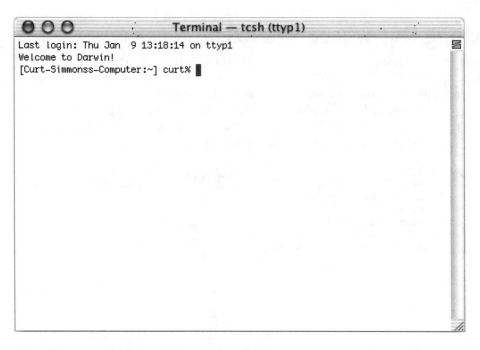

Now, if you're thinking, "Wait a minute, where are icons, menus, and an interesting looking interface?" you'll have to think again. UNIX is a command line interface only. This means you work with strings of text, issuing commands to UNIX and getting information back from it. You see no graphical user interface, no pretty colors, no icons—nothing but text. This fact alone may be enough to bore you to tears and send you running back to the OS X interface. That's fine—and most people use the graphical interface over the UNIX terminal—but you can do plenty of cool things with Terminal.

Notice first of all the name of your computer in brackets (it may also say "localhost"), then you see your username and a % sign. The % sign in UNIX works like a colon. You also see a color block. This represents your cursor (but it doesn't blink). Notice that your mouse doesn't do anything in this box. You use your keyboard if you work with Terminal because it responds primarily to keyboard commands only.

Checking Out Where You Are

One of the first things you can do with Terminal is find out where you are in the Mac operating system and what folders are around you (in UNIX, they are called "directories" instead of folders). You can do this with an easy command called pwd, which means "print working directory." At the command prompt, just type **pwd**, as you can see in the following illustration. It will show you the current location, which is the Users folder and your personal account folder.

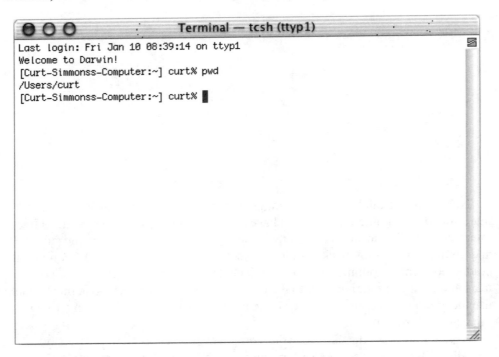

Once you know where you are, you can find out what is there by simply typing **ls**, which means "list." As you can see in the following illustration, you see a list of folders in your location, such as Desktop, Documents, Library, and so forth.

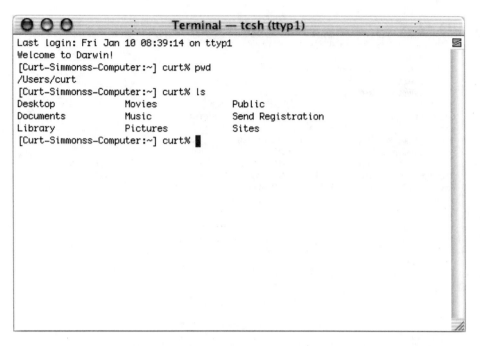

```
                    Terminal — tcsh (ttyp1)
Last login: Fri Jan 10 08:39:14 on ttyp1
Welcome to Darwin!
[Curt-Simmonss-Computer:~] curt% pwd
/Users/curt
[Curt-Simmonss-Computer:~] curt% ls
Desktop            Movies            Public
Documents          Music             Send Registration
Library            Pictures          Sites
[Curt-Simmonss-Computer:~] curt%
```

Another common command for moving around is the **cd** command, which means "change directory." You can think of it as changing folders. For example, let's say that you want to see what is in your Pictures folder. Since you are already in the User folder holding the Pictures folder, all you have to do is type **cd pictures** and then type **ls** to see what is in the folder, shown in the following illustration.

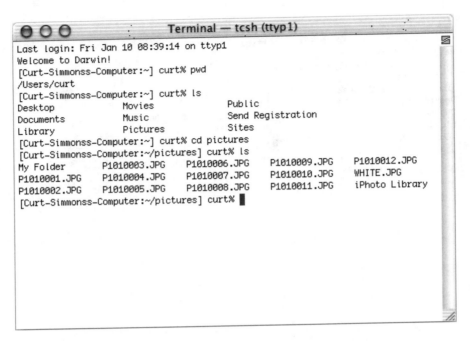

However, what if you want to move to a completely different directory? You simply type the path to that directory. For example, if you wanted to go to your Movies folder, you could type **users/*username*/Movies**. One important point to note here is that Terminal doesn't see spaces in terms of words—it sees each space as a separation for a command. If you have a folder named Cool Photos, you need to type it as **"Cool Photos"** using the quotation marks, or UNIX will tell you the directory doesn't exist.

*If you want to back out of some directory, you can use the **cd ..** command (note the space between cd and ..). This takes you back up one level. You can even go multiple levels back up by using cd ../.. and so forth.*

Working with Files

Aside from moving around in directories on your Mac, you can also use Terminal to work with files. Specifically, you can copy, move, create, and delete files. Obviously, these actions can be serious, and you can't go back and drag items out of the Trash once you delete them in Terminal. If you want to play around with these features a bit, consider logging on with a Normal (not Administrator) account or turning Administrator privileges off on your own account before proceeding.

Copy (cp)

The cp command allows you to copy files and folders. There are a couple of different ways you can do this, and the UNIX command prompt can be a really efficient way to make copies of a bunch of files or directories.

The basic command for copying and pasting a file is **cp** *file1 file2*. For example, let's say you want to copy a document called Vacation. You want the new file to be called Vacation2. Navigate to the directory where the file is located and type **cp vacation.doc vacation2.doc** and press RETURN. That's all there is to it.

> TIP
>
> *You must use the file's extension, such as .doc, .jpg, and so on.*

Let's say you want to copy Vacation.doc as Vacationcopy.doc. In this case, you use a backslash to specify the two works. The command is **cp vacation.doc vacation\copy.doc**.

If you want to copy a file from one location to another, you simply specify the path and use a tilde symbol. The command is **cp vacation.doc ~/*foldername*/vacation2.doc**.

If you want to copy the file from one folder to another without giving the file a different name, all you have to do is specify the path. The command is **cp vacation.doc ~/*foldername*.**

> TIP
>
> *There are many other command variations you can use when using the cp command, but these will get you started!*

Move (mv)

The mv command allows you to move a file or folder from one location to another. The mv command works a lot like the cp command. You can also rename files and folders at the same time you move them, which makes life a lot easier. Basically, to move a file or directory, the command is **mv** *file1 file2*. This command moves the file and renames it as you wish. For example, let's say you want to rename a file called addresses.doc as personal.doc. All you have to type is **mv addresses.doc personal.doc**. The old addresses.doc simply becomes personal.doc.

In the same way you copy a file, you can move a file to another directory by typing **mv** *file ~/foldername*.

Create (touch)

You can create empty files quickly and easily using the touch command. Using touch, you simply specify the command and the file name along with the extension. For example, **touch addresses.txt** creates an empty text file called addresses.

Delete (rm)

The rm command (which stands for "remove") enables you to delete files and entire folders from your Mac. However, before you use this command, keep in mind that there is no Trash and there is no Undo command—once you run an rm command, the deletion is permanent, so be careful!

To delete a file or directory, just type **rm** and the name of the file or folder that you want to delete. For example, **rm addresses.txt** deletes the stated file.

> **TIP** *To give yourself one more shot to back out, type **echo** in front of rm, such as **echo rm addresses.txt**. UNIX will spit the command back at you once to proof before you make the change permanent.*

As you can see, I have just given you a few things here to either whet your appetite or send you running back to your beautiful Mac interface forever. Regardless, if you want to learn more about UNIX, consider picking up *UNIX Made Easy* by John Muster (Osborne, 2002).

Appendix D

Web Sites for More Help

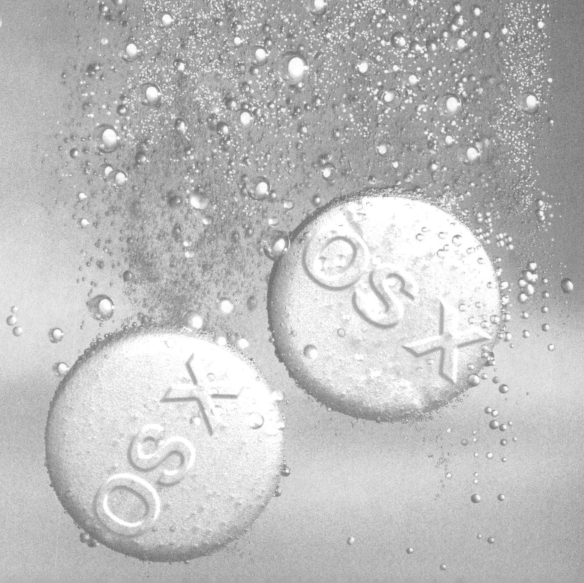

Still struggling with an OS X Headache you just can't cure? The Web has a wealth of information for fixing problems and for generally using Mac OS X. Check out these helpful sites.

Apple's Help Site

www.info.apple.com/usen/macosx/tshoot.html

This is the official Apple troubleshooting site for Mac OS X, shown in the following illustration. Here you'll find plenty of categories, problems, and potential solutions you can try. You can also search the AppleCare database at this site for problems and solutions. Also, check out the Apple KnowledgeBase at kbase.info.apple.com and the Apple Support page at www.apple.com/support.

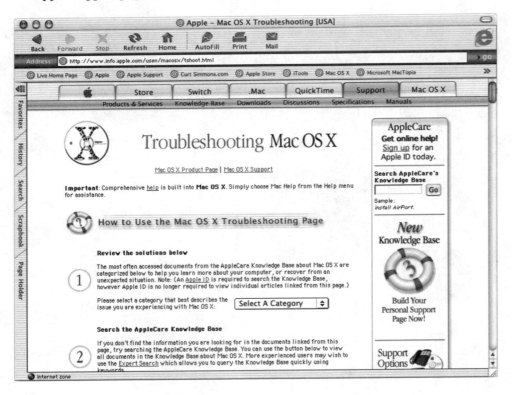

Mac OS X Hints

www.macosxhints.com

The Mac OS X Hints site, shown in the following illustration, is full of tips, tricks, and troubleshooting solutions. You can literally find thousands of helpful hints about all areas of OS X.

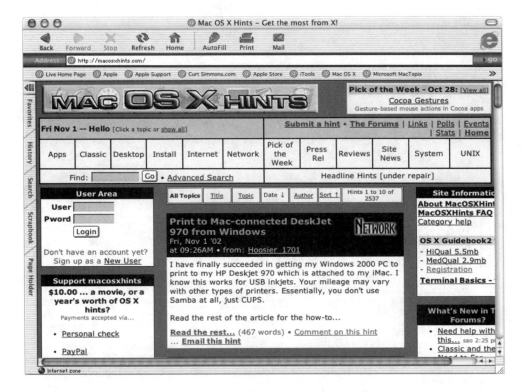

MacAddict

www.macaddict.com

MacAddict is a great site for keeping up with all things Macintosh. You may not find a lot of troubleshooting solutions here, but this is a great site to just keep up with all that is going on in the world of the Mac. Built from the popular magazine, this one is worth checking out for general news and info. See the following illustration.

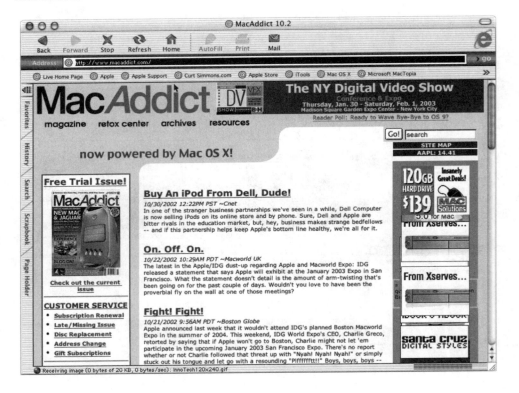

MacFixIt

www.macfixit.com

MacFixIt, shown in the following illustration, is a popular and great site you should check out. It is full of problems and solutions and troubleshooting discussion boards with tons of information; you are sure to find what you need.

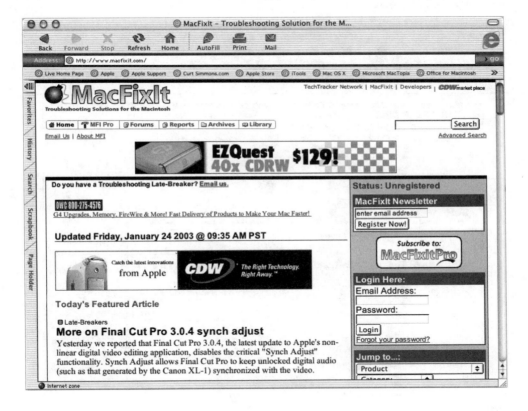

Mac Observer

www.macobserver.com

The Mac Observer site, shown in the next illustration, is another great general information site where you can keep up with the latest developments and issues concerning OS X and Apple computers. You can also find helpful tips and a tech support section here as well.

Macworld

www.macworld.com

Maworld, shown in the following illustration, is perhaps one of the most popular Mac sites, and certainly the most popular Mac magazine. It gives you a full plate of information about the Mac. Here you'll find news, articles, reviews, forums—and you can subscribe to the Macworld newsletter here.

OSX Zone

www.osxzone.com

OSX Zone is about everything OS X. There are tons of articles, FAQs, links and all kinds of stuff, as you can see in the following illustration. Some of it is admittedly high level, but if you are having problems of the OS X kind, you might try a quick search here for possible help.

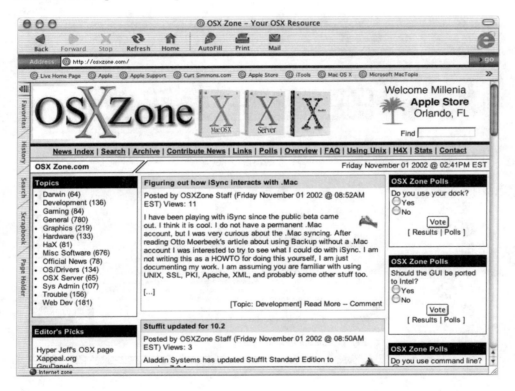

MacintoshOS.com

www.macintoshos.com

The MacintoshOS.com site, shown in the following illustration, has a lot of shareware products you might want to browse through. You'll also find a discussion forum that may be useful to you.

Macinstruct

www.macinstruct.com

Last but not least is the Macinstruct site. At this site, shown in the next illustration, you'll find helpful articles and even some good troubleshooting information that can make your day. Be sure to check out the forums and the tech support sections.

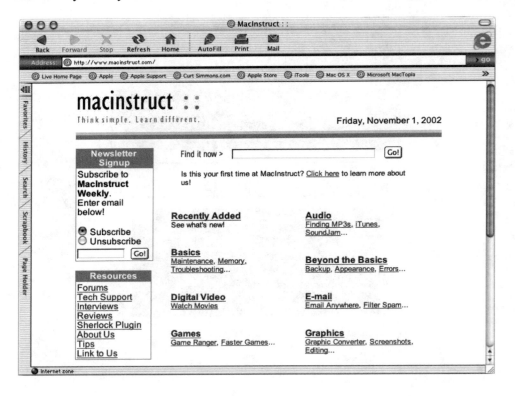

Index

INTERNATIONAL CONTACT INFORMATION

AUSTRALIA
McGraw-Hill Book Company Australia Pty. Ltd.
TEL +61-2-9900-1800
FAX +61-2-9878-8881
http://www.mcgraw-hill.com.au
books-it_sydney@mcgraw-hill.com

CANADA
McGraw-Hill Ryerson Ltd.
TEL +905-430-5000
FAX +905-430-5020
http://www.mcgraw-hill.ca

GREECE, MIDDLE EAST, & AFRICA
(Excluding South Africa)
McGraw-Hill Hellas
TEL +30-210-6560-990
TEL +30-210-6560-993
TEL +30-210-6560-994
FAX +30-210-6545-525

MEXICO (Also serving Latin America)
McGraw-Hill Interamericana Editores S.A. de C.V.
TEL +525-117-1583
FAX +525-117-1589
http://www.mcgraw-hill.com.mx
fernando_castellanos@mcgraw-hill.com

SINGAPORE (Serving Asia)
McGraw-Hill Book Company
TEL +65-863-1580
FAX +65-862-3354
http://www.mcgraw-hill.com.sg
mghasia@mcgraw-hill.com

SOUTH AFRICA
McGraw-Hill South Africa
TEL +27-11-622-7512
FAX +27-11-622-9045
robyn_swanepoel@mcgraw-hill.com

SPAIN
McGraw-Hill/Interamericana de España, S.A.U.
TEL +34-91-180-3000
FAX +34-91-372-8513
http://www.mcgraw-hill.es
professional@mcgraw-hill.es

UNITED KINGDOM, NORTHERN, EASTERN, & CENTRAL EUROPE
McGraw-Hill Education Europe
TEL +44-1-628-502500
FAX +44-1-628-770224
http://www.mcgraw-hill.co.uk
computing_europe@mcgraw-hill.com

ALL OTHER INQUIRIES Contact:
Osborne/McGraw-Hill
TEL +1-510-549-6600
FAX +1-510-883-7600
http://www.osborne.com
omg_international@mcgraw-hill.com

New Offerings from Osborne's
How to Do Everything Series

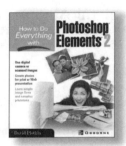
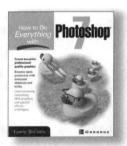